The Last Fighting General

The Last
Fighting
General

The Biography of
Robert Tryon Frederick

Anne Hicks

Schiffer Military History
Atglen, PA

For my sons and daughter

Book Design by Ian Robertson.
Copyright © 2006 by Anne Hicks.
Library of Congress Control Number: 2006923026

Printed in China
ISBN: 0-7643-2430-6

We are interested in hearing from authors with book ideas on related topics.

Published by Schiffer Publishing Ltd.
4880 Lower Valley Road
Atglen, PA 19310
Phone: (610) 593-1777
FAX: (610) 593-2002
E-mail: Info@schifferbooks.com.
Visit our web site at: www.schifferbooks.com
Please write for a free catalog.
This book may be purchased from the publisher.
Please include $3.95 postage.
Try your bookstore first.

In Europe, Schiffer books are distributed by:
Bushwood Books
6 Marksbury Avenue
Kew Gardens
Surrey TW9 4JF, England
Phone: 44 (0) 20 8392-8585
FAX: 44 (0) 20 8392-9876
E-mail: Info@bushwoodbooks.co.uk.
Visit our website at: www.bushwoodbooks.co.uk
Free postage in the UK. Europe: air mail at cost.
Try your bookstore first.

Contents

Acknowledgments

I am indebted to a considerable number of people who generously gave of their time to provide comments or recollections. Chief among them are dozens of World War II veterans who served with Frederick, and without whose graphic and colorful accounts, and enlightening glimpses into Frederick, this book would be like a gourd—hollow of any human traits and reactions. Most of these people are listed in the selected bibliography, but due my particular thanks for their frank and lengthy interviews are General Albert C. Wedemeyer, Bill Mauldin, General Paul D. Adams, General William W. Quinn, and General Kenneth G. Wickham.

Sadly, these five men have since died, as have several from the World War II era in other countries, including Finn Roll, who resided in France and, by his amusing stories, helped me immensely.

Grateful acknowledgment also goes to the dedicated staffs at the National Archives, at Hoover Institution on War, Revolution, and Peace, at the State Department Records Division, and at Carlisle Barracks. In addition, my thanks go to Charles E. Minihan, from the Staunton Alumni Association, and Joanne E. Eriksen, chief of graduate records at West Point.

Lastly, I count myself lucky to have had ready access to some of the Frederick family letters and records, which was not only beneficial, but made my task measurably easier.

A Life Heroic and Legendary
An Introduction by Way of Retrospect

As much as he did not die unmourned, so too would his military record not go unsung. In the past three decades, memorials to Robert Tryon Frederick have been erected both in Europe and North America. The tourist in Rome, Italy, might spot the handsome bronze plaque on a wall outside the United States Embassy that tells this building was used by Frederick as his command post during the liberation of Rome. In Le Muy, France, citizens and visitors alike motor along the General Frederick Traffic Circle, and not far off in La Mitan learn from the plaque on a farmhouse this was Frederick's *Quartier*, his CP, during the airborne invasion of southern France. Thousands of miles away in Ontario, Canada, at the entry to Canadian Forces Base Petawawa, stands the large, stately Frederick Gate. Nor has America neglected one of its proven leaders. At Fort Ord, California, on the now closed army base there remains Frederick Park housing community, and at the home of Special Forces Command, Fort Bragg, NC, troops work out at the Frederick Physical Fitness Center.

No less a tribute to the young general was when in 1981 President Ronald Reagan, in a speech to Canada's parliament, reminded its members:

"In World War Two there was something called the First Special Service Force, a unique international undertaking...composed of Canadians and Americans...famous for its high morale, its rugged abilities, and tough fighting."

He was referring to the bi-national unit which, formed and trained and led by Frederick, became a paragon of nations integrating to provide world freedom.

Such is the telling of history, a bit gleaned from here, a bit there, to build a frame of reference. But that alone fails to convey the aggressiveness, initiative, and independent thinking Frederick so ably manifested. He was a military activist. He was a master of human relations. In peacetime as well as in war he demonstrated courage and valor, and inspired such fanatical loyalty that, as his troops put it, "We would have followed him into the bowels of Hell." One of the most decorated men in World War II, Frederick believed in personal command. He led from the frontline, and would likely not easily accept today's technology that allows commanders to see, with computer tracking, the location of troops.

I have tried to discern the makeup and personality of Frederick by looking beyond the legend, and found as he undeniably shaped history, some of his life was quite remarkable, and some more commonly characteristic. Yet what stood out were his values—and the value of such a soldier.

"If we had a dozen men like him, we would have smashed Hitler in 1942."

Prime Minster Winston Churchill
Janaury 1944

"I would have died a thousand times for him out there. He means more to us foot soldiers than all our fathers put together."

A G.I. returning from a bloody battle in Italy
June 1944

"He won many honors, awards, and decorations, but the only thing that was meaningful to Frederick was the love and great respect we had for him as an officer and gentleman."

General Albert C. Wedemeyer
February 1986

1

"A Hopeless Case"

As a boy of nine in San Francisco, California, Robert Frederick tried devilishly to bring the wild Old West back into the city. Doing so, he nearly brought on the death of a citizen. He sprang from behind a bush, the same time shrieked an Indian-like war whoop, and caused a shocked horse to bound sideways and topple a cart carrying a vegetable grocer. The grocer lay sprawled in the street, gasping and clutching his chest, when the culprit high-tailed it home, certain the entire police force would be hunting for him.

So for months the boy tried to avoid city streets, and to create his wild and wooly west headed, instead, into the U.S. Army Presidio of San Francisco. A short five blocks from the Frederick house high on a hill, the Presidio had tangled groves of tall pines and berry bushes where he could easily keep his phantom frontier alive. At the time he had no other ambition. The cavalry on the Army base knew him as a flitting nuisance sneaking behind shrubs and tree trunks, with a leap and a holler charging out at their horses, only to end up with irate soldiers in hot pursuit of him and supplying, inadvertently, the dash of realism and excitement he wanted. What the soldiers never caught on to, "which," claimed a childhood pal later, "saved his hide," was that Robert could run fast, for miles, and he knew every short cut to safety.

But if it had been up to his parents, young Frederick's undrooping energy would have been fueling efforts at becoming a fine musician and linguist; instead, in a constant state of disappointment, they were finding their son hell-bent on shaping his own path to adulthood. Numerous attempts were made to dissuade him. In the evenings nine year old Robert, atop three books on a chair to be taller, was made to practice the cello an hour, then cap the ordeal with a forty minute stab at conjugating verbs in German or Latin—depending on whether it was an even or odd date. German on odd numbers, Latin on even. It was all part of his parents' unflagging and ofttimes blinding desire to have him follow in a string of talented paternal footsteps.

"That goal felt like boulders on my back," said Frederick later, "and I kept trying to prove I wasn't cut out for any part of it. But this was never easy, because I lacked the imagination to keep thinking up ways to show I was actually rebelling."

Which was why he often resorted to his romantic version of the old West, where there were thousands of beleaguered settlers and—a seagull feather tied in his hair—one cunning Indian. He succeeded in being a constant source of annoyance to others, and almost as frequently felt whippings with a razor strap at home. But sad to say, it was all in vain.

"As a means of rebellion," he said, "it was as useless at that as it was stupendous at forever getting me in trouble. But then, without question, I deserved it."

San Francisco was the birthplace of Robert Tryon Frederick, who arrived uneventfully on March 14, 1907, on the heels of the city's resurrection from the infamous "'06" earthquake. His parents, Dr. and Mrs. Marcus White Frederick, had lost nothing in the quake, but were made to struggle, at the time, with a much deeper despair, when just hours before blocks of San Francisco tumbled down, their firstborn, a boy, died at the age of two weeks. It was their healthy new son, Robert, who brought sunshine back into their lives, and in another eighteen months, the addition of a baby girl, Marcia, rounded out the family circle. But for however much the children were welcome, the Fredericks had no desire to hear babies squalling and jabbering.

Robert and his small sister were relegated to the third floor of the family home to be reared by a governess, and they tramped up and down a back stairway oblivious—until Robert turned five—that the people living below were their parents. When the startling fact was finally revealed it might have cheered the boy had he not been overcome with indignation. As far as he could tell, the downstairs couple had confessed a kinship only so they could barge in with lectures on obedience, demand his loving attention, and insist he take a slew of unappreciated lessons in music and language.

Dr. Frederick and his wife had married barely two years before the birth of their second son. They had met in a hospital room where the doctor had been called to treat a teenage nurse dying, purportedly, from typhoid. It so happened the young nurse, Pauline Adelaide McCurdy, was also pretty, her illness detracting not a bit from the green of her eyes, or her long red hair covering her sickbed pillow. Dr. Frederick was then forty-four years old, divorced, childless, and it appears certain of his patient's survival. For in ten days he had proposed marriage; and as soon as her health improved, Pauline had abandoned her job as a nurse to join, on a trot, in her new husband's "posh" lifestyle.

But while Dr. Frederick was indeed prosperous at the time, he had taken a far flung meander through professions that he relished, and was determined any son of his would repeat. With a business degree from Harvard, he had owned a saw mill in Maine for three years, sold it, gone to Germany and been master violinist in the Berlin symphony orchestra for six years, quit, and, fluent in six languages, had taught four of them for several years in New York, after which, back in Berlin, he had enrolled in medical school. Finally, at age thirty-nine, he had set up practice as an eye, ear, nose, and throat specialist in San Francisco. Both of his parents, who were teachers, had laid the cornerstone of his quirky transatlantic hopping when he was young. As newlyweds they had emigrated from Prussia to jobs in New York, then sallied westward, in 1861, to cash in on the gold rush mania, and ended up in Virginia City, Nevada. There they built the lucrative Frederick Hotel, only to realize, as their family grew, that Virginia City would not ever be, by European standards, a hub of cultural, much less academic, endeavor. So each year they shipped their son to Germany for ten months to study science, languages, and music. They could hardly fault him when, as an old salt at continental commuting, Dr. Frederick simply repeated the trek while taking his sweet time finding his professional niche.

But for his wife, Pauline, no halcyon cavalcade east to west and back as a youngster had spared her from neighbors mad with rage over goats crazy with hunger. Her father, Francis McCurdy, had run off from his family's farm in Canada when he was twelve to be a drummer boy in the Civil War, and he had beat a drum for Union Forces marching on northwest Virginia. He was still there a decade and a half later, in 1880, when he met sixteen year old Catherine Tryon as she stood criticizing his failing enterprise, a withering sweet potato patch. Catherine Tryon's family was haughty, rich, and, they proudly told anyone, descended from a long family record of government service. Most notable was that of Lieutenant General William Tryon, who in colonial days had been England's governor of both North Carolina and New York. By contrast, Francis McCurdy's family tree had sprouted only dirt poor farmers in Ireland, who had, of late, had no better luck in Canada. Nonetheless falling in love, he and Miss Catherine—after she quarreled two years with her father over her choosing a penniless man—eloped and lit out hastily for California.

At a crossroad fifty miles east of San Francisco it seemed their true destiny had arrived, as friendly settlers gave them two goats to persuade them to homestead. Yet by the time their daughter Pauline was thirteen, no man or woman among those same settlers was not harboring thoughts of killing off the McCurdys. For while their goats by then had multiplied into dozens, they seldom reinforced the goat pens the critters routinely bashed down to reach, and devour, every neighboring farmers' crops. On a day the feud escalated to bullets slicing through walls of the McCurdy house, Pauline had fled the homestead, never to return. A score of odd jobs had got her through nursing school, whereupon marrying Dr. Frederick she was catapulted into society; and took to it with gusto, also agreeably going along with the idea of raising their son in an astounding pool of musical and linguistic opportunity.

It nearly drowned the boy. At age five little Robert was taught Italian, French, and to strum a pint-sized mandolin. And by his ninth birthday every Saturday was bringing a parade of teachers to the house to give lessons, as already mentioned, in German, Latin, and the cello. "I have krule [sic] Saturdays," he complained in a grammar school composition, "while my friends get to play." Worse were the long evening hours of practice, while he sat atop three books and under the tutoring ears of his father.

It was true that Dr. Frederick was one of San Francisco's most jovial, well liked, and quick-witted citizens. But his son tended to know him better for his quick temper, and bore the marks to prove it. With one too many horrendous squeals from his cello, his father whisked the cello bow from him, and grabbing his hand sawed the bow across his knuckles till it drew blood. Should he stumble over a foreign word, which was often, it brought a stinging slap to the back of his neck, at times in concert with a tongue lashing from his mother. Many an evening then ended with Robert bolting to the third floor or through the nearest door leading outside, undaunted by his father's familiar yell of anguish. Good God! He won't amount to anything! He hasn't a whit of talent!

But how to convince his parents he did not care?

His sister, Marcia, admired his knack for vanishing fleet footed from their parents, especially when—within a year—he'd climbed out every first floor window one time or another to escape Saturday lessons, and outrun his father trying to chase him down in the family Model T. He had even disappeared an entire night, which to Marcia was the crowning act of defiance, and Robert could not bring himself to tell her it really had been a leanwitted mistake. He had been absolutely terrified as he hid through the night in a nearby park.

The insufferable upshot of his sister's admiration was that she demanded he take her along one Saturday, though after sneaking out he planned, with two pals, to race downhill to the city's piers. The more he insisted she was not welcome, the louder Marcia, with clenched fists, stamped her feet and screamed, until forlornly her brother hoisted her through a window.

He and his pals were out to settle a dare made among themselves; they would verify that, with the U.S. embroiled in World War I (it being 1917), it was easy to get a look at a battle raging overseas. Out on a pier, eyeing a ship being loaded with freight, they inveigled Marcia—by threats of drowning her—to distract a sailor on a gangplank with fake sobs of being lost, while they whistled past in an attempt to stow away. All were caught, hauled home shamefaced in a police wagon, and Robert fingered, by his sister, as the ringleader.

"Of course, I was the one who got a whipping," he remembered years later. "But just as painful was being told I had steered us up the gangplank of a ship that happened to be going to Hawaii. My friends never would let me forget I almost had us blithely sailing off in the wrong direction."

That same week his father, responding to a note from a relative, wrote:

"Thanks for asking about our son, but in honest reply, he is still only adept at wearing out the soles on his shoes. We are not at all consoled that his last report card from Spring Valley School shows in class work he is 'satisfactory,' considering in everything else he remains a hopeless case."

From a front hall window in the Frederick house was a splendid view of the waterfront, where a great many ships coasted past, midst a usual crowd of fishing boats left bobbing helplessly. Robert, as if taking a long wistful look at the view, stood at the window hours one afternoon, as around him rugs were rolled up and the furniture carted off. It was moving day, to a larger house across town, and he was trying to be as inconspicuously useless as possible.

Earlier he had dawdled on the third floor, dredging up memories and in the process tagging them good or awful. Up there, with his sister and, for over a decade, their governess, he had celebrated birthdays, Christmases, and held lively impromptu feasts he catered by sneaking food up from downstairs. When fog and rain kept them all indoors, they had spent hours weaving tales of wild adventure, or reading from the hundreds of books sent up, over the years, by his parents. These were his only "good" memories of childhood, and now at age thirteen and a half, he had blown a change to ever remember his quantum jump to teenager as being anything but awful—and seemingly getting worse.

He meant only to test the scrappy power of adolescence when on his thirteenth birthday he had impetuously threatened to run away rather than endure another lesson at home. Since then there had not been even a whispered reference to music or a foreign word, and some credit goes to Dr. and Mrs. Frederick, who already had been worrying why their son seldom smiled. Had they been too relentless, too harsh? But in turn they had declared he would indeed have to leave home "and sleep in streets" if, at the end of six months, he did not identify, and begin to pursue, his own interests.

Alas, he hadn't the slightest idea what these might be. While he stared out the window at the waterfront he decided, however, to see what lay beyond soon as he figured a way to get there; meanwhile, he had to be content with leaps in the dark at quickly finding an interest on solid ground.

One, vaguely plausible, was in school, where freshmen boys had the option of taking gym class or Junior ROTC. Admittedly, he based his choice on nothing close to interest in anything military, but on merely what was least degrading—a baggy gym suit, or an itchy wool uniform that reeked of gun lubricating oil. And too late, he then discovered the wool leggings on his uniform were a mortification all their own. Each time he laced them tight, to stay up, the circulation in his legs petered out, yet with laces loosened his leggings crawled sideways, backwards, never made it around front again, and repeatedly earned him an upbraiding for "sloppiness."

In charge of the uniformed bunch was a captain from the Spanish-American War who had since been shifted to Army Reserves, to incubate boys in the art of soldiering. Neither ROTC nor the school's junior edition (which had no career benefits; it led to nothing) was viewed those days as treacherous—no peaceniks or anti-militaryniks around cussedly jeering at civilians being taught to defend the country. Thus, whenever the captain sent his perspiring, itching "troops" wheeling around the school grounds on marching drills, admiring girls lined the field's edge and crammed at classroom windows to watch.

To boot, Robert had been put on the rifle team which, toting .22 caliber guns, was herded once weekly to firing ranges in his favorite old stomping grounds, the Presidio. But though appreciating that all the repetitive drill was in fresh air, and most seemed equally appreciated by young females, not a thing about Junior ROTC gripped him with interest. Excepting, as he mulled over his predicament, the fact that it had a heap more appeal than testing the validity in his parents' threat to evict him.

It also, perversely, was what led Robert Frederick to commit an act of grand perjury.

His fingers were crossed deep in pockets of his winter jacket as he strode into the office of a National Guard unit the week he turned fourteen and announced, sober faced, he was eighteen. Sworn in, he walked out as Private Frederick. What had got the better of him, he admitted later, was the sight of cavalry soldiers on their mounts when he was at the firing ranges with the rifle team. All he desired, since not once succeeding in his young days of horse chasing, was the opportunity to get up in the saddle. And he could honestly say at the time of enlisting, he had no idea it entailed spending two weeks of summer at a military camp over a 150 miles from home.

Nonetheless, he had a whale of a good time those weeks, learning while fighting mosquitos and spurring a weary Army horse, he enjoyed the commiserating comraderie. But nothing was going to placate his already disappointed father, who on hearing his son's enthusiasm for camp life burst out in protest. Did Robert think he could keep frittering his life away on whims like—God forbid—wanting to sit on a horse! And get away with dishonesty?

Well, it did appear so, Robert had to confess, in light of the fact he soon would be crossing the Pacific Ocean. He had at least thought of a scheme to see what lay beyond the waterfront, and it required another fib; exaggerating his age two years, he had claimed to be sixteen and in dire financial straits. As a result, the Maritime Union had hired him to be polisher of all brass railings around the decks of a passenger liner, the *Sonoma*, during the ships' six week summer run to Australia. With that news, his father threw up his hands, alleged to giving up hope entirely, and his mother wept.

In the bargain of going to sea, young Frederick was quartered with a crew of men seven to fifty years older who were in a blackhearted mood, due to an unsuccessful seamen's strike that left them vying for jobs. When out at sea, they badgered him to reveal how he got employed "and instantly detested him," a seaman recounted later.

"Yet we were perplexed," he added, "by Bob Frederick, deckboy, lowest form of maritime life. He was not properly awed by our seamanship or his lack of it, and instead performed his lowly duties with dignity. On top of that, we suspected he had unusual confidence, but preferring to view it as hubris, we went out of our way to shun him, and he was totally unaffected by this."

Not quite; but he saw no way to improve his situation. For on board ship, the crew talked about women, on shore they talked about ships, and he didn't know beans about either. Given plenty of time alone he kept the brass railings gleaming, and in the port city of Sydney he made scrupulous lists of his expenses; the lists included a laundry charge of a half cent to clean his handkerchiefs, and nine cents for a shirt, and indicate he saw little of Australia outside the laundry, one restaurant, and a "bleak" hotel room. But if attempting to be frugal with the first large sum of money he had earned, just as likely he was not too sure what one did all alone in a strange country.

It was only when the ship again dropped anchor in San Francisco that he took a chance to get on better footing with the crew. He invited one of them home for dinner. Unluckily, the seaman recognized the Frederick address was nowhere near his rough-edged neighborhood in town; and as he put it later, he shot back, "What for? So you can show rich folks what you are up against? Hell no! I'm not going to be exhibit A!"

"Then come tomorrow night," Frederick gamely suggested, "and consider yourself exhibit B." And just as abruptly rebuffed a second time, he gained no ground whatsoever in the maritime world.

Frederick himself remembered the incident late in life only as having made him aware of a need to occasionally stand in another's shoes, to think from that person's perspective. He did not elaborate on the durability of this "lesson." But in the reminiscences of legions of men who later served with him at varying stages in their careers, there runs consistent reference to how he seemed intuitively to sense their needs and concerns.

As for the immediate upshot of his voyage, he woefully found his parents had decided he would attend the Naval Academy. This because of his brief fling at sea; and never mind as a student in high school he was solidly mediocre. His father had persuaded a local senator to meet their son and arrange, prematurely, his appointment to Annapolis. It was futile, Robert thought, to argue he flat out opposed the idea. So, failing to appear at the senator's office, he hid out in a movie theater where doors were unlocked but no movie was being shown. He sat there hours, undisturbed, pondering the one nemesis in his life—wherein others kept making plans for his future. And albeit slowly, the notion hit him he could, perhaps, staunch this ongoing problem if he showed a modicum of ambition.

It was, thus, nothing noble that goaded him to go home and declare he would attend West Point and carve out a career in the Army. After all, he was not galvanized by any march and drill regimen, nor did he own a shred of longing to one day lead others. Besides, he had recently processed a transfer from California's National Guard to the Army's Enlisted Reserve Corps, which he had heard offered a greater number of weekends on horseback.

Obviously, he made his decision under duress, and may have hoped no one would hold him to his word a year later. But his father, not giving up easily, had reawakened his fierce drive to get the best, of whatever it was, in his son to surface. For this a military school seemed imperative, and one in particular—Staunton Military Academy in Virginia—fit the bill; it had spawned many a boy qualified for West Point. So it was in late August 1923, after he unpacked his gear from a stint at an Enlisted Reserve Corps camp and repacked, Frederick, sixteen, rode the train east alone.

The town of Staunton, Virginia, nestles in the Shenandoah Valley amid patches of grazing land and orchards, dwarfed by the Blue Ridge Mountains. The streets rise and dip steeply along routes once used by Indians and covered wagons, one street winding uphill to the wood-trimmed stone buildings of Staunton Military Academy. The school no longer operates, but it is easy to imagine how the valley's heavy fragrance of blossoms in spring, and in autumn the cidery smell of ripening apples, drifted in what used to be open dormitory windows.

When students trudged downhill, they were confident their brass buttoned uniforms would stir the hearts of townfolks, and facilitate getting to know their daughters. For so like the southern cult—especially in the first half of the 1900s—Virginians took seriously their military past and any item related. Or, as Robert soon found, they asked first the history of your ancestors, then your name, and conversation turned instantly to the War Between the States.

His classmates were less fervid, though steeped southern style in the glory of anything smacking of military, they too were interested in one's heritage. Right off he erred by mentioning his grandfather McCurdy had beat a drum for northern forces in the Civil War, and afterward, there is the Shenandoah Valley where others prospered, darn near starved to death trying to grow sweet potatoes. His classmates gasped. What had the Yankee just said? Was that his ignominious background?

It was hardly a brilliant beginning for the one newcomer in the senior grade. But he showed them a thing or two in the Military Science classroom by using the earthy reasoning he picked up at summer camps. Then, within weeks word arrived he'd been promoted, at sixteen, to the rank of corporal in the Enlisted Reserve Corps. Yankee or no, classmates could now not ignore among them was a "seasoned" soldier due their trust and respect. They showered him with friendship.

Even so, life at Staunton was disposed to breed competitive animus, both in class and on the field. It may have been such competition from peers—or this coupled with freedom from home—which fed the sudden bug that bit Robert to do well. He simultaneously took biology, chemistry, geometry, history, English, military science, Spanish, and mandatory training. Plus he volunteered as a reporter for the school newspaper, and with his marksmanship helped the rifle team get to the National Championships.

But his efforts paid off. Before June rolled around he had been accepted to West Point. In the Staunton yearbook below his photograph, he is called "Fred" and "Bob":

"...the original military ringer. He has attended so many government camps he actually found out what they are all about. The sad part is...he is going to leave. We have a sort of sneaking sensation...he would make...a busting good officer."

With graduation on 7 June, it allowed three weeks for him to get to San Francisco by train (his parents did not attend graduation) and return in time for West Point indoctrination. Instead, he begged off a visit home, and holing up temporarily in a boarding house, he was as much trying to avoid a session of his parents' discipline as he was wanting to recuperate from a year of hard work. But compared to either, as someone might have said, "Boy, you ain't seen nothin' yet!"

2

"1928 Has its Mainstay"

So brutal was West Point's program for cadets in the 1920s, over a half century later, brimful of rancor they roar, "It was licensed slavery!" "Cruel inhuman purgatory!" And indeed swiftly and assuredly, cadets were robbed of freedom, dignity, bravado—and left feeling lower than a worm's belly.

But, alack, no school a young man previously attended bore one iota of semblance to a dry run. Certainly Bob Frederick arrived dimly cognizant of the dreadful ordeal when, climbing the steep hill to the main entry, he steamed by a crowd of new students; for which observers must have muttered, "There's an eager fool." But in truth, Frederick's lone urge was to reach the dark shadows of tall grey buildings rearing up before him. It was 1 July, the morning blazing hot and, making it worse, nearby in teasing paradox was the cold Hudson River. Miserable in his obligatory civilian suit and hat, it did not occur to Frederick to savor his last chance for eighteen months to be on the hill on his own and slouch, laugh, and lollygag at will. Nor did the Academy deem it dastardly that lying in wait in the shadows were senior cadets—Firstclassmen—proficient in merciless hazing.

Insults rolled off their tongues like oil. In mere seconds Frederick was called "subhuman, wooden idiot, Mr. Dumgard" and a "beast" to, henceforth, spend two months in "Beast Barracks." Shrieked at, snarled at, ordered to run doubletime, he raced to and fro, to be measured for uniforms and to collect gym wear, bedding, a mattress, seven pairs of shoes and boots, and mounds of gear. Running to his assigned room with each new armload of provisions, in between times, ordered to stand "braced" (at exaggerated attention), sneering seniors screeched out at him a litany of rules.

More galling seniors stalked the barracks, screaming how to dress, fold clothes, and stow each heap of gear. Web belt here! Gun oil here! Sabre belt here! Cross belt here! Brass polish here! And on it went, "blurring," as Frederick later said, "into a numbing spiel of tyranny." Afterward, sent bolting back out to scorching sunlight, drilled ruthlessly three hours to march with West Point precision, at dusk his class was marched off to mess hall, where harangued new cadets had to "brace" on the front three inches of chairs and, with eyes lowered, in silence eat "By The Numbers."*

Frederick half-listened. He was thinking for nine hours he'd been run ragged, scolded, and bullied; seen new students crumble from sheer fright or fatigue, some sob openly, their spirits pulverized already. Surely, he told himself, there won't be another day like this—there can't be.

That night, after "lights out," in the darkened barracks Frederick sat slumped on a side of his cot, talking in whispers with another newcomer (later Major General) Frederick J. Dau.

"I had mentioned," Dau would recall, "that West Point admitted new students (plebes) as old as twenty-two. Then I asked Bob his age, and as he was barely seventeen, proceeded to inform him he was probably the baby in our class. With that, he sighed and said he'd 'at least had some prior experience in drill and discipline.'"

So Dau asked, "Where?," and after dead silence heard a loud thud. Frederick, falling asleep sitting up, had crashed to the floor.

"Headfirst," Dau continued. "But he had crawled back onto his cot and had dozed off again when, wondering if he had a concussion, I decided to periodically check on him. Because we were not permitted out of bed after lights out, it required creeping soundlessly on all fours in the pitch black to his cot, and each time I did this he was okay, and why I kept repeating that trip—I was exhausted—puzzled me. But though it still

*It meant all arm and hand movements to be made at right angles; and between bites hands lowered and placed in their trouser pockets.

does, I have enjoyed claiming I must have been the first to come under the spell of whatever made men later follow Bob through hell and high water."

What is certain, before dawn seniors stormed into each room, and like jackals eager for prey, rousted and verbally mauled their groggy victims; and one day, Frederick now began to realize, was as bad as another.

From two months in Beast Barracks, new cadets gained "a smartness in drill and duties," their handbooks read, "the end of which they are sent on a hike": sort of. Chaperoned by the ubiquitous seniors, Frederick and his classmates were led over countless mountain ranges, to each day pitch their shelters at a different campsite. For three days it poured rain, and they floundered through grasping mud, their skin wrinkled like prunes and gear blanketed with mildew. And when finally sunlight pierced the dreary sky, Frederick had a flash of inspiration. If he staked just half his shelter, draped the rest on top—That done, sunbeams fell on both it and his gear, and his sodden patch of ground. But if thunder and lighting ever showed on a face, a Firstclassman wore it as, midway down a row of peaked little tents he came upon an unconforming, sagging apparition. He let out a roar of fury, and then demanded, "Who is the idiot!"

Frederick was no miscreant; but neither was he willing to let the reason for his action get shot down by salvos of rebuke he was sure to get anyway. He squared his shoulders and, readied mentally, took in a deep breath.

"Sir," he called out, "this idiot knows that in a regulation to stop proliferating mildew, it says that when in the field we can use whatever heat is available." Quickly gasping in air, he added, "The regulation is in our Army Hygiene manuals."

The upperclassman glowered at him. Yet without a word, pivoting on his heels, he strode away, stymied by Frederick's inarguable claim. Among his classmates struck dumb with astonishment, one later recounted: "Frederick had set the tone for his entire cadet career, and soon we all knew that, independent by nature, he was perfectly comfortable doing what he wanted if he didn't like how things were done."

In a significant way, the teenager who sat in a movie theater rather than meet a senator had not changed. Surprisingly, given that demerits were affixed to even tiny infractions of rules, Frederick received no more than average. But then who better knew—from past lessons—that to skirt sanctioned behavior successfully required a reason making as much, or more, sense. Even so, as demerits accumulated for his petty misdeeds (they included "laughing out loud" and "belt too long"), he often wound up marching in the punishment yard in solitary for hours. And as displays of affection were forbidden, after caught "arm in arm" with a gorgeous young lady.

"Who he had, as yet, to meet, fortunately," a classmate later said; adding, "For with plebe life prison-like, just thinking of girls made it more wretched."

As did, Frederick found, the start of academics in September, when Second- and Thirdclassmen returned from summer camp or furlough. Now it was three to one. Now, on top of drill and studies, imperative was that he memorize the answers to nonsensical questions all upperclassmen asked plebes in the mess hall. To respond incorrectly was to be denied a meal, and he already had lost twelve pounds, and regretted his errors, as his stomach rumbled at him furiously.

It was while he frantically memorized the answers from his handbook that he read "few men" had experience in fencing, and always "on the lookout for men" was the annual cadet variety show. Whereupon, he took up fencing and volunteered to help with the show. From the one he became adept with the épée and saber, and from the other launched into a host of extracurricular activities, and by the end of his first year, he also ranked above average academically. Save for in one subject. In Military Tactics, indicant of his future, Frederick had pulled in the highest grade in his class.

But nothing guaranteed he would survive. That was an unremitting challenge, best proved when later, due to a lack of constant zeal or intelligence, of the original 457 cadets in his class a whopping 193 would fail to graduate. But for the moment, he wrote jubilantly to his sister, "Am still alive and kicking here at Hell-on-the-Hudson."

That summer, in the hilly outback of the Academy, along with his class Frederick practiced maneuvers, surveying, and firing weapons. Honors had come to him; he had been made an Acting Corporal, and with this went a responsibility to discipline others. Giving no outward sign he detested the shrieking of upperclassmen, privately he resolved to try the opposite; to be soft-spoken. But always expecting a fierce reprimand for his indulgent break with tradition, as a diversion he kept thinking of the happier prospect of a week off at Christmas. It would be the first time in a year and a half his class could leave. Since it would not be long enough for him to get to San Francisco and return (commercial aircraft back then flew only in daylight, stopped often to refuel, and in snow flurries or heavy rain sat immobilized), on the chance his family came east, he sent home the dates he would be free, and took the opportunity to share: "I wonder if someone has written about peoples' responses to discipline. From the little experience I get [as Acting Corporal], I am convinced if a person's self esteem is constantly bashed, he does only what it takes to avoid more of that, but if treated decently he works hard to do his best to get more of that treatment."

It was an insightful view from one so new at exercising authority. But back came a letter from his parents with only the news they planned to tour China all of December, with his sister to be farmed out to friends.

The first cold of winter had brought freezing wind howling off the Hudson, and a sky grey as the Academy's walls when, Christmas week, Frederick hiked snow covered hills, watched movies in the gymnasium, and polished his boots, buckles, and shoes mirror bright. Despite the fellowship of others stuck there it was the gloomiest week he ever endured. For he now had acknowledged his parents never had offered any support or praise—much less affection. It was about this time, he later said, he "felt at home at West Point"; where at least as a judge of his competence he was measured against his peers, not someone's high-minded ideals. "Except," he laughed, "when pitted against the orneriest of cavalry groups."

As the cavalry meant horses (not yet outmoded by tanks), cadets had to learn Roman jumping, which entails leaping off and back onto a horse running full throttle. But more troublesome, the horses made it clear they were there to race each other rider-be-damned. If a cadet's hands tangled in the reins as he dismounted he was dragged along, his body bopping horse flesh, his boots raking the dirt; and if failing to swing back up on his steed, he was knocked silly by horses pounding up behind him. One photograph taken at the time shows a handsome young man on a horse, but he wears an expression of such sober misgivings over jumping down, it is barely discernable this was Frederick. As for his earlier infatuation?

"The only reliable thing these horses do," he told a friend, "is to keep persuading me not to join the cavalry."

Otherwise he coasted through his second year, his top grade again in Military Tactics. At nearly five foot ten, he was now a muscular 152 pounds, and though not coincidently, in the embryonic stage of being a military activist. In his cadet Company C and his class, he had become the conduit for gripes and suggestions to the staff; "Because," one ex-student put it later: "...he commanded respect, even from the Tacs [martinet Army officers who levied punishment], though when he challenged them about procedures on our behalf, he would not accept their answer 'That's the way it is.'

You see, Bob was beyond his time, and that of most Army officers, who wouldn't dare voice an original idea. It was go by the book always in those days. But, if something could be improved upon, he went for it. Like rather than get three demerits for an unauthorized book on his desk, a cadet write a report on the book to give some relevance to the punishment and the crime. Plus, that way we could finish reading books we liked. Though he lost that one, the Tacs did admit it made sense. Too humble to take himself seriously, Bob did everything in a spirit of fun. And as he was an eloquent speaker, if the staff was not buying what he proposed, he'd give them a big smile, and switching to a sales pitch for another idea, get them confused about just what to turn him down for. How often he succeeded escapes me, but I know he was intelligent, definitely facile, and innovative."

And soon, madly in love.

Her name was Ruth Adelaide Harloe, and as for flirting, Ruth had skills that left men enthralled, and women pouting and scowling. The daughter of an eminent surgeon in Brooklyn, once a month Ruth took the train north to attend a cadet dance. And though in the social cocoon of West Point the arrival of any young lady was a welcome sight, with alacrity crowds of cadets lined up to sign her dance card. She was stunningly pretty, with auburn hair and sparkling grey-green eyes, "and the way she looked at you," said one smitten fellow, "you felt you were the most important person in her life." At least temporarily. As one cousin of Ruth's described, "Being the bell of the ball at West Point was icing on her cake. Not only was Ruth a sought after fashion model, she had a teaching degree and taught third grade, and able to play anything by ear on the piano, she was constantly asked to parties. She was already popular and busy."

Bob Frederick had been checking on decorations he helped obtain for a dance when, fox-trotting past in the arms of a classmate, Ruth had smiled at him. The next time she danced by she smiled again, and needing no further enticement he had asked around, "Who is she?" But with a snaking line of contenders—a cadet could cut in only after the seventh dance—his interest had fizzled when, the following month at a dance, Ruth approached him.

Now she gave him her full attention, driving others away with a wave of her hand. Afterward, Frederick returned to his barracks grinning: Ruth Harloe had requested that he escort her to the next dance.

"Whatever did you say to her?" his friends asked.

"Not much," he replied, honestly. Ruth had chatted about how the year before, when nineteen, she had wed a young banker who had insisted they live with his parents; that after thirteen weeks of their hounding her to be a stay-at-home cook and laundress she divorced him; and while many of her relatives disapproved, as they lived in upstate New York, she saw them only in summer and was not perturbed.

"But you must have said something right to snare her!" persisted his friends.

"All I got to say was she was interesting." Frederick smiled. "Maybe she liked that."

Actually, this was partly true. Although he was not aware of it, Ruth was "sick" of cadets trying to impress her, who "proceeded," she said, much later, "to impress themselves, while ignoring what I had to say." She had decided to let no one male hog her time at a dance when, "thinking

Bob was good looking, my resolve unraveled as this quiet, reserved cadet listened to me." It helped, perhaps, when next they met, she learned both their fathers were doctors; both had had a sibling die;* and she and Mrs. Frederick had the same middle name, Adelaide. At any rate, by the end of that evening Ruth just knew she had found the right person with whom to spend a lifetime. And very soon after, so did Frederick.

Meanwhile, he felt the impending grip of the Academy's creed— Duty, Honor, Country. For two years taught to obey, he was now being taught to command. America's top general of the day, John J. Pershing, had likened cadets preparing for Army careers to men who "consecrate their lives to service of the Church; [they] yield the hope of wealth." The Army, moreover, ensured being a nomad—waiting in perpetual readiness for events to demand transforming into a warrior; to with flesh and blood protect the nation's freedom. These were hardly recruiting come-ons, Frederick had reflected—not amazed it had heightened the fact each day got him closer to when committed to with "Duty" well-performed, "Honor" untarnished, guard the "Country."

Yet, in his Military Art course his instructors pontificated on trench warfare, as if so devoted to old ways they saw potentials for airplanes and motor vehicles as sacrilege. And in Military History, the feats of battle captains filled his textbook, but he had not entered West Point to emulate a past leader; he had no heroes. By a paragraph on one Civil War great he scribbled in the margin, "Had this nitwit used logic, not gone by the book, he would have trapped the enemy."

Still, it was the Academy's aim to build strong character, not independent thinking. And as exemplary cadets repressed individual ideas, Frederick now appeared reformed (as he later said, "to insure I graduated"). The bonus was the start of his senior year, the staff and his peers concurred that he had plenty of proper character, and elected him to be a cadet captain. It was the highwater mark of his student life; and part of an elite cadre of cadets in command of their companies, he now discovered one of the pleasures of leading others; that of seeing men respond smartly to his orders. "March!"..."Pass in review!"... "About face!" But something kept nagging him that had everything to do with his chosen profession.

*Ruth's sister had succumbed to diphtheria at age seven.

It was a time when civilians were having a collective attack of ambivalence about the Army. An offshoot from nine years before, when at the close of the Great War pacifists had demanded the U.S. disarm, ever since, Congress had voted the Army a skinny budget in reaction to the popular outcry. Had not the end of the war brought lasting peace? Why give the Army anything! It has piles of old equipment and supplies it can use!

Frederick was resigned, when getting his commission, there would be no better chance of the Army modernizing. Convinced of the value of soldiering, he could live with that. What nagged him was there also was no prospect of a junior officer's meager salary improving. A second lieutenant, on scarcely a living wage of $129.00 a month, had to pay for his own supplies, uniforms (a winter overcoat cost $60.00), food, housing, and civilian clothes (a suit was about $55.00), leaving nothing for extras. Ruth had come up for a Sunday visit, when sitting a prudent foot away from her, he said, "You know, the Army has so few resources it can't replace aging weapons, and hasn't a prayer of changing the pay scale either. I imagine," he was patently hedging, "those married to servicemen find the low income a hardship."

"But look what they get," Ruth replied. "They get to live in different places and meet new people. I happen to think that's a great tradeoff."

"You do?" Frederick laughed, suddenly rid of his nagging worry; and continued, "Well, I happen to know I love you." With that he proposed marriage, and Ruth quickly accepted, making it plain she was anxious to join him in the trials, joys, and suspense of military life. They set the time to wed for six hours after he graduated on June 9, 1928.

Cadet Captain Robert Tryon Frederick had much to feel good about as he marched his company on parade one last time. He not only had brooked the crushing system, but more than just survived. He was the managing editor and business manager of the yearbook; treasurer and business manager of the Dialectic Society; was on the Equipment and Camp Illumination committees; had been on the fencing team, school newspaper staff, and for four years helped run the variety show; was a rifle sharpshooter and pistol expert; plus had become a company commander; all the while remaining in the top half of his class in academics.

Described by others in the academy yearbook as having "a modest personality," and "inherent ability to make friends...and get things done," as later notated by a colleague (onetime Adjutant General of the Army) Kenneth G. Wickham: "Frederick had displayed diversity, competence, leadership, and creatively involved in numerous activities, achieved what most cadets would not even consider undertaking."

Or, as more concisely summed up in the yearbook: "every class [has] one guiding hand...1928 has its mainstay in Fred."

When it had come time to choose a branch of service he had picked the Coast Artillery Corps, "because, overall," he told his friends, "Coast Artillery bases have the best housing." It was the least he could do for his beautiful bride-to-be.

The wedding took place in the Dutch Reform Church in Brooklyn. Ruth, recycling her bridal gown, was all in white—as were Frederick and his classmates-cum-ushers, in their spanking new tropical dress uniforms. Ruth's parents were there, of course, as were an approving Dr. and Mrs. Frederick, and daughter Marcia. But noticeably missing was Frederick's best man, a fellow graduate who had hitched a ride with friends and got royally lost. They were still circling frenziedly around Brooklyn when the newlyweds drove off in a sporty Auburn car, a gift from the senior Fredericks. The bridegroom carried with him orders to report to Fort Winfield Scott in San Francisco on 16 June; thus, by decree the young couple had just six days to honeymoon, and by necessity, had to keep heading west.

Still, Frederick was eager to start his career. Schooled in the art of peace and discipline of war, and since boyhood steadily honing his ability to make the best of circumstances, although the peacetime military demanded conformity, he felt sure he could serve the Army well as an officer. And a "mainstay" is, by definition, a principal supporter.

3

"Suitable for High Command"

That August 1928, the U.S. signed the Kellogg-Briand Treaty, as did fourteen other nations. It outlawed war, and stipulated finding peaceful ways to solve international rifts. But among U.S. Army personnel, with a rolling of eyes heavenward, rose the groan, "God, what next." For it gave politicians a further excuse to starve the Army of money, while clearly the rest of the country was enjoying prosperity. Farms and businesses were thriving, and not even Prohibition dimmed the good times, as much of the populace was consuming alcohol anyway. And while Bob Frederick had no strong view about the treaty or people drinking, it was in this national atmosphere of thumb-a-nose at the law and military that he would soon encounter a local malfeasant citizenry.

Reporting to the 6th Coast Artillery regiment at Ft. Scott, Second Lieutenant Frederick was posted to a battery of coastal guns (cannons) guarding San Francisco's harbors. Within a week his unit held a "live fire" drill, every gun roaring as a thunderous fusillade of live ammunition was shot out to sea. He had been interested to note beforehand the great effort made to warn civilians when firing would start, and "to open all windows in advance"; if not open, the blast from guns would blow a window out.

But, as usually gunners trained with dummy ammo, now in August his unit spent three days in the field loading, and unloading, dummy shells; and Frederick was dumfounded when soon after dozens of bills for broken windows flooded the post headquarters. Yet his immediate superior, a captain, was plainly bored by it all: "My only opinion," he offered, "is that it's your turn, Lieutenant, to sign affidavits no live ammo was fired."

So, trekking over to the headquarters, explaining his mission Frederick was handed the affidavits, to which had been stapled the bills for damage. Thumbing through them, one bill caught his eye; it was for 184 panes of glass. Curiosity led him to check the address, and at the end of the day, still in uniform, drive out there.

"It was a palatial house," he remembered, "and behind it sat a small shed consisting of new wood beams nailed in a grid pattern with open spaces. But I had seen no damaged windows when, still looking over a side fence it hit me that was not a shed out back, but framework for a new greenhouse. Counting each space where a glass pane would go, I came up with one hundred and eighty-four."

Feeling more than a little outrage, he rang the front door bell.

"It was not official, but I wanted the homeowner to hear firsthand that his duplicity was contemptible. Except, before I got out one word, seeing my uniform he swung at me with his right fist, missed, tried unsuccessfully with his left, and after I ducked his second right jab, he told me to go to hell and slammed the door."

It was an indubitably wiser young lieutenant who decided henceforth to ignore the not infrequent attempts by civilians to bilk the U.S. Army,* only to get another lesson that swiped away at his naivete.

Four months later, Frederick found his name on a list of those assigned to take a course in Mess Management at the School for Bakers and Cooks in the Presidio of San Francisco. Reading further, he noticed the other students would all be first lieutenants and captains. "Which made my position already precarious," he recalled. "But what fixed that for good, because our orders read 'no expense to government to be incurred,' it cost those officers something to get to the Presidio from their permanent stations, while I could walk there from Fort Scott."

---

*Not that he forgot the incident; years later, when contending with a land developer who stole government bulldozers ("cause my taxes pay for 'em," the thief argued), Frederick kept referring to him as "a son of a one eighty-fourer."

The result was, the others kept up a running joke about the "'rookie second loot'" getting a free ride.

"That I could do nothing about," recalled Frederick. "But, thinking maybe if I looked older they'd drop the 'rookie' angle, I started growing a moustache. And though it had no effect, as they were using rank to bolster their egos, I determined to never allow rank to blind me to the feelings, merits, and value of a man."

But it would be a soberer event that, the following summer, caused Frederick greater angst. Ruth's parents had come west to visit when, on arriving, Ruth's mother suffered a fatal stroke. Dr. Harloe had left immediately to arrange the funeral, and Ruth had then forlornly accompanied her mother's body to New York on a train and, upon her return to California, to console her father, she had gone east again. Now back with her husband once more, she hoped to repeat the trip in six months. Full of sympathy, and deeply in love with his wife, Frederick would not have denied her this. But, as he already felt the pinch of poverty, to pay for another round trip on his salary spelled financial calamity— and kept him awake nights with worry. So, it was certainly timely when about now the Army reassignment board decided come the first of October, Second Lieutenant Frederick should serve in the 62nd Coast Artillery regiment. The 62nd was based at Fort Totten, New York.

Historically, that October 1929 conjures up the crash on Wall Street— from where America wobbled into the Great Depression; yet for Frederick, the only vexation that month was his own professional unsettledness. Assigned to a battery of anti-aircraft guns at Fort Totten, he was spending long hours practicing defending the sky over New York City. He enjoyed the technical part of figuring wind speed and direction and air temperature (all effect speed of bullets), and with slide rules and firing charts, gauging the correct angle and aim of gun tubes. Not that the approach of enemy planes was a concern. It had been barely two years since Charles Lindbergh's famous flight across the Atlantic, and of the few aircraft that hove into view, most were Army Air Corps planes flying around to sell the public on the value of air power. But on these rare sightings, watching them, Frederick longed to be up there skimming along on that frontier of new technology.

Still, it took him all of October until—sparring mentally between enticements: Stay with artillery he knew and liked? Go to flight school?—he chose his course of action. He would be a pilot. At least, he assumed he would be.

The cottage on the outskirts of Brooks Field, Texas, was a ramshackle eyesore. Peeling paint and soiled wallpaper hung off the walls, and the kitchen was in great disrepair. But it was the best a married flying officer could afford. It had taken Frederick five months to get there. For, while he was waiting for an opening in flight school, he had been assigned to teach French at the West Point Preparatory School at Fort Totten; only to then get a message informing him he was being sent to Paris for a year as a military liaison to gain more skill in the language. To which he instantly had wired back: "This must be a mistake. I was approved for primary flight training, and not even remotely does that relate to if fluent or not in French."

Finally, reassigned, and not unnaturally expecting Ruth to stay with him in Texas, he was dealt two huge disappointments. For starters Ruth, saying she could not stand the derelict cottage, caught the next train back to New York.

The trouble was, Ruth Frederick had grown used to being pampered. Perhaps being a doted-on only child most of her life played a part, but mainly fostering it was all the attention danced upon her by many who found her quite fetching. Whereas Frederick, unexpectedly now facing this problem, could only resort to sending her a stream of letters. They are, however, a handy chronicle of his spare time, in that he wrote:

We couldn't fly today because of foul weather, so after ground instruction, I repaired the front steps, replaced the broken door hinges, and washed some windows. This evening I finished painting the walls.

He could hardly be having much fun, in another letter describing:

...got to San Antonio today and bought new kitchen fixtures, and am having a heck of a time installing them—which pretty much explains what I'll be doing all of tomorrow (Sunday).

Meanwhile, his colleagues, knowing he was married, good-naturedly kidded him about his "invisible" wife. "Where's she at today?" they kept asking the first week.

"Still in Brooklyn, seeing old school chums," replied Frederick.

"Now where'd she go?" they asked the next week.

"To Poughkeepsie, to stay with a relative," he said.

After this continued for three more weeks, suspecting his young marriage was on the rocks, some said as much; and Frederick was just about to entreat Ruth to shorten her visits, when now the Air Corps dealt him a blow. Most of his colleagues, in fact, were bowled over.

Up until then all had gone smoothly for the fledgling airmen. With only six hours of ground school they had begun to fly solo, and no accidents had occurred, despite their planes having few instruments and no brakes. When a wannabe pilot landed his plane, he had to put down far enough back on the grass field (paved runways nonexistent) to coast to a stop; and when disoriented in the air, his only beacon home was a hangar smack in the middle of the field. Frederick, finding the risks invigorating, had performed efficiently. But now, on a hot April day an instructor lined up his class in the shade, and commenced to call the names of those going on to advanced training. When he finished, there was stunned silence; an unprecedented 75 percent of the flying officers, Frederick included, were being washed out.

"It was the highest rate on record," wrote a later pilot. "A lot of capable airmen fell by the wayside in 1930 because the Army could not get adequate funds to build up, or even sustain, its air corps."*

Frederick was in a slough despair as, bracketed by disappointments, he awaited word of where to go. But, almost immediately after told to report for duty at Fort Barrancas, Florida, he heard from Ruth. She had

---

*Which at the time amounted to less than 11,000 officers and men.

telephoned to say that she was over two months pregnant, was losing her slim figure and yen to gad about, and would head to Florida straightaway. And six months later it was an elated and proud lieutenant who not only had his wife by his side, but a baby daughter, Jane. Meanwhile, the reassignment board had been gearing up to issue him new orders; the message that reached Frederick in January 1931 read: "Proceed to Fort Amador, Panama Canal Zone."

This is not the place to dwell on America's involvement in Panama, but because it influenced Frederick's growth as a soldier, it helps to know why the Army was there. When the U.S. declared war on Spain in 1898, it had then found it direly needed all three of its first class battleships in the Atlantic Ocean. But as one ship, the U.S.S. *Oregon*, was floating about the Pacific, months were wasted (and the war nearly over) before the *Oregon*, churning 13,000 miles around Cape Horn, reached the Atlantic. At which point thoughtful Americans asked the obvious—wasn't it time to build a canal to link the two oceans?

Such a Herculean venture had been already tried in Panama in 1881 by the French, who after seven years of cave-ins, and laborers dropping like flies from malaria and yellow fever, had run out of funding. By 1903 Panama (then a province of Columbia) had itched for independence, and in a bloodless revolt had declared itself a separate republic. But to survive it needed money. The stage had been set whereby, paying $10 million that guaranteed Panama's self rule, the U.S. got to construct and control a canal, as well as a ten by fifty mile zone around it for military installations to guard America's investment.

By the time Frederick arrived the canal, built with the know-how of the U.S. Army Corps of Engineers, had operated for sixteen years. Yet he was instantly greeted by disquieting tales about life among the palm trees. Fort Amador was a steamy outpost at the west end of the canal, and had no highway access, and as all goods came by boats, when storms delayed them "everyone goes without food and medicines," said fellow officers. Plus, from the nearby jungle there flowed into living quarters "deadly scorpions, hideous lizards, and monkeys prone to leap from roof edges and scare the wits out of anyone going out a door." And furthermore, they warned, the always lurking danger of boredom from garrison life was exacerbated by the "wet" season—up to seven months of rain.

· "For anecdotal proof," said Frederick, later, "the sky was spilling rain, when initially entering our quarters, I saw two scorpions on a wall. Ruth then checked out the kitchen, and tore out of there yelling because a good size lizard was lounging in the sink."

As for his job, he had been posted as personnel officer for the 4th Coast Artillery's railroad battery. The battery was armed with a behemoth 105 ton, sixty foot long gun which, mounted on a flat bed car, could be hauled on rails zigzagging through the jungle near the course of the canal. Not having worked with railway guns, he spent his first day asking, "...dumb questions, like, what keeps men from tripping over each other on the flat car and falling off? And no doubt the sergeant who was stuck with me was ruing his fate."

In early spring, his unit was ordered to move the gun across Panama, to conduct a live-fire drill on the east coast. With its convoy of men and equipment, the gun train was chugging up to the drill site when a tropical storm blew in: "...and for four days," recalled Frederick, "prevented laying curved track the gun car had to sit on during firing. But on day five we were set up, and we presumed, ready to fire."

As each projectile for the big gun weighed 1560 pounds, it took a crane run by a generator to hoist each shell onto a loading tray, where gunners could shove it into the gun tube. But on this particular day, the crane lifted its hefty cargo and stopped, dangling the huge shell in mid-air. Whereupon a not unusual reaction of alarm ensued—when in danger, when in doubt, run in circles, scream, and shout. Frederick, unsure the crane would sustain its grip, was himself yelling, "Stand back!" when he noticed:

"The corporals were aimlessly running around, the sergeant was engaged in a fulmination against all things mechanical, and my superior, Captain Somebody-or-other, who had earlier lost his shoes in a mudhole, was still sitting in a train car a ways off. Figuring I had to take over to restore discipline, I ordered some of the gunners to turn the hand cranks used in emergencies to gingerly lower the crane, and told the maintenance crew to check the generator and power cables. Just a cable leading to the crane was loose, and soon completing the drill, loading everything onto the train, we rode back through rain to Fort Amador."

One month later, having nearly forgotten that day, Frederick was amazed when the 4th's commander issued: "A commendation. The following to be commended for successful conclusion of the drill: 2nd Lt. R. T. Frederick, for his superior initiative, and for his conscientious and diligent attention."

Though pleased, of course, Frederick was greatly surprised. Yet he had acted decisively and with valuable steadiness in an emergency, plus shown he was adaptable; and shortly after he was made the S-3 of his battery, in plain English meaning that he was now in charge of plans and training.

He then got another surprise that spring. As neither the best nor worst about Fort Amador alleviated a lack of things to do, sending $9.00 to a New York bookstore Frederick requested "several military history books," to read on weekends. Arriving at his quarters one evening, he opened a carton from New York, and inside were twenty books, along with a note from the bookseller: "The extras are free. The subject isn't selling." It was an obvious reflection of the mood of Americans; but, on the one hand, made uncomfortable by this, on the other hand Frederick was not sorry he received such a fine collection. Trying Ruth's patience, he began to study the books nightly; "So in case of war again," he told another officer, "I will have a stronger grasp of past mistakes."

This officer, Brigadier General William Harris, was to later say, "If in Panama, Bob had had to pick to be social or a loner, he'd have been a loner. He was always studying, and besides teaching himself to reupholster a used chair he and Ruth acquired, had no other hobby. He hated golf, and when cajoled into playing bridge, didn't enjoy it. Oh sure, he partied, but unlike most young officers who did all the clubby pastimes of the old Army in hope of becoming indelible in the minds of their superiors, Bob wasn't interested."

Which caused more than a few officers to wager that Bob Frederick was destined for obscurity before he even rose to the rank of major's gold leaves. But precisely the opposite would happen.

In January 1933, Frederick was posted back to Fort Winfield Scott. By now, the country was gripped in the Depression, bringing as an offshoot inauguration the Civilian Conservation Corps. The CCC was a scheme the newly elected president, Franklin D. Roosevelt, had lifted when—during the term of his predecessor, Republican Herbert Hoover—congress had proposed "a chain of camps" run by the U.S. Army to feed, house, and train some four million unemployed youths. But as that idea had been hooted out of existence by Americans who called it "fascist," Roosevelt had revised it so the Departments of Interior and Agriculture would run the camps.

Fine and dandy; except neither Department had the experience or manpower. So again the obvious was to have the Army establish and administer hundreds of camps nationwide. Thus, in April 1933 a directive to supply personnel was sent to all Army Corps commanders, one of whom was Major General Malin Craig at the Presidio of San Francisco; and with that Frederick found himself headed for the Stanislaus National Forest, as commander of the 191st Company CCC.

"He led an advance party," recalls (then lieutenant) Armen Mardiros. "I had been ordered to Camp 82, and was met by a snappy looking second lieutenant named Frederick. He impressed me because he had such shiny boots and was impeccable in dress. He'd planned the layout of the camp to house one hundred sixty boys and, since military training wasn't allowed, he then had to spend two months shaping those boys up into a group that functioned."

His job there done, Frederick was sent further into the wilderness, to mountainous woods between Medford and Klamath Falls, Oregon. This time with three jobs; he was detailed to be the Finance Officer, Signal Officer, and Adjutant of that entire CCC district. Starting his day at 5:00 AM and finishing past midnight, as Finance Officer he wrote reams of checks to government agencies, "for everything from coal to pickles, and in the process got a lot of writer's cramps. But more tedious," he remembered, ruefully, "was being Signal Officer."

For though he had been told to set up a communication network to link all the camps in Oregon, "to begin with, the plan mandated crews of soldiers install telephone poles in the woods to hold phone lines. But someone down at the Presidio of San Francisco kept failing to execute an order to send the crews north, and instead, I had to keep making numerous trips over the mountains to each camp to retrieve and deliver messages." Moreover, every U.S. Army car and truck had been already requisitioned, leaving him with one mode of travel—a horse.

Which resulted in an unfortunate mishap, as we shall see.

Yet it was "as Adjutant," said a co-worker later, "that Frederick had the most tremendous burdens. He had to constantly have his finger on the pulse of supplies, contracts, and health and sanitation, and he had to interpret the tons of regulations that spewed out of 'New Deal' Washington. The district commander made some of the big decisions, but it was Frederick who ran the district."

All the while squeezing in his "numerous trips" to each camp.

One day, carrying a bundle of messages, he rode out from Medford with his sergeant toward a camp twenty miles east. Halfway there, having paused to water their horses, as the sergeant stood by his mount, the beast bit off half of his left ear. Frederick used his own shirt to bind the wound, and elected they try a shortcut back to Medford for medical aid. Riding at a gallop, they were plunging through a forest when Frederick's horse, displaying no will to trailblaze, stopped, and with a titanic buck sent the bare chested lieutenant flying headlong into a clump of blackberry bushes.

Extricating himself from the thorny web, with hundreds of prickers in his face, hands, arms, and torso, he climbed back on his recalcitrant horse, wincing each time he blinked as the thorns in his eyelids dug in deeper. And by all accounts, it was a sorry sight when late that night, the horses plodded into Medford with their woebegone passengers. The sergeant, alas, faced permanent damage. But of no less note, it took Frederick and a medical orderly, working in unison non-stop, twenty-four hours to tweeze all the thorns from Frederick's skin.

It was not until December 1933 that Frederick returned to Fort Scott, and to a joyful reunion with his small family. Upon departing from Oregon he had assumed that, for his colleagues there, the lasting impression of him would be as the only man to get hurled off a horse. Yet had they been asked, "What will you remember Frederick for?," their answer would have been, "Rare organizational skills." For the fellow who replaced him was so overwhelmed by his multiple duties it required two additional officers be sent north to help fill Frederick's shoes.

Receiving several swell commendations for his work with the CCC, Frederick was lauded for his "energy ... intelligence ... initiative," his "ability to keep smiling when everything went wrong" and "sense of humor": the latter, however, fading fast, as now he learned he was the object of high echelon wrath. At IX Corps headquarters in the Presidio of San Francisco, General Craig had inquired into his past performance and was demanding the lieutenant serve as Assistant Adjutant General of IX Corps Area CCC—though Frederick already was posted as Property Officer for the 6th Coast Artillery at Fort Scott. The first clue of his dilemma came when Craig telephoned the 6th's commander and fumingly asked why Frederick had failed to appear at Corps Headquarters. And not put off by the explanation that he had been assigned elsewhere, Craig now had fired off a wire. ARRANGEMENTS HAVE BEEN MADE FOR LT. FREDERICK TO GIVE A REASONABLE AMOUNT OF TIME TO HIS OTHER DUTIES BY COMMAND OF MAJOR GENERAL MALIN CRAIG.

Given that these "arrangements" simply allowed Frederick until 2:00 PM daily to report in as Assistant Adjutant General, for one and a half years, beavering away day and night, he held both positions. Later he called this "inconsequential." But he must have known it was noteworthy—especially when whoever canvassed officers' records, to find those deserving recognition, proved it so in 1938. In the meantime he had two consolations. He was promoted July 1934 to first lieutenant, and the following February became a proud father of a second daughter, Anne. His two years of juggling varied duties in Oregon and California were benchmarks in shaping him as an administrator and manager of men, only to have his next posting make no use of this.

For, despite that Frederick now had orders to attend the Coast Artillery School at Fort Monroe, Virgnia, IX Corps' coast artillery commander, a General Sherwood Cheney, demanded that he, instead, serve as the General's aide. Cheney persisted, won out and, for the next two years, adamantly refused to release his aide when asked, first by the War Department, then by the Chief of Engineers.* Thus, drifting along with his fate, having moved with the general from Fort Scott to the Army Base in Boston, Frederick had begun counting the days on his calendar until, in August 1937, Cheney was forced to retire at age sixty-four.

Hoping now, however, to get to soldier with troops, Frederick was dismayed to be again ordered to the Coast Artillerymen's school. Yet it turned out to be one of his most enjoyable postings, in part due to the fact Ruth was enthralled by historic Fort Monroe, and ecstatic her husband had regular workday hours. And, whether frolicking with their daughters on the beach at Monroe, taking car rides to explore Virginia, or gathering friends for an evening in their small quarters, the Fredericks were a picture of happiness.

"I distinctly recall," said a neighbor of theirs later, "everyone considered them the 'ideal military couple,' as both Bob and Ruth were sophisticated, extremely attractive, and loads of fun to be around."

As a student Frederick was no slouch, either. Finishing the school year on June 8, 1938, with ratings of "superior" in all his classes, he had been rated overall "Of highest value...Suitable for training for high command." Then one day later he was promoted to captain.

Before him glowed a breather from worrying over money, what with a slight raise in pay. When the Depression had hit, military salaries had been cut 15 percent, and while in Oregon—his bank balance sinking to nine cents—he'd had to cancel his life insurance and sell all his military history books. But more important, his future looked brighter careerwise, too. For though it was not unusual in the '30s that a first lieutenant wait fourteen or more years to move up to captain, he had done it in four years, and was still marveling at his triumph when informed he was now being sent to the Command and General Staff School at Fort Leavenworth.

"It can't get any better," he told himself deservedly; as not only was it an honor to get chosen to be a student there, he was the first from his West Point class to attend the elite school. Which, according to one West Point classmate, Paul D. Adams:

*With increasing technology in airplanes, Frederick—figuring that coastal artillery was soon headed for extinction—had applied to transfer to the Corps of Engineers.

"Maybe surprised a few from the Academy, but caused outright consternation among older Coast Artillery captains, majors, and lieutenant colonels who, senior to Frederick, aspired to get that choice assignment."

"Choice," but draconian. Students, themselves, were constantly studied by the staff. Did they get along with others? Display leadership? The intent was to assess and prepare them to command divisions or work in critical headquarters in time of war. Using examples from history to plan hypothetical battles, they had to maneuver and supply imagined warriors to prove, in the yearlong test of their proficiency, that they could follow the accepted method for waging war. But early on Frederick missed a week of study. Sitting in class one morning he was summoned outside, and told his father had died of heart failure. Dr. Frederick had quit practicing medicine three years before, and retired to a 250 acre walnut ranch he had bought in Brentwood, California; and it was to there Frederick rushed to assist his mother, only to find she was serenely overseeing the harvest of tons of walnuts she planned to sell. With the same pioneering spirit that had led Mrs. Frederick, Sr., to set out on her own as a teenager, she was determined to manage the ranch alone. It was her son who was disconsolate.

All his adult life, Frederick had hoped to someday hear his father approved of him. Though the emotional bonds between them had been brittle, robbed now of even this hope, he felt shortchanged; and yet for the better, enlightened, upon his return to school. In the past, never sure if his motive to do well professionally was simply to win his father over, it was now crystal clear to him he was just being true to his character. He did splendidly. And just once was to be disappointed the remainder of his stay at Fort Leavenworth.

It had to do with the one big social event for students, the commandant's reception—the last week of school. The required uniform was dress blues, and Frederick, dropping his uniform off at the cleaners, had asked Ruth to pick it up the day of the party, while he worked with schoolmates on a project. Late that afternoon he bounded up the stairs to his apartment and, swinging open the door, called out, "I'll be ready in half an hour."

"For what?" Ruth Frederick asked, perplexed. She had forgotten about the party, and worse, forgotten to retrieve his uniform from the cleaners, which by then was closed.

"That was the first time Bob got mad at me," she later remarked. "After sharing a year of intense study with his classmates, while they were celebrating their imminent transition into graduates, Bob sat at home twiddling his thumbs."

But at least at long last he was given leave, and two whole months of it. In September he was to report—his orders designated—to the 64th Coast Artillery at Fort Shafter, Hawaii, to assume command of an anti-aircraft battery. So, leisurely driving westward, the Captain and his family visited Yellowstone Park, Salt Lake City, and his mother's walnut ranch prior to boarding a military transport at San Francisco. That evening, the ship's loudspeakers blared out the news early that morning, German time, Adolf Hitler had invaded Poland.

The fuse of a world war had been lit, as France and England were committed to come to Poland's aid. The date was September 1, 1939.

One note of interest: exactly one year before, when the Fredericks were heading to Fort Leavenworth from Fort Monroe, they had spent two days at a cabin by the Greenbrier River, in West Virginia, where they had found an abandoned, malnourished puppy. Ruth had hoped to nurse it back to health, and was watching the pooch when it tumbled down the river's bank. Alerting her husband, he ran after it and tried soothing the pup as it died from distemper. Then, laying the dog in a small box, for an hour after he sat beside it, tears running down his cheeks. While he never spoke of this, Mrs. Frederick later did: "That was part of Bob's nature few people knew about, but always close to the surface of his emotions was an excruciatingly acute sensitivity to suffering."

What seems, then, a mystery is: How did Frederick keep his balance when later surrounded by, and a player in, the absolute horrors of war?

4

"Bunch of Ostriches"

For the moment, Bob Frederick was not so much worried that Japan was swinging its martial sword around Asia, but that he seemed to have just sailed in the wrong direction. Yet few Americans were spoiling to fight the Nazi tide, and on 5 September, with vote getting speed the U.S. administration declared America's neutrality in Europe's war. But with Germany hogging the headlines, it was now easy to ignore Japan's expansionist rampage; that—nabbing China's major ports the past year, then attacking Russian troops on Mongolia's border—Japan wanted dominant economic power in east Asia. Besides, President Roosevelt recently had announced U.S. intentions to withdraw from a commerce treaty with the Japanese, to cut supplies of fuel and metal needed to equip their military. So much for Japan's war machine: doomed—the Asian bully was, wasn't it?—by the U.S. treaty ban.

Such was the general thinking when the Fredericks disembarked at Oahu with a swarm of shipmates, all dog weary from days of rough sea. Save for one young lady who, carrying a huge box of Kotex, flounced by Ruth Frederick and hissed "It's too primitive here to get these things." Staring inland, and desperate to confirm Hawaii's reputation as the best duty station, Ruth refused to budge, until swayed by her husband's uneducated guess, "There are no inconveniences here."

True, as they reached Fort Shafter it looked idyllic; around a sun bathed parade ground sat officers' quarters that were breezy bungalows shaded by hibiscus trees. But no inconveniences?

"Hah!" later exclaimed Ruth Frederick. "Those bungalows had been inhabited by cockroaches and termites as long as by man, and to keep them from overrunning the place you had to mop, scour, and sweep three times a day."

Yet Fort Shafter was the heartbeat of the U.S. Army in Hawaii, and beyond the rim of a deep gully stood Hawaiian Department Headquarters. Across the gully were offices of the 64th Coast Artillery where, after a day, Frederick reported in to his boss, Colonel "CK" Wing. Wing, a man with a sour visage, had, in addition, a streak of timidity that Frederick later unhesitatingly would chastise him for. But what he was interested in now was to find his unit, which Wing explained was "rehearsing its wartime placements on a bluff overlooking Pearl Harbor."

Frederick drove to where at a distance he saw rows of .50 caliber anti-aircraft guns pointing skyward. And, on foot crossing the bluff, each half dozen yards closer to his unit he grew more discouraged. He had expected his battery's guns to be World War I vintage, but not, he estimated through the glare of the sun, over half to be wooden dummies mounted on tripods to resemble the real thing. It was a sorry sign of Army shortages. Introducing himself to a crew of gunners, and wanting to get a handle on their states of mind, he asked, "Do you like your jobs? Any complaints?"

"Yes, sir," proffered one soldier. "Our ammunition is getting so old, a lot of it probably won't detonate if it hits something."

"So what?" quipped his buddy. "What guns we got are so old, even when they don't jam, we couldn't shoot down a damn thing 'less it's flying awful low and slow."

Frederick nodded, fully distracted by the troubling thought, Good Lord, let's hope we never have to defend this island.

Now that he commanded a battery, his job was to balance training and maintenance while, by his leadership, motivate men to perform well in any circumstance. For this Frederick had one advantage; he had been an enlisted man, and was keenly aware that without a weapon he respects a soldier is hard put to believe his value—unless given another reason.

"Right away, Captain Frederick," related one of his gunners later, "improved our training greatly by increasing the tempo, stimulating our interest in what we were doing. He did it with gentle understanding, a firm application of discipline, and setting high standards for himself required the same of all, whipping up in us a feeling we were mentally and physically top notch."

Night and day at unpopulated beaches the air was ripped by the rat-tat-tat of Frederick's battery firing blanks at targets. Then, his men hot, dusty, and exhausted, he drilled them on racing to and back from battle positions. Overtly seeming to enjoy command, he was unsparingly, however, testing his ability to lead others; or so he thought. It took fellow officers to point out he had "an intuitive flair," said one, "for getting the best from men," as they watched his battery build quickly into a proud— and weapons notwithstanding—punitive force.

The year 1940 began ominously. In January, German U-boats sunk seventy-three allied ships: in February, Japan fashioned a budget over half of which was for military buildup. But no far off event elicited so much anger in Army personnel on Oahu as did wealthy American tourists who, arriving to board Japanese ships for cruises to the Orient, were told "by aloof Jap sailors" they must bow to the Rising Sun flag. Insensible to Japanese etiquette that *everyone* show respect for the Emperor by acknowledging the flag, the offended tourists were hounding U.S. officers to speak out against the act. But wasting no sympathy, the officers coolly responded they too were governed by rules of etiquette, some equally annoying. And while left unsaid, topping the list was having to make formal calls on senior ranks twenty-four hours after reporting to a new post. On Oahu, this irreverently was called "Oriental torture."

"The required attire was a tropical tuxedo," recalled a former lieutenant. "But as few of us owned such a thing, it meant scrounging up a cummerbund, cuff links, shirt, tie, and money to buy a jacket and pants at the Liberty House. Personally, I was terrified to enter the commander's quarters, and as he made no effort to relieve my tension, when the legal fifteen minutes expired I dashed outside. My next visits were not as bad, but the bright spot was my last duty call to the quarters of Captain Frederick. He put me at ease, offered me something to drink, and chatted with me well beyond fifteen minutes. I have always considered he was someone special—very thoughtful, and urbane."

Also, colleagues of Frederick were heard muttering at times, "Damn sure of himself." For either as witness or victim, they all had observed Frederick exhibit unlicensed wry humor.

"Oh, it was pure rascality!" later commented a Colonel Diestal. "I commanded another battery and saw it often. I particularly remember headquarters often sent us bulletins requesting we report all plumbers, electricians, or carpenters in our batteries, depending on what job needed doing. But I kept noticing Frederick never claimed to have a workman of any sort in the more than two hundred men he commanded."

Yet, not until several months passed did Diestal at one point say, "Bob, you're not playing fair. You never volunteer anyone from your battery."

"Well, heck," Frederick answered. "I read those bulletins, you don't."

"I do too!" Diestal retorted.

"Then get out the last one and read it again," replied Frederick; so Diestal did: "Battery commanders to report all carpenters in their batteries. Negative reports to be submitted."

"See?" said Frederick, grinning, "I am just doing what someone stupidly keeps telling me to do, submit negative reports."

And one day, Diestal would remember thinking, Bob will get a purpled dressing down by the brass. "Because in the Army," he was to later say, "a shrewd mind was not appreciated."

Which Frederick painfully, within a year, would learn; the U.S. Army, meanwhile, strained by definitely more serious mischief.

In mid-May 1940, prodded by the Army's recently named Chief of Staff, George C. Marshall, Roosevelt asked the U.S. Congress for $900 million for military rearmament. But no sooner done then a Roosevelt scheme was exposed. In response to pleas from British Prime Minster Winston Churchill to help England fight the Nazis, Roosevelt planned to subvert U.S. Neutrality Laws by "selling" old army weapons to steel factories that would "resell" them to England. Was the same wily deal, worried top Army leaders, the future of longed-for-soon-to-be produced new aircraft and weapons?

Only a month before, the U.S. Pacific Fleet had glided into Pearl Harbor for a temporary stay—but with a quick change of mind the Navy Department decided the fleet remain there, to deter Japan's aggression. Then the War Department got a bee in its helmet that because Japan now had a puppet government in China and had quit fighting Russia, it was no longer preoccupied and *might* raid Hawaii. On that basis, the U.S. Army on Oahu was ordered on immediate alert to protect the fleet and islands— with its seventy-six crotchety old coastal guns, thirty-six obsolete pursuit planes (half usually under repair), aged machine guns, and ammunition so old much of it failed to detonate, and fell to earth with a thud.

But like most of his peers, Frederick felt that, even if a false alarm, the alert was a superb exercise. Sprinting to field positions, with nothing thundering into view, his troops had time to rework radio nets and underground phone routes to Pearl Harbor. Then, too much time as the alert dragged on through summer, and stuck at battle positions, soldiers grew bored.

"To ease the monotony," later said Frederick, "I had some men recheck phone and radio nets, dust off tripods, had the gunners keep ringing alternative ranges on maps and, twice a day, made everyone do strenuous calisthenics and shave." Almost as a self-deprecating afterthought he added, "At least I had the best groomed bunch of adversaries an enemy could have met."

In the meantime Coast Artillery chiefs noted his resourcefulness and when, at the end of summer, the alert dissipated like a croak of ballyhoo gone hoarse, Frederick was no longer with his battery. He had been chosen over a number of older captains to be Assistant Plans and Training Officer for the 64th, and in two months, in December, was bucked up to Director of Plans and Training.*

---

*It was the same job George C. Patton, when in his forties, had held at Schofield Barracks on Oahu; but unlike the flamboyant Patton, who had been relieved in three months for being "too abrasive, overeager, and savage," Frederick would be remembered for "his great sense of decency."

But though it scotched what he would have preferred—to again lead a field unit—assuaging this, he was now a peg closer to those higher up. He had a batch of ideas for defending Hawaii that he had methodically jotted down. On these occasions, he took his family to the shore where, bent over a pad of paper, he wrote out his thoughts on defense needs, and how Japan viewed Hawaii. Ruth Frederick would beg him to join the family in the surf, or to play bridge with friends on a beachmat.

"You killjoy!" she once fumed, in chorus with a friend, who from a mat nearby chidingly asked, "Chrissake, Bob, aren't you ever off duty?"

"Sure," Frederick said, "But I feel like someone whose relative has a terminal illness. There is little I can do about it, but I can't stop thinking about it." Whereupon he returned to his project, and Ruth, gnashing her teeth, played a three handed game of bridge.

Deep in thought, Frederick was unaware at the beach that he made a dashing figure. Trim, with a tan setting off his dapper mustache and dark hair, if envied by some men he was noticeably admired by their wives. He was no dolt at parties either, where he "danced like a dream," one woman recalled. At a Halloween dance in the Officers' Club that year he appeared as the scarecrow from the Wizard of Oz, and for days after the female grapevine had buzzed with flattery for him. He had won first prize for his costume, and with straw jutting out of his hat, shirt, and pants, at others' behest he had done a hilarious pantomime of a scarecrow trying to do the Charleston.

But dull he could be. And mulishly engrossed in work off duty. Even so, unlike some officers who, assuming self-importance, hustled for recognition, Frederick used his mental percipience for his own enjoyment; and not once in his life would utter a word of self-sell. Which, ironically, is what worked in his favor.

On February 4, 1941, Frederick got word that he was promoted to major. He was thirty-three years old, had been an officer twelve years, and a captain just two—in an institution where one languished decades at one rank. Clearly somebody in Washington was reading his efficiency ratings; at every posting his commander had written he was "thorough," "trustworthy," "[his] present and future value of highest order." Then, within days, a new Hawaiian Department commander, Lieutenant General

Walter C. Short, arrived, and because Short's career was top heavy with training assignments, as Frederick stood on the parade ground watching the General accept the commandant's flag, he held the thought Short would soon improve defense readiness—and that his own ideas fit that concept.

Indeed Short, instantly requesting "joint" Army-Navy meetings, one of which Frederick was told to attend, had immediately realized the need for interservice cooperation regarding defense. For while the U.S. had rung in 1941 with hopes of peace, it had been over the din of Japan banging a loud war drum. Japanese troops now occupied French Indochina, and Japan had signed an alliance with Germany and Italy. The big question was: Would it next try to nab the U.S. commonwealth, the Philippines?

In Washington the Army's Chief of Staff, General Marshall, did not believe Japan would "attack fortified Hawaii," although a plethora of facts suggested otherwise. From Japan's consulate on Oahu, spies were spewing out to photograph Army equipment, and track comings and goings of Naval ships; plus, a Japanese code had been broken, and from it was discovered that Tokyo had requested its spies report all U.S. military activity in Hawaii. Meanwhile, in preparation for the "joint" Army-Navy committee meeting, Frederick had begun typing up his report. Dated 24 February, he presented it that day, in his opening remarks adding a stinging critique at the last minute.

"This committee has made no recommendations that solve the problems—that coordination of Army and Navy anti-aircraft artillery is impossible due to absence of communication between Navy ships and Army units—that recognition of enemy aircraft can't be done by prescribed visual procedures...[it] requires supplementary devices on planes and on the ground. And this committee has expressed itself against use of barrage balloons because air officers object to their use, but your concerns should be the broad problem—the defense of Oahu—and not confined to lesser problems."

Frederick saw the committee chairman, a Colonel Picket, stonily glaring at him. But on he went, to now read his report.

"While no anti-aircraft protection is provided for Kenohoe Naval Air Station, or Ammunition Station, protection of other vital areas varies from wholly inadequate to barely reasonable. This committee must recommend the War Department furnish troops and equipment without delay, as reenforcement will be impossible when most needed, [for]with the trend of recent years, there will be no formal declaration of war prior to opening hostilities."*

At this point, Bob Frederick's report became an exceptional piece of work:

"If Japan," he continued, "engages in war with the United States, her most lucrative target will be the ships of the U.S. Navy. It is probable the initial attack will be a surprise air raid—the ships at Pearl Harbor, and the airdromes on Oahu the objectives. A hostile raiding force including aircraft carriers can remain out of sign of Navy patrol planes, then steam toward Oahu during the night, releasing its planes about daylight for the attack...a dive bombing attack, with a torpedo bombing attack." (As exactly was to occur.)

A wall clock loudly marked time as Frederick, pausing, took in a deep breath, to then launch his blueprint for defense:

"When lacking positive information enemy forces will not attack within twenty-four hours..."; and for ten minutes he outlined his agenda of defense measures, among them:

- No ships to be in Pearl Harbor; ships to pull out to refuel and to take on stores and ammunition by use of barges.
- All antiaircraft batteries and air corps antiaircraft weapons to be at war position with one day of fire, and at readiness "2" (five minutes), except from one hour before daylight until one hour after, at which time they be at readiness "1" (ready fire).**

---

*Although General Marshall had stated bomber planes would be dispatched from the mainland in event of war, they would, of course, take up to 10 hours to reach the Hawaiian Islands; and Marshall had no plans for how, if ever, troops and arms would arrive.
**Unduly fearing sabotage, General Short was refusing to issue live ammunition, insisting it remain locked in storage; and on the "day of infamy," not one antiaircraft battery had bullets to fire at the enemy.

- All aircraft on the ground, except fighter planes ready to take to the air, to be dispersed to the maximum limit.*
- Navy patrol planes, supplemented by Army reconnaissance if necessary, to search the sky to the maximum limit consistent with long range operations.**
- Barrage balloons in sufficient numbers to protect Pearl Harbor should be obtained to, if necessary, supplement defense.***

Frederick ended his report with, "Does anyone here know when a Coast Artillery radar set is coming?"

Feet shifted. But save for the clock madly ticking away there was heavy silence until, finally, as chairman, empowering himself to unify the committee, Colonel Picket said, laconically, "Major, we're not impressed with your ideas."

Frederick felt like he had been punched. Abruptly leaving the room in disciplined disgust, afterward he was troubled that by departing he fluffed a chance to pry loose at least one supportive voice. "But I was darned if I would give up," he later said, and so on the thin hope of being taken seriously, he mailed his report to the War Department, "directing it to the War Plans Division."

But as yet, few who filled high official boots recognized that the U.S. Fleet at Pearl Harbor was not deterring aggression, but was baiting Japan. One good swipe at the congested ships, and the tiny nation would feel safer prowling the ocean on its expansionist quest. Frederick had also discerned that hobbling the thinking of many was the mindset war would be declared before an attack. He had no access, of course, to top official communications or scenarios of war being thwacked out in Tokyo and Washington, but pragmatic he was, and—sometime later—tagged a "ruthless analyzer."

*Instead, airplanes were kept parked wing tip to wing tip, making a plum of a target, as Japanese fighters swooped down and easily pinned them to the ground.
**Neither occurred: Short never did offer assistance, and the Navy commander never did institute long range patrol.
***Up to the final moment of attack, Japan's warriors fretted these bloated obstacles would be tethered over Pearl Harbor and greatly hinder bombing U.S. warships. None, though, were ever obtained.

Yet he would never be credited for his prophetic report. For instance, the most famous document on defense needs and likely attack on Hawaii was produced by the Hawaiian Air commander Major General Frederick Martin, and Naval Air commander Rear Admiral Patrick Bellinger and their staffs. Strongly resembling Frederick's report, the well-known Martin-Bellinger paper was written one month after Frederick presented his report (and while uncoincidentally, many months after the "killjoy" at the beach had homed in on the magnet effect the fleet would have on Japan).

All the same, in Washington, General Marshall clung to his bias Hawaii "is so well fortified, the Japs won't dare to attack." Among those in the War Department frustrated by this was forty-three year old Major (later General) Albert C. Wedemeyer.

"I know Marshall read Frederick's paper," Wedemeyer would recall later, "because daily I reported to Marshall, and had opportunities to exchange views. He brought up the subject, said he was not particularly taken with it, but I told him I was."

As did, more intently, one of the Army's top intelligence men, Colonel Rufus Bratton. An expert on Japan's militarism, Bratton swooped into the chief's office to urge him to see the viability in Frederick's paper. But Marshall fobbed him off. Thus, Frederick's report was slipped into an obscure file—and much too late, hindsightedly retrieved.

But to Mrs. Frederick, her husband's warnings merited being in a tailspin.

"Bob looked ashen when he arrived home from that committee meeting," she remembered. "But when I asked if he was ill, he said no, he just didn't have the clout to influence preparations for what was inevitable—that Japan would sink our ships, and bomb our planes so they couldn't retaliate. I asked him, 'How do you know?'

He told me militarists controlled Japan, but posing as forecasters in Hawaii and Washington were 'a bunch of ostriches with their heads in the sand.' Which scared me, and that night, pacing the floor, half the time crying, half the time venting anger at being deemed expendable, I got so worked up I could have had us packed and off the island in an hour."

Instead Ruth volunteered as an airplane spotter. Using a pamphlet that had pictures of Japanese aircraft, she sat on the parade ground most mornings, scanning the sky through binoculars, and flipping pages of the pamphlet when a plane came into view. Though futile as a means of defense, Frederick interrupted her only once, to say he was taking their youngest daughter on a walk: he left unsaid that his motive was to find a site suitable for building air raid shelters for dependents. His daughter later wrote:

"We had wandered through tall grass and bush in back of Fort Shafter when Dad spotted a low hill. Telling me to stay put, he was walking toward it when he hollered, 'Holy Moses! Don't move!,' and with his arms pumping the air he raced off away from me. Right behind him were two wild boar, their tails rigid with anger as they chased him until all I could see of this running, leaping figure was an occasional blur of his shirt as he sped through a clearing. Eventually he returned and said, 'Now two men are running fast.' I was more interested in the animals and asked what they were. 'Wild boar,' he said, 'and when defending their territory, they are not only mean, but smart.' I thought that was the end of the story, but then he added, 'and it wouldn't take much to convince me man is the dumbest animal.'"

There is no evidence Frederick again sought a shelter area for dependents, or that one was even contemplated by those able to enforce it. But by spring 1941, war clouds were closing in on the U.S. For now, on top of Nazi armies stampeding through Europe, Roosevelt had embargoed iron and steel to the Japanese who, feeling the pinch, were hopping mad at America. In a collective frenzy, every U.S. military base had begun feverishly readying to receive recruits, National Guard, and Reserve troops. But not so roused were government attempts to fill out the scintilla of equipment; not one new antiaircraft gun had arrived in Hawaii. True, Frederick felt better when a radar set for the 64th Coast Artillery showed up and was positioned on a hill to scan out in a wide arc. But the set was so novel, and its operators novices, that weeks passed before it was discovered that all it was picking up were cars driving around Oahu.

But now, laboring to bring the Army in Hawaii up to war standards, General Short had requested the 64th write "upwarding" plans. That was

Frederick's job, and in the 64th's plotting room he burned the midnight candle as he rewrote every stereotyped plan for artillery batteries so it included all accouterments needed for defense. Although up to his superior, Colonel Wing, to present the plan to Short, Wing requested the young major accompany him, and as they started off Frederick was heard telling Wing, "When we get there keep your mouth shut and I'll do the talking. The way you pussyfoot around we won't get anything." Wing nodded compliantly.

"Not long before, he had reneged on organizing a drill," recalled Colonel Diestal, "and that time I heard Bob tell him, 'Damn it, Colonel, when will you learn to take charge of things!' That Frederick got away with such insolence had to be due to Wing appreciating his professional integrity. And while Frederick had no patience for timidity or stupidity, he was not impatient with ignorance, which has room to absorb teachings."

However, whether Short would act on the "upwarding" plans was dicey; he could only, he candidly told the two coast artillerymen, "do so much."* Frederick hardly felt buoyed up, but commented to Wing as they departed, "At least Short was honest." And, as if by divine intervention, Frederick would be spared seeing the eventual debacle. For no sooner had he returned to the plotting room when he was summoned instantly to Wing's office. There waiting for him were orders to Washington D.C.

In the workings of the War Department, which now was clamoring to expand its staff of bright young officers, his name had popped up. "Major Robert T. Frederick," his orders relayed, "is to report for duty September 3, 1941, as a member of the War Plans Division." He reread the message, this time savoring that after the chastening snub by the "joint" committee, he now felt atoned.

Ruth Frederick rushed aboard the military transport headed for the mainland, like many another anxious to leave the tropical playground. Expressing relief quietly, as if too much joy might bring attention to the unarmed grey vessel plying dips and swells—and make it a target for a wanton Jap bomber—passengers subduedly played bridge, soothed fretful

*To his credit Short soon begged the War Department for more guns and equipment and men for the Coast Artillery, though it was to no avail.

children, and after two days out, dug through steamer trunks for warm clothing, as unseasonable cold air gusted across the sea lane. Frederick stood alone at the rail for hours.

"He only looks absentminded," Ruth felt a need to explain to a shipmate, "but really he's visualizing the worst of futures, and right now feels useless."

Before departing, on the pier he had told his friend Diestal that at the War Department he intended to illuminate how "a myopic mentality of some on Oahu obstructs defensive planning." He felt optimistic that whoever influenced decisions in the Chief of Staff's office would then react constructively, and heading up the gangplank, as a parting shot to Diestal he called out, "Boy, I sure hope they come twist the tails of the jackasses out here."

5

"Mission...Suicide"

No tails were twisted. As would be clear in three months, those in top positions in Washington, failing to heed warnings, did not feel uneasy enough about Hawaii to ensure it was on guard.

So far as Frederick was concerned, he had reported to the War Department in the Munitions Building on Constitution Avenue to find a mound of projects on his desk in War Plans offices. And a week passed, "...before I spoke to several members in the Chief of Staff's complex and, pulling no punches, graphically described weaknesses in command and defense on Oahu, and how the status quo begged disaster. Then I had to focus on tasks piling up on my desk, all of which dealt with Hitlerism in Europe."

For while the War Department had concentrated for years on strategies of war against a foreseen enemy, Japan, that had changed when Germany successfully seized Denmark and Norway in 1940, stomped into France, gravely threatened Great Britain, and invaded Russia in June 1941. It had necessitated adopting a "Germany first" policy, and on this huge sphere of operations Frederick and his co-workers ground out contingency plans. With his typical introspection Frederick assimilated hundreds of facts—production of war materials, climate, geography, anything to do with war—before coming to a decision.

"He made an excellent impression on all of us...sound judgment, an inspiring leader," said General Al Wedemeyer later. But meanwhile, if Frederick felt a particular misgiving, it must have been that with the mushrooming of events in Europe, it spelled even less of a chance of Hawaii being adequately prepared.

It was just past dawn, 7 December in Washington, when in the Fredericks' rented house at 33rd and Oliver Streets, Frederick headed into the basement. Halfway round the world, Japanese carriers were sneaking over the dark Pacific Ocean as he began sawing wood to make shelving for storage; and stopping for lunch in the early afternoon, he was upstairs when the phone rang. He listened to the caller and, replying "What time did it happen? - Thank you," his body sagged as he dropped into a chair "and asked me," remembered Ruth Frederick, "to turn on the radio." As sketchy reports came over the air Frederick was silent, digesting, he was to say, "the enormity of the truth, that Japan had achieved a total tactical surprise."

There was no sense of his going anywhere; a call he was needed at the War Department would come soon enough. Later Frederick wished he had napped while waiting, for when the call did come it was the start of a grueling sixty-two hours straight of desk work. In the meantime, he had unpacked his uniforms. Customarily, to keep a low profile, the staff in the Munitions Building wore civilian suits. But now America was at war.

As shock and fury swept through the U.S., so did dark suspicions about Pearl Harbor. Had Roosevelt goaded the Japanese with his embargoes and when, just that summer, he initiated a boycott against Japan? How derelict were U.S. commanders in Hawaii? Later every aspect of 7 December would undergo fervent scrutiny, yet questions still linger. Hadn't shortages of men and munitions plagued the effectiveness of defense on Oahu? Why weren't commanders there told the contents of a Japanese message decoded in Washington that signaled the fleet at Pearl Harbor was marked for an attack? And how could they have been on full alert 7 December when, in late November, General Marshall and his naval counterpart sent them a "war warning" dispatch, but instructed they do nothing "to alarm civilian population or disclose intent?" A pall of guilt lay over Marshall's head; he had failed to ensure he had an able commander in Hawaii; and 7 December at 10:30 AM Washington time, shown a Japanese missive that war was imminent and urged to instantly telephone General Short in Oahu, Marshall had chosen to write out a note to Short to be sent by teletype—which was delayed.

In twenty-four hours the United States had declared war on Japan; then, on 11 December, Germany and Italy declared war on the U.S. In a crisis atmosphere, Frederick and his colleagues in the War Plans section faced the grim need to plan for global conflict. Each day decisions had to be made about troop dispersal, weapons supply, and establishing bases; and "working eighteen hour days, we were fatigued, worried, and on occasion," Frederick later said, "somebody would lose his temper, rupturing everyone's concentration."

No one, however, was to quite match the hotheadedness of the new Deputy Chief of War Plans soon to arrive, to replace the former deputy, who was assigned a field command. Brought in to take over the job was fifty-two year old Brigadier General Dwight D. Eisenhower. Who had, as Frederick quickly would learn, "a very short fuse."

At this stage, flowing into the War Plans offices were suggestions from inspired citizens on how to wage war. Some were thought provoking, some goofy, and it was one of the latter Frederick read one morning. It was from a well known politician; he had proposed the Army use animals to lessen the human toll in combat; that by strapping explosives onto horses, dogs, and camels, and sending them charging off into enemy emplacements, they could then be detonated from a distance. In addition, the politician theorized, the enemy would waste bullets trying to bring the animals down.

It struck Frederick funny. He was chuckling when Eisenhower walked up to his desk, "and asked what had made me laugh. And, looking down at me regally as I told him, he stormed out. He had a demanding attitude, and was," Frederick recalled thinking, "absolutely humorless."

Nevertheless, overlooking these traits, Frederick grew to highly respect Eisenhower's abilities. And the feeling would certainly be mutual, as will be seen.

Again, Frederick was promoted in an amazingly short span of time when, on 9 February 1942, at age thirty-four, lieutenant colonel's gold oak leaves had been pinned on his shirt. It was now early spring, and while Americans looked to the military to rapidly stop the Nazis and Japs, the mood in the War Department was growing desperate. Men and materials were needed everywhere as plans for a European invasion took shape. To that end, General Marshall had flown to London to confer with Winston Churchill on launching an attack across the English Channel into France; and the War Plans Division had been renamed. What had been needed was an agency to gather all strategic information, and produce and edit plans that Marshall could base his decisions on. With Eisenhower its chief, it was now called Operations Division—which Frederick assumed had no effect on his job; accordingly, he figured he might end up chained to a desk throughout the war.

However, in London, Churchill was hoping to divert Marshall from the pie-in-the-sky idea of a continental invasion. Strategically it was unrealistic: the U.S. lacked enough trained troops for the job. Visualizing British blood flowing in the English Channel, Churchill had arranged that Marshall meet with England's head of Combined Operations, Lord Louis Mountbatten, who was acquainted with a rash new concept of warfare that required a small number of troops traveling in motorized snow sleds on missions of sabotage in remote areas.

If America was so eager to get a toehold in Europe, why not accept it? Churchill proposed.

Pushed along by the Prime Minister's enthusiasm for the concept,* Marshall returned to Washington and circulated among his key staff a memorandum.

"In London, Vice Admiral Lord Louis Mountbatten...brought to me personally a man who is deeply interested in the development of a motorsled.

[A] considerable area of Europe, especially in Norway and certain passes out of Italy into Germany, are covered with snow for periods of

*When first hearing about it, the eminently quotable Churchill had waxed gushingly, "Never in the history of human conflict will so few immobilize so many!"

the year varying from 60 days to 250. If a snow vehicle, armored, carrying adequate guns and a small crew can be developed, it is possible that it may be used to considerable effect against critical points. They have in mind establishing a glacier base from the air in Norway, from which to operate against the critical hydroelectric (power) plants on which Germany depends.

The civilian concerned is to come to this country in the near future...(It) is necessary that some particular officer of ours be designated to go into the matter.

       G.C.M.

       Chief of Staff"

Frederick was writing a summation of a military plan when, entering his office with a handful of papers, Eisenhower plopped them down on his desk.

"General Crawford (an assistant to Marshall) asked that you assess the feasibility of this as a military operation," Ike said. "There's a sort of rush to get it done."

Frederick glanced at the top page. It was titled "Mastery of the Snows"—and as he recalled later, "My initial reaction, frankly, was 'that's a wacky idea.'"

But for twelve days he examined each germane facet of the "Snow" thesis Marshall had carried back from England, and that had assumed the code name PLOUGH PROJECT. How many hydroelectric plants were in Norway? How many in German hands? What was the terrain? What type snow vehicle would it take? What explosives worked in cold weather, and how many would saboteurs have to carry? It was a wearisome round of research, as he interviewed anyone he could find who knew something about Norway, arctic warfare, or equipping cold weather troops.

And, getting the answers he needed, Frederick typed out a single spaced, fourteen page analysis. PLOUGH PROJECT, he had concluded, was impractical. There was no way to transport snow vehicles without lessening the chance of surprise; no proof a handful of U.S. men would better succeed destroying vital installations in Norway than would native Norwegians; and the project would only rob the U.S. Army of resources needed elsewhere. But what most concerned him was there would be no way to retrieve the crews of saboteurs in motorized sleds. Their mission would be suicide, each man sacrificial.

With a sense of relief, he turned his report (that became known as the Frederick Memorandum) in for Eisenhower's signature. Two days later Ike returned from England, where he had gone on Marshall's behalf, and summoned him into his office. His face flush with anger, he held out Frederick's negative analysis.

"I can't sign this!" he exploded.

"Oh...." Frederick paused. Seldom revealing any emotion, his eyes were wide with surprise. "Why not, General?"

"Because in London," Ike steamed, "I told them we were going ahead full speed with this."

And also he may as well have added, Marshall had begun to see the value of having a small, swift striking, mysterious unit on the roster of fighting strength.

Swallowing hard, Frederick demurred from responding he had done what had been asked of him. To do so would be paramount to an insane act of insubordination. Besides, he was now free of the project—or soon to be, after one conference that afternoon, and one meeting the following day.

Churchill and Lord Mountbatton had just arrived in Washington, and Frederick was told to accompany Mountbatten and Ike to the Russian Embassy, as the Russians were anxious to acquire a snow vehicle.* Frederick's contribution at the embassy was to state that "any vehicle" developed for traveling steep slopes or snow fields was "vulnerable to breaking down." The next day, gathered at a high level meeting with Eisenhower were Lieutenant General Joseph McNarney (the Deputy Chief of Staff), Lord Mountbatten, and the Englishman who had written "Mastery of the Snows," Mr. Geoffrey Pyke. As ordered, promptly showing up was the man most knowledgeable about the military aspect of PLOUGH PROJECT, the very junior Lieutenant Colonel Bob

---

*Already the allied triad—England, Russia, and America—was fraying at the seams; the Russians, backed by their leader Joseph Stalin, were demanding the U.S. give them everything available in arms and equipment.

Frederick. Mountbatten and Pyke, discussing in depth their projected uses for a small commando-like raiding force, wanted assurance the U.S. would proceed with "Plough": in fact, Ike said, to prove the U.S. Army's commitment, he had been directed "that an officer be selected this afternoon to activate it." Frederick, his patience waning during the dignitaries' dialogue, quickly departed. Now, finally, he was rid of the project.

But in three days, the officer chosen for the job had met with Mr. Pyke, and it had been a positive calamity. Pyke felt the officer, a Colonel H.R. Johnson, was not dynamic enough to command his concept of saboteurs scurrying around snow clad Europe in motorized sleds. In turn, Johnson had informed Pyke it was a military matter, and his opinion was not welcome. In a high dudgeon, on 8 June 1942 Pyke complained to Mountbatten, who then telephoned General Marshall and relayed, "That officer has to be replaced."

As it happened, Mountbatten was a man of fertile imagination, self assuredness, and daring, and liked that in himself, and in others. At the meeting with Eisenhower he had observed that the man who tried to bury PLOUGH PROJECT had an orderly mind, was quietly confident, and was not afraid to attempt changing things to get better results.

"But I found another one for you," continued Mountbatten.

"What's his name?" asked Marshall.

"Colonel Frederick."

"If you're satisfied, I agree," Marshall replied.

Yet if he would have so readily agreed had he sensed beforehand some recognition of Frederick was open for question. When slowly working his way up the ladder of rank, as a captain, Marshall had been posted to the Presidio of San Francisco in 1912 and, likely as not, been one of those irritated soldiers pestered by the nine year old lad who kept jumping from behind trees to scare their horses, then racing off to safety.

In any case, that evening the telephone rang at the Fredericks' house. On the line was an officer in the U.S.-British Combined Chiefs of Staff office. "I was instructed to tell you, Colonel," he said, "you were appointed to take over Plough Project, and arrangements made for you to fly to Canada with Admiral Lord Mountbatten and Mr. Pyke tomorrow evening."

Stunned, Frederick felt like he'd had the wind knocked out of him. "I see," he managed to reply quietly, after a pause, adding, "Thank you."

Even in fiction it would have seemed outrageous—the one negative critic of PLOUGH named to form and command the military force.

The phone rang again. The caller this time was the man who would one day be U.S. president. "Frederick, you are now in charge of that Plough scheme. You've been over the whole thing and know it well. Let me know what you need."

There was a long silence.

"Did you hear me?" inquired Eisenhower.

"Yes, General, and I already received word of this seconds ago. I am just trying to absorb it." Frederick answered.

Presently, Ruth Frederick came to her husband's side. "What was that all about?" she asked.

"I have got to fly to Canada tomorrow night," Frederick said. "I have to build a new unit, and at a meeting the other day, it was mentioned it might include Canadian as well as American troops." What he would not tell Ruth was what he earlier had determined—the mission slated for him and those troops would be suicide.

Although wartime called for untested theories and action, the U.S. Army thrived on conformity, and Frederick not unaware he was risking his career. If the project failed, all censure would fall on his neck. A shawl of humidity cloaked Washington the next day, and beads of perspiration were on everyone's brow in Operations Division as, clearing off his desk, he doled out his stack of other projects-in-progress. By dusk he was headed toward Ottawa with Lord Mountbatten and Mr. Pyke to discuss including Canada in PLOUGH. Mountbatten was carrying the ball for Winston Churchill, who had suggested the Canadian involvement as an ally binding act. Canada needed U.S. help to jointly protect North America; and, of course, nothing is so comforting in wartime as having a grateful neighbor.

In Ottawa, they met with Canada's Governor General and with top defense officials, and Frederick only briefly alone with Mountbattan. At which point, Lord Louis related the tale of a close call he had once had sailing a boat. Courteously amused, Frederick replied, "My lord, Lord

Mountbatten," made a mental note that sounded silly, and vowed to henceforth stick with Oh, golly.

It was heady company for the young lieutenant colonel, and yet he considered it lucky his visit lasted but five days. The Canadians were enthused over supplying troops for PLOUGH, so Mountbatten had departed the third day, leaving Frederick and Pyke to iron out the details. But by now Frederick had found that coping with the Englishman was taking every ounce of his patience and tact. For Pyke, beside being a visual nightmare—he wore slacks four inches too short, wore spats to eliminate needing socks, and seldom bathed or shaved—talked incessantly.

"He never shuts up," Frederick wrote in his office diary. "In a dictatorial tone he spouts his ideas, but has no knowledge of how the military structure must be developed. Then the end of each day, when I'm trapped in a hotel room with him, he keeps on talking, talking...."

Returning to Washington on 14 June, Frederick spent the evening composing a ten paragraph directive on what he needed to mold his unorthodox force of fighters. He had been told to have the unit ready for combat by mid-December—six months off. With haste the shadowing mover, and knowing any request could be rendered impotent in quagmires of governmental bureaucracy, in his directive he gave himself hugely unusual authority to procure personnel and equipment; to requisition facilities; to expend funds; to deal directly with foreign government officials; and that commanding generals and all army agencies were to "cooperate with and assist" him.

He took it to Eisenhower, who signed it under the official "By the direction of the Commander-in-Chief" on 15 June.

"It was a masterstroke of administration...a remarkable directive" as was later noted; for what Frederick had got for himself was a *carte blanche* ticket from the government.

Pyke was the visionary; Bob Frederick now had to bring that vision raging from a theory into reality—to build, with no guidelines, a force of guerrilla-like fighters. This was not just an evolutionary step forward in the U.S. Army. Frederick was about to revolutionize the way America conducted ground warfare.

"It was absolutely astounding how fast he grasped the job before him," later wrote General Paul Adams, who would serve under Frederick.

It was not quite that amazing. To the casual observer, Frederick appeared soft spoken, almost shy*; but the bedrock of his character was independent thinking, a quick decisive mind, and organizational genius. And, beneath his reserved demeanor breathed a firebrand. By the end of 15 June, combing the Munitions Building, he had begun to gather his staff, and in one day, had a Logistics and Supply Officer, Intelligence Officer, and four stenographers. In far flung places, others were notified much the way as was Kenneth G. Wickham, who was one unperturbable young major.

"I got a phone call from Bob Frederick asking 'Did you get orders?' I answered, 'Yes, what in the world is it about?,' but all he said was 'You will find out when you get here.' I had barely known him when he was Plans and Training Officer of the regiment I was in on Oahu, but he had struck me as very active, and a very gracious individual. No one who ever met Bob forgot him. At any rate, he said he expected me to be in Washington in twenty-four hours, and I was."

Wickham's task was to write an organizational profile of how many men Frederick envisioned for Plough force. Lacking precedent, he had decided on about 2,400 troops, of which the combat element, made up of three undersized regiments, would have 1,704 enlisted men and 94 officers. The rest of the troops were to be in a separate Service Battalion, an innovation that Frederick—showing no reverence for Army doctrine, which dictated service troops should be in combat units—felt was necessary. He wanted his fighters to be free of K.P., guard, and supply duties. There was little enough time to train them to be arctic-ski-demolition-paratroop-mountain climbing commandos.

But in the load of responsibilities he now shouldered, the one Frederick felt heaviest was the lives of men. Unlike soldiers in large divisions with supporting units, his brigade of saboteurs would be working alone or in pairs, relying on individual skills and cunning, and thus "had to be given great consideration for being fragile," he said later.

---

*On first meeting him in the early chaotic days of 1942 Eisenhower was heard inquiring, "Is he just being polite, or does he always border on bashfulness?"

"A soldier can break as much from the fear of getting lost or ill as from fear of enemy threats. The one edge that I could give them was they be trained under the most rigorous conditions, so that they knew every trick of survival, and attained top physical endurance."

In six days, next to arrive in Washington was his Operations and Training Officer, whom Frederick instantly sent off to find a base to assemble and train the force—which in its combat echelon was to be one third Canadian. And which already, U.S. Army Department heads were convinced would be too oddball an outfit to understand. They would not be disappointed.

As PLOUGH was a code name, Frederick was being deluged with titles Army Public Relations thought he should call the unit. Positively wincing at each fierce sounding name sent to him, he wanted to shield the secret nature of the unit. The fact it was special, the first of its kind; "That's bland enough," he remarked to Wickham; he decided to call it the First Special Service Force (FSSF). This alone was to flummox Department heads when, soon, the Army's entertainment branch was named Special Services. It resulted in some vexing but hilarious mixups.

On 7 July Frederick informed his staff he had chosen a base. His Operations Officer had been wildly exuberant over an unused post, Fort William Henry Harrison, outside Helena, Montana. There were mountains nearby, snow came early and left late, and plenty of flatland for an airstrip and paratroop training. Only a few derelict buildings stood at Fort Harrison, yet, while puzzled by Frederick's insistent "Act with utmost speed," on 9 July the commander of the Corps of Engineers agreed to contract civilians "to rebuild the camp in haste." That same day, Frederick then received word he had been upped to the temporary rank of full colonel, followed by some not so good news. Meeting with an arctic specialist who worked for the War Department, he asked the fellow, "What is the best clothing for cold weather operations?"

"[R]eindeer clothing made by Alaskan Eskimos," the expert answered. "The required number of suits is ordered about two years ahead of time."

"Two years!" echoed Frederick.

Excusing himself hastily with, now, less than six months to get his unit combat ready, he fired off a communique to the commanding general of Services and Supply:

"Request clothing for First Special Service Force be secured with least possible delay.... Equipment for the base echelon to arrive no later than July 24, that for the combat echelon not later than August 1."

Up to then, only one issue had frustrated him. On 6 July he had flown to South Bend, Indiana, where production of the snow machine proposed by Mr. Pyke was going on at Studebaker Corporation. Frederick's force was to get 600 of the snowmobiles, which he had determined must be parachute dropped with his troops to achieve the maximum surprise. But in South Bend, he had learned the dimensions of the vehicle were too large to fit through the bomb compartment of any U.S. aircraft. He was told only one British plane, the Lancaster, "is big enough."

Left no choice but to hope England supplied the planes, even so, Frederick felt little cause to worry there would be a hitch. After all, had not the whole Plough scheme germinated in England? And its warlord, Churchill, soundly embraced the concept and the inclusion of Canadian troops? What could possibly go wrong?

Fortunately soon, at least, Mr. Pyke would no longer be a burr in his side. The unwashed Brit, returning to Washington from Canada, had been telephoning Frederick at all hours, demanding to be told the latest set of developments. He also had disclosed, to everyone he had met, the plans for the FSSF, which had necessitated that Frederick write to him, warning:

Success of the project depends greatly on the secrecy in which planning and training are carried out. To disclose the fact that such an operation is contemplated or even being investigated may cause its failure.

But Pyke had kept blabbing. And saying that he alone should control the Plough Project, accusing the War Department of kidnapping his "snow" thesis, he had threatened to "get a big broom and sweep the place clean." As word of this reached the White House Roosevelt's close advisor, Harry Hopkins, notified General Marshall, who in turn contacted Bob Frederick on 10 July and asked, "How essential is Mr. Pyke?"

"Not at all," replied Frederick; thereby furnishing the incentive needed by Marshall to request the eccentric Brit be instantly recalled to England.

About the same time, the Air Corps relayed to Frederick that six pilots and C-47 airplanes called for in his operational blueprint, for paratroop training, would reach Fort Harrison, Montana, in five days. That evening in his office diary he wrote, "Now every army branch and service in the War Department is working on some aspect of the project."

The ball was rolling, and momentum building.

"Lumberjacks, Prospectors, Hunters, North Woodsmen, Game Wardens, Explorers"—read a notice sent to Army camps. Frederick had visited military psychologists and, explaining "I need tough men afraid of nothing," had asked for guidelines. And beside the occupational requisites, due to the slated high-risk missions for his unit, each man had to be unmarried, age twenty-one to thirty-five, and "completed," Frederick stipulated, "three or more years of grammar school."

Some U.S. camp commanders, however, viewed the notice as a way to empty stockades of troublemakers, by offering to prisoners the choice to finish their sentences or "volunteer" for Frederick's unit. These jailbirds would cause him uncountable problems, but certainly most all American volunteers were not ne'er-do-wells; and, meanwhile, in Canada a search was going on for disciplined troopers experienced as woodsmen, mountaineers, skiers, or with some winter training. As for junior officers, Frederick wanted men not conditioned by other commanders, and had sent his adjutant, Wickham, off to scout out graduating classes at officer candidate schools. Then, with three of his staff, leaving Washington on 19 July Frederick moved to Fort Harrison to await arrival of his troops.

Churning up clouds of dust, bulldozers were carving out streets and leveling ground for tents, and making a thunderous racket sawing and hammering workman were everywhere, putting up temporary latrines, mess halls, classrooms, a post exchange, and a parachute packing shed and drying tower. Frederick was elated: "Such quick action"—he wrote to Ruth. And when one of his junior officers soon arrived, greeting him Frederick gestured at the chaos of construction surrounding them. "This is the Force's home," he said, cheerfully. "Isn't it great?"

The fellow's mouth fell open, nearly to his chest.

They came pouring out of trucks and train cars on rail sidings at Fort Harrison, baffled by the unfinished camp. Cloaked in secrecy, few volunteers knew where they were, and compounding their bewilderment was the wide variety of insignia and uniforms on other volunteers. Yet most were obstinate and high spirited—exactly the sycophants that Frederick needed to weld together troops from two nations. Those lacking brashness or tenacity were quickly weeded out if, after forty-eight hours of physical conditioning, told to make a parachute jump and one the next day, they froze at the door of the airplane. Standard Army policy was to devote five weeks to paratroop training, but Frederick did not have that luxury of time.

In fact, setting a record for brevity, Frederick listened to ten minutes of instruction on how to land, went up in the first plane, and was first out the door.

Asked afterward, "Were you nervous?," he said, "A little," paused, and added, "No, more than a little. But my purpose was twofold: to lessen qualms others might have, and to let them know I won't be sitting on my haunches."*

It would not be long before his men would learn what the Force's executive officer, Paul D. Adams, was to depict in an interview: "Frederick was unusually fit, both muscularly and in coordination. Kind of like a cat. During training at Fort Harrison, we fought each other with bare bayonets, [and] he was tough. He nicked me in the neck. When he got in combat—same thing. Mountain climbing, carrying a big load on his back, which he had to do lots of times, he'd just go sailing along."

With his parachute jump, Frederick had set the tenor for training; and now he hoped to rapidly build a cohesive bond between his American and Canadian troops. "Who," he later said, not too ruefully, "acquired each others' bad habits almost immediately."

---

*Adding to his legendary leap, because his paratroop boots had yet to be shipped to him, Frederick wore his street shoes when he jumped.

6

Shuttled and Shuffled

There was plenty to worry Bob Frederick that summer of 1942, as his bi-national force took shape, and soldiers from Canada mixed with American G.I.s. The Canadians' military system was quite different, as were their uniforms, and both were an instant stimulus for arguments and brawling fist fights over who had "the best army."

But in little ways, Frederick began to nullify their differences. The Canadians marched with their arms swinging wide, while the G.I.s kept their arms at their side; thus, as a middle ground, he ordered everyone to swing his arms slightly; "and if the Americans don't like it," he instructed his training officers, "tell them it's good for them, as it will teach them to use their arms the way they'll need to in cross country skiing."

As for uniforms, the entire First Special Force was to wear U.S. issue. But Canada's troops were accustomed to shoulder ropes (lanyards) that represented their various regiments, were of numerous colors, and hung from their shirt tab buttons in a loop under their left arms. So flying off to Washington, Frederick purchased red-white-and-blue lanyards at a uniform company. Carrying them back with him, he assembled his men and announced, "From now on, this is the only lanyard I want to see, and it will cost you ninety cents."

"Hey!" shouted one indignant trooper. "You can't make us buy that thing!"

"True, I cannot," Frederick responded, "but I can tell you nobody leaves this post unless he is wearing one."

It so happened, several men planned to head into nearby Helena come Saturday night and—reluctantly plunking down their money—wore the shoulder ropes into town. On their return to camp they disclosed to their buddies that Helena's girls said the ropes looked "swell," and within days, every soldier expediently came up with ninety cents and proudly sported a red-white-and-blue lanyard.

It was these sorts of devices Frederick used that helped rapidly unify his North Americans. As did when the first 1,200 who qualified as paratroopers lined up under a blistering sun and received their jump wings—and horrific sunburns. Frederick had insisted on pinning on all 1,200 wings, and slowly worked his way down the line, "to make personal contact, which is important," he told his staff, "as I won't always be here with the men." And not simply because he had to witness tests of the snow machine being developed, or in Washington select supplies and equipment for his force, or nail down its arrival dates at Fort Harrison. Thrown into building an untried concept, he intended to sculpt it his own way as much as possible; and it meant being at the War Department to put on pressure, or if need be fight, for unsanctioned gear and supplies.

One such item was a medical pack. His force, working alone, unsupported by a medical group, would have to take care of itself. But the standard pack held only gauze and sulfa tablets. So, going to the Surgeon General's office, Frederick demanded the packs for his troops also hold Benzedrine, to ward off sleep or exhaustion as they skied their way or rode snow sleds out of enemy territory to safety. And for his officers, he demanded even more radical a departure; that each pack contain morphine, sutures, and a few surgical instruments. Meeting stiff resistance, he argued, "It is better an amateur doctor try to save a life than a man die from lack of aid"—and won his case.

But though his foresight on his part gained his subordinates' approval, it was as much a reminder of the solitary warfare they were being trained for as when his officers gathered one evening at Fort Harrison to watch a demonstration on how to cut off a leg, during which one major bolted to the street and, vomiting, choked out, "This is a godawful outfit! What did I get myself into!"

The FSSF was, however, fast becoming the closeknit, aggressive force that its commander wanted. But at times the mass of details he had to attend to seemed suffocating as he shuttled between Montana and Washington. On one trip east, Frederick sent back to camp the picture of an obstacle course to be constructed: "as it is higher, longer than any other." Next he went in search of gear for arctic-airborne-mountain warfare. He needed gun oil that would not jell in frigid air; insulated canteens; mountain stoves; lightweight compact tents; long range radios his paratroopers could jump with; and as his force was not connected to any army branch, an insignia for the unit. Aided by one of his staff, he chose an old Indian scout insignia—crossed arrows. And, for a shoulder patch, a red spearhead with USA-CANADA embroidered on it in white. (The Force would also have the first and only North American flag, made of red silk with a black dagger on a white shield.)

Meanwhile, his forcemen were learning armed and unarmed hand-to-hand combat. Frederick had brought in an Irishman, "Pat" O'Neill, and put him on the payroll, ignoring the fact he was not a U.S. citizen. O'Neill had been a member of the Shanghai International Police, and knew how to barehandedly render a man useless. Taking the training himself Frederick, then observing his soldiers practice their new skill on one another, described it as "legalized assault, battery, and mayhem." The men, moreover, were no less enthusiastic once demolition exercises commenced. Using to full advantage his self-made *carte blanche* ticket from the government, Frederick had procured a limitless supply of explosives, to train the men as saboteurs. But, by his own admission, "We messed up part of Montana."

Two of the more notable incidents involved a bridge and a mill. Assigned to blow up the bridge, one unit of soldiers used so many explosives the blast took down most every chimney in a nearby town. As to the mill, the owner had offered to let the Force blow up the mill's machinery, so he could sell it for scrap iron. Yet, not only did the machinery get torn apart, the entire mill soared 200 feet in the air, fell earthward in bits and pieces, and the surrounding woods caught on fire.* One group of daring-dos even went so far as to put a stick of dynamite in

*The U.S. Government, meantime, kept getting bills for the destroyed civilian property, ultimately paying them, of course.

a hot stove in their living area, whereupon, along with the stove, all the windows and part of the roof disappeared.

But unquestionably Frederick was psychologically acute to the men; he shrugged off the hell raising "as showing the spirit of self reliant characters who get restless"—unlike some commanders, who impose rigid discipline to compensate for their own lack of influence. When forming plans for the bi-national force, Frederick had determined to make allowances for men chosen for their rugged individualism, from whom would be demanded superior skills and versatility—and he would not waver.

"As you make a decision," he had told one sergeant serving in his headquarters, "the picture in your mind should be as clear as a printed map." Later that sergeant, Ben Gray, commented: "When Frederick got a picture in his mind he was an artist. He painted it to perfection. We had the best specialized gear and training, becoming, as historians say, the 'elite' of the elite."

However, it also helped that Frederick was a good picker of men, and surrounded himself with highly capable officers.

Undergoing the severest training in the U.S. Army, his unit marched 140 steps per minute instead of the normal 120; doubletimed everywhere; hiked up to sixty miles with packs weighing 100 pounds; learned to use carbines, pistols, rifles, grenades, submachine guns, and light machine guns; and did much of its training in the dark. Emphasizing, "In combat, operating at night is the best way to surprise the enemy," Frederick was a night person anyway. ("No one could work as late at night as him" his executive officer, Adams, later said, sighing, "and be ready to go the next morning.") All of which greatly disconcerted a War Department staffer who, briefly visiting Fort Harrison, reported back to General Marshall, "It is hard to tell what is this unit's principle weapon! And they train in rain, even in darkness!"

It was now mid-September, and to Frederick, imperative to now pin down England's cooperation in loaning the airplanes needed to launch the snow vehicle and his men. He also wanted to directly speak with Norway's government-in-exile in London about the mission for the FSSF. But first, flying to Washington, he selected one more weapon for his men to carry; examining samples of knives, he ordered custom made stilettos with menacing long, narrow blades, and skull cracking pommels at the end of the handles. Then he met with the Deputy Chief of Staff, General McNarney, to relay the purpose of his trip—and was told that when the Force reached its staging area prior to combat: "...neither I [McNarney] nor Marshall will have control of how it is used. It will operate under Eisenhower [who was now based in London]."

From Washington, taking the train to New York and departing from La Guardia on 15 September, in his diary Frederick noted:

"Refueled at New Foundland. The plane is a Sikorsky, quite comfortable. Berths made up at 11 PM. Ireland visible 4:15 AM (Sept 16). It looks like a toyland—many farms, each with a small cottage surrounded by a stone wall."

Landing at Foynes, Ireland, he boarded a British Overseas Airways plane:

"...the windows blackened, flew at low altitude for recognition by air defense. Arrived London 4:30 PM. Went to Bailey's Hotel, ...not comfortable, not expensive (Sept 17). Breakfast at hotel, consisted of oatmeal, no sugar, milk or cream available. To meet with Eisenhower this AM."

Going to Ike's headquarters, Frederick conveyed to him the status of the FSSF's development and training, later noting, "Eisenhower was very interested, until...": repeating what McNarney had told him, "Now scowling, Eisenhower's mood changed. He responded he had received no inference 'the Force is to operate in my domain.'" Frederick left with a distinct uneasy feeling.

Next he went to the headquarters of Lord Mountbatten, and after cordial chit chat, Frederick broached the subject of England supplying the airplanes for PLOUGH PROJECT. Mountbatten stiffened. What was this about needing aircraft? "When the project was proposed to General Marshall," he said, edgily, "it was agreed it would be American only." He then invited Frederick to lunch with him and Lady Mountbatten at their home where, making quick work of the meal, the American hurried off to now meet with the commander-in-exile of Norwegian armed forces, General Hansteen, to cement plans for blowing up Norway's hydroelectric stations.

"But for two hours," Frederick recalled, "Hansteen discussed the project, and only then did he reveal that he and his government, though originally endorsing it, had since done a volte face. They had decided blowing up the stations would be more inconvenient to their countrymen than to the occupying Germans, as it would deprive Norwegians of power for industrial use, and to heat their homes."

So far as Frederick was concerned, that was reasonable; but he was now more disturbed. If neither McNarney, Marshall, nor Eisenhower knew under whom the FSSF was to operate, who did? Without the support of U.S. high command—and suspicion over unorthdox units, over individuals acting individually in war, was running rampant in Washington—his force would have no mission.

It had been a long, disheartening day when Frederick arranged to again, that night, see Mountbatten, to press him to pursue the loan of aircraft. But now Mountbatten, saying it put him "in some difficulty," confessed he had never even mentioned PLOUGH PROJECT to the British Chiefs of Staff. Frederick stared at him in languid silence, one line from a poem he'd had to memorize at West Point having slipped into his mind, "Wink no more in slothful overtrust."*

As if feeling he needed to fill the void, Mountbatten offered, "But they are to convene tomorrow morning. Perhaps if you present to them personally...."

On hand at that meeting were Britain's Chief of Navy Staff, Chief of Air Staff, and Vice Chief of the Imperial Staff. Regarding the U.S. colonel as a mere intermediary, they exerted parsimonious courtesy; or as Frederick wrote in his notes: "The Chief of the Navy Staff sat frigidly mute. The others questioned me in detail, obviously antagonistic to the plan, particularly use of their aircraft. In a supercilious tone the Air Chief suggested I submit the plan for him to study to see if it *justified* use of England's planes."

*From "Ode on the Death of the Duke of Wellington" by Alfred Lord Tennyson.

Soon after he departed for Washington; but his plane hit turbulence and rattled and bounced its way to Ireland, where pelting rain had grounded all flights west. Stuck in a dreary hotel for four days, he ruminated how, at present, there was no tactical need for his force anywhere. So once the weather cleared he flew back to London to settle one last issue—was Mountbatten willing to fight for continuance of PLOUGH PROJECT.

In a nutshell, no. For now, revealing a campaign was being waged against Combined Operations which Mountbatten commanded—to shrink its influence on British Chiefs of Staff, "I am not in any position," he said, "to fight for Plough."

Frederick's professional probity kept him from seeking excuses to keep the project alive when, finally arriving in Washington, at McNarney's office, he dropped off a report of his trip that generated an amazing amount of official communication that reached into the highest corridors of power.

To begin with, McNarney quickly dispatched a message to Marshall:

It appears that the Pough Project had never been presented to the British Chiefs of Staff prior to Col. Frederick's recent visit. Their attitude is quite unsympathetic. In view of [this], we must make a prompt decision on the future of the First Special Service Force....
  a. continue the force on its present mission
  b. disband the force and turn its special equipment over to the Army Ground forces
  c. prepare the force for operation in another theater

Accordingly, Marshall immediately issued a response that read in part:

[T]he First Special Service Force has received considerable publicity, and to disband it now would have highly undesirable results on the Canadian public. This force, composed of picked fighters of high morale, on [which] much effort and considerable funds have been expended, should not be allowed to go to waste. Possible uses...Send the force to the South Pacific...Or send the force to the British Isles to await pending need of it in Europe. Action recommended. The force to be sent to the British Isles.

Actually Marshall, in a reflex to steady advances being made by German troops toward Moscow, had in mind using the Force in the Caucasus mountains, southwest of Russia. Thus, among numerous memos about the FSSF classified Secret being briskly routed around Washington, was one to Frederick that said in essence "continue training." Marshall then notified England's representative to the U.S., Sir John Dill, of the situation.

> Dear Dill,
> The nonavailability of air transport during the coming winter has necessitated canceling the operation of the First Special Service Force as originally conceived. Decision has been made to retain it...with a view to its possible employment in the Caucasus area early in 1943.
> Faithfully yours,
> G. C. Marshall

As a matter of routine, Sir Dill related Marshall's missive to Lord Mountbatten, who then passed it on to Winston Churchill; who, no less passionate than before over a highly mobile unit traversing snow, received the news with furrowed brow, and doubtlessly his fleshy jowls aquiver. For he instantly fired off a cable back to Dill:

> ADDRESSED BRITMAN WASHINGTON
> ON NO ACCOUNT DISSIPATE PLOUGH FORCE. NOTHING COULD BE MORE IMPROVIDENT. THEIR CHANCE WILL COME AND MAY ALTER THE WHOLE STRATEGIC POSITION OF THE WAR WHEREAS TO BREAK THEM UP IS TO BLOT OUT LARGE STRATEGIC POSSIBILITIES IN THE FUTURE. UNLESS YOU CAN ASSURE ME ALL IS WELL I WILL TELEGRAPH THE PRESIDENT WHO HAS ALWAYS BEEN THE PATRON AND PROTECTOR OF THIS IDEA.

But Dill had yet to compose a reply when Churchill, his impatience stirred up, went ahead and telegraphed:

TO PRESIDENT ROOSEVELT FROM FORMER NAVAL
PERSON MOST SECRET AND PERSONAL
ALTHOUGH I UNDERSTAND FROM MOUNTBATTEN
THE PLOUGH SCHEME AS ORIGINALLY CONCEIVED IS
NOT A PRACTICAL PROPOSITION THIS WINTER I AM
CONVINCED IT IS OF UTMOST IMPORTANCE AND THAT
DEVELOPMENT OF THE VEHICLE SHOULD NOT BE
DELAYED....SO WE SHALL BE FULLY PREPARED TO
GRASP OUR OPPORTUNITY WHEN IT OCCURS AS IT
CERTAINLY WILL
PRIME

But whether Churchill knew of his country's refusal to lend the needed planes seems in question, as it appears he believed, or had been led to assume, developing the vehicle was in jeopardy. (Actually, the snowmobile was being successfully produced.) In any case, the person most definitely having lost his way in the maze of military planning and buildup was Roosevelt. Reading Churchill's telegram, he turned with a quizzical look to his Naval aide, who was standing nearby.

"What do you think he means?" asked Roosevelt.

Subsequently the aide sent out a: "Memorandum for the Joint Chiefs of Staff. The President directed I refer to you for the appropriate action the attached dispatch from the Prime Minister. The President is under the impression that 'plough' refers to snow plows."

Which, of course, necessitated Marshall send a memorandum back to the White House:

I recommend the following transmitted to the Prime Minister.
REFERENCE YOUR COMMUNICATION CONCERNING
PLOUGH THE VEHICLE WILL BE READY ON SCHEDULE
AND THE SPECIAL SERVICE FORCE WILL HAVE THE
VEHICLE FOR USE THIS WINTER. STOP. TRAINING OF

THE SPECIAL GROUP OF U.S. AND CANADIAN
SOLDIERS PROCEEDING VIGOROUSLY.

If Roosevelt did or did not know that snow plows were not involved
was a moot point to Marshall. He had vastly greater concerns right now,
primarily over amassing tons of equipment for U.S. Army troops gearing
up to join British units battling Germans in North Africa. Frederick,
meanwhile, had returned to Fort Harrison; with his force still alive, but
its Norway mission dead, he needed to restyle the training from sabotage
to sustained combat. For this, he had secured as additional weapons flame
throwers and bazookas—plus lightweight but unauthorized Johnson
machine guns which, skirting Army officialdom, he got from the Marine
Corps in trade for two tons of a new explosive, out of seventy tons
allocated to his unit.

And now (late autumn), also on the training program was mountain
climbing. Then, with the first snowfall, ski training began, and with it,
harrowing episodes as the uninitiated, dangerously out of control,
cartwheeled and tumbled down the slopes, their packs and rifles flying
around on their backs. Viewing this, Frederick went to bed one night
thinking they were such a threat to each other on skis "it won't take an
enemy to stop them in their tracks." Fortunately, however, there was a
quick remedy.

For while in London, he had got from General Hansteen the okay to
import twelve Norwegian ski instructors. And under their tutelage, the
entire Force could soon stay upright down the slopes, and make a thirty
mile cross country ski trip in one day. But not its commander. Waiting
until dark, and heading to a remote area to try just once to ski, and calling
it a "disaster," Frederick later described, "Ninety percent of my effort
was spent landing on or getting up off my backside." In the meantime,
100 of the snowmobiles had been delivered, and every man in the combat
echelon had learned to drive and maintain the little vehicle. So in one
respect, at least, Frederick could now relax. The FSSF was ready, as he
had been ordered, for deployment to a combat zone in mid-December.

But to where?

Of course, until War Department inspectors checked his unit's combat readiness it could go nowhere. But Frederick, with a self-made ticket to get the job done, did not welcome these "experts" who, he and they knew, were unqualified to pass judgement on what had never been done before. So, he made himself scarce when first a chaplain arrived to inspect the "soul" of the Force. Frederick, his religion a commingling of his father's Roman Catholicism and his mother's Protestantism, was not a churchgoer. Yet he kept a rosary tucked in his wallet ("I'm covering all bases," he once explained): he believed in the power of prayer; and most important, for the moment anyway, he was a stickler about the Force chaplains always being available to minister—and hopefully to be moral examples—to his soldiers.

As a result, the inspecting chaplain glowingly reported to Washington "There is a remarkable team, Protestant and Catholic chaplains, especially assigned and adapted to uniqueness of this U.S. and Canada force."

But when next appeared a colonel who was an "expert" on arctic training, Frederick's patience narrowed. He instructed the colonel be billeted in one of the officer sleeping quarters—a square the size of a tent, with one board thin walls—and be given just two blankets and wood to make his own fire in the stove. That night the temperature fell to -22°F. And in the morning, as the colonel, shivering, prepared to make his rounds Frederick instructed the windshield be put down on the jeep that would take the colonel to the training area. With wind lashing at him in the back seat, by the time the "expert" reached the training grounds he was too cold to move from the jeep. His report to Washington: "Training appears good."

But in contrast, Frederick went to exceptional lengths to assist his own men. Like when he learned one Canadian soldier's mother back home was ill. Penicillin was a new "miracle" drug, hard to get, but could help this woman; thus, postponing chores he needed to do, Frederick spent over four hours telephoning to clinics nationwide to find penicillin for the woman, whom he had never met. Word gets around. And, as with his snubbing inspectors—which revealed to his forcemen that he was fully confident in their abilities—his aiding the soldier's mother unveiled aspects of him as a leader, and they now knew their CO would help anyone in a crisis.

They did not, however, know that their unit had no mission, for Frederick had not divulged this. His troops were chafing to get on with the business of war, and the fact they had no job would create tremendous morale problems. To forestall that, he granted everyone ten days leave staggered from Christmas to the last day of January; at which time, carrying a few gifts for his family, he flew east, and after a half day celebrating a belated Christmas with his daughters and Ruth, he began to search for a job for his brigade, again managing to provoke a protracted series of messages. Only this time, they were so maddeningly contradictory one would think the War Department was trying to confuse the enemy.

Briskly patrolling the hallways of the huge new Pentagon building that had just been opened for use, locating his office Frederick had found his Intelligence Officer waiting for him with news of a message to General Marshall from Eisenhower (who was now chief of land forces in Europe). Dated 2 February, Eisenhower had written:

"First Special Service Force is desired for participation in Husky [code name for an invasion of Sicily]. Winter training should cease immediately, and intensive course in amphibious operations begun. Unit should be shipped with organizational equipment for a beach landing and warfare in semi tropics only."

While Frederick sat impotently in wait for definite word, Marshall sent a message to "Commander of U.S. forces Europe, Lieutenant General Frank Andrews, for attention Mountbatten.":

Eisenhower has requested Special Service Force be dispatched to his theater. It occurs to me that the Force might be desired in the UK [United Kingdom] for operations. It can be given its amphibious training here and then dispatched to the UK, or it can be dispatched to the UK as soon as shipping becomes available and receive its amphibious there.

Well and good; except what Marshall had proposed fell with a thud. On 12 February, General Andrews replied:

"Subject matter [is] under study by British Chiefs of Staff and Lord Mountbatten. No use of First Special Service Force contemplated for this theater in near future."

But Marshall kept pushing, responding to Andrews three days later:

"[I]t would seem that this force should either go to the United Kingdom for possible use by Mountbatten this coming summer, or for Minute Jupiter [a proposed invasion of Norway], or for use in Husky as desired by Eisenhower. Please discuss this with Mountbatten.
Marshall"

So now Norway was back in the picture. Kept informed about each pending option, Frederick laughingly commented to a colleague, "I am getting so many different directions that it is, actually, becoming amusing."

Then, on 18 February General Andrews responded to Marshall, "As stated, no use of Canadian First Special Service Force contemplated in this theater in near future."; and he followed this up on 20 February with another message:

"Mountbatten, with authority of Prime Minister and Chiefs of Staff, earnestly asks that Canadian Special Service Force should continue their [sic] training in snow warfare in America...but be held ready to come over to the United Kingdom directly if any prospect of employing them in operation such as Minute Jupiter."

Obviously Andrews, having twice called the Force "Canadian," was confused; as was now the War Department's message center—which was forced to add at the end of his second missive, "Unable to identify reference."

Meanwhile, Marshall had responded "To Andrews, for Mountbatten: To prepare and equip 1st Special Service Force for employment in Jupiter it is necessary to know nature of mission of special force. If force is to be airborne and snow vehicles to be used what type of British aircraft will be employed for transporting forces and vehicles?"

Yet not waiting for a reply, Marshall sent off the following to Eisenhower.

"Special Service Force of U.S. and Canadians will continue snow warfare training in America, and be held in readiness for shipment to UK for use by Mountbatten."

Some men may have damned Marshall for handing use of the Force over to Lord Louis, who had not bothered to inform Britain's Chiefs of Staff of its existence. But Frederick did not waste emotions. Returning to Fort Harrision, and for two days overseeing training and maneuvers, he then flew in his C-47 to Alaska. Nine months before (in June 1942), Japanese troops had occupied Attu and Kiska islands in the Aleutian chain, stretching west from Alaska. And as it was feared Japan might use the islands as stepping stones to North America, preparations were underway to invade the islands. To Frederick that seemed a promising chance of a job for his force; the cold weather and mountains in the Aleutians were suited for the skills of his troops.

"With the proper assignment, my men can pound the will of any enemy," he told the head of Alaska Defense, Lieutenant General Simon Buckner, who—having been looking around for additional assault units— abruptly wired the War Department, urging that the FSSF be attached to his command.

But in the meantime, a frustrated Dwight Eisenhower had cabled to Marshall:

THE SPECIAL SERVICE FORCE OF US AND CANADIANS REQUESTED RE[my message] OF 2ND FEBRUARY IS URGENTLY REQUIRED FOR HUSKY. PLANS HAVE PROGRESSED BASED ON EMPLOYMENT OF THAT

FORCE. REQUEST RECONSIDERATION OF YOUR DECISION.

None of which settled where Frederick's force was to go, but at least it was now popular; and within the month Frederick got word to move his bi-national brigade to Camp Bradford, Virgnia, in mid-April to commence amphibious training.

At Camp Bradford, Frederick's troops began instantly to practice scrambling down rope ladders from ships to landing craft, and making beach landings on the Chesapeake coast. The first night was cold and rainy when, heading to shore in a mock attack, one soldier heard a voice in the dark ask, "Well, how do you like it?"

Grumbling that "It was 'not worth a damn,' that I'd like to have Frederick out here and see how he likes it,' lo and behold," recalled the soldier, "it was him. But soon I was well aware whatever he asked us to do, he did first. Then, watching us, he would rapidly get rid of slackers because, he'd say, he was only as good as his men." (Who happened to shatter all records for scuttling down rope ladders. The best of Army platoons had been timed doing it in one minute; the Marines, 52 seconds; whereas loaded down with full packs and weapons, Frederick's "North Americans" did it in 32 seconds.)

"This is the best combat unit in the world," boasted Frederick to the training camp's comander, a General Taylor.

Replying with a huff, Taylor wordlessly conveyed his disbelief.

"Okay, to prove it," countered Frederick, "I bet you ten dollars my men can breach all the security safeguards you have on this post."

The two agreed to meet the next morning; at which time, leading the general around his own post, Fredrick pointed to where his forcemen had placed simulated explosives under each building, barracks, and gun emplacement, and had even planted a stick of fake dynamite under Taylor's bed. "See?" said Frederick, a satisfied grin broadening his face, as he readily pocketed the general's ten dollars.

Due to its superb skills his unit finished amphibious training a week early, and now, to perfect its inland raiding, Frederick moved it to Fort Ethan Allen, Vermont, where he received orders to prepare his men to embark for the UK on 25 July. His thoughts were *the Force will sit in England waiting for Mountbatten to use it, and will grow stale, and morale will plummet like a boulder*. Not unnaturally, he was feeling anxious over the ambiguity of going to England. But not for long, thanks to others.

"We were nearly completely packed," he later said, "when on 9 June the orders were changed, which General Marshall, because of political and military pressure, had been forced to do."

For though by then U.S. troops had ejected the Japanese off Attu island in the Aleutians, they remained on Kiska Island, and U.S. politicians, thinking of upcoming elections, had been railing, "They're still on American soil!" as simultaneously, gearing up to attack Kiska from Alaska, General Buckner kept hounding both war planners and Marshall to use the FSSF.

Thus, it came about Frederick's force would lead the assault on Kiska, and hold the beachheads as the main landing units came ashore. Revealing the destination to only four of his staff, Frederick called together all his troops.

"They were pumped up to fight, but being near the Atlantic coast they were fired up to 'Get the Krauts!' So, hoping to diffuse their disappointment when troop trains carried them west, I told them that in the place they were going, there was a girl behind every tree—which was not a lie. At our Aleutian base camp there was no vegetation taller than eight inches."

By the time the Force was loaded onto two Liberty ships in San Francisco Bay, however, beautifully less important to his troops was who the enemy would be. Finally, they were to get in on the fighting.

Or so they and their leader—and all concerned—assumed.

7

"Use the Back Door"

Flying on ahead to the Aleutians to arrange for his force's bivouac area on Adak Island, Bob Frederick was not happy. Adak was teeming with units training for the invasion, plus one glance at the soggy tundra covering the available area convinced him that seventy miles west the island of Amchitka offered, if not better terrain, plenty of uncrowded space to set up a base camp. Informing the campaign's overall commander, Admiral Thomas C. Kincaid, of his decision, Frederick then went on an Air Corps bombing mission so that he could reconnoiter Kiska; and, keeping a sporadic personal diary, in it he wrote that he "was pleased that the close AA [antiaircraft] fire did not frighten or bother me."

But he could not say the same about the bickering between Army and Navy commanders that was ongoing and "downright childish, and," he added, "delaying planning." For instance, the U.S. Navy wanted to change every sector name on maps of the Aleutians already printed by the U.S. Army. And when Frederick requested his troops be allowed to land on Kiska to scout out enemy positions before the attack, the Navy denied his request—although its intelligence data was guesswork.

Nor was he happy with plans the head of Army operations, Major General Charles H. Corlett, laid out. The plans had one Force regiment landing on a beach where boulders shot straight up to nests of Japanese defenses. "There is a great lack of concerted thought by all the headquarters involved, and a certain amount of jealousy...." he noted in his diary. But willing to fight the high echelon, he told Corlett to his face that the plans were unsuitable, and that he would devise his own. (Thinking first of the well being of his troops, this was to often irritate his superiors throughout the war.)

Arriving at Amchitka to spend a week in shakedown training, his soldiers were full of confidence, for during their voyage they had made exacting studies of maps of Kiska, and memorized its profile shapes. Frederick's plans called for a double envelopment in which, 600 men strong, one regiment acting as the spearhead would lay beach markers for the main landing units, and then proceed to hold a high ridgeline; another regiment would land on a more westerly shore, and move in to effect a pincer grip on the Japanese defenders; and on D-day +1, the remaining Force regiment would parachute into Kiska, if needed.

The mission was fraught with danger. At a minimum of five hours— until the main infantry came ashore—Frederick was to carry out an independent operation, his force fighting alone against an estimated 12,000 Japanese. To Frederick the odds unmistakenly augured his force could be eradicated, and the mission nearly as suicidal as the defunct Norway plan.

Surprise was paramount.

At 0:30 AM on 15 August 1943, a Naval destroyer ferrying the first wave of Frederick's troops drifted to a stop. As the grey hulk bobbed up and down in the frigid Bering Sea, the forcemen, their faces smeared with camouflage paint, climbed down the nets into rubber boats and, in the inky black of night, quietly paddled toward Kiska. Following in two six-man rubber boats—instead of the usual twelve-man size, were Frederick, four of his staff, and several radiomen and Alaskan scouts. Frederick had let himself be swayed to use the smaller boats by one of the occupants, Lieutenant Finn Roll who, claiming to know good seamanship, had said that way they would get to shore faster.

Yet, weighted down with radios, generators, and assorted gear, the smaller boats sat barely above the water line as they got underway; and by now an outgoing current around Kiska had picked up in velocity, and despite paddling furiously against the ebbing tide, instead of a swifter trip it took Frederick and his boatload two hours longer than he planned—

until 4:40 AM—to reach the island. As for the second little boat that held two of his staff, the radiomen, and generators, it never arrived. Drawing in water, it had been carried out to sea, and it was daylight before those men, paralyzed by the 31°F waters, were spotted by a U.S. Navy ship, hauled aboard, and unceremoniously dumped on deck. In the meantime, quelling a deep worry for the missing men, Frederick was bird-dogging through the hilly terrain to connect with his troops, accompanied by the scouts, one sergeant, and Lieutenant Roll.

"But he wouldn't speak to me because he was madder than hell at me," said Roll, "for suggesting we use the small boats."

So far, however, not one shot had been fired. Creeping forward and climbing up the ridgeline, his troops had met no opposition, and there were signs the enemy had hastily departed. Uneaten food lay on mess kits and on stoves. But had the Japanese simply dug in further north to launch a surprise attack? Frederick was not ready to rule this out when his concern came to full vent, as offshore rose a great clanging and clunking of unraveling chains from Navy landing craft lowering their ramps, then the destroyer blew two sharp whistles as, under the cover of darkness, the second wave of forcemen set out in rubber boats.

If trumpets had blasted, they could not have better served as a warning to the Japanese. Still, no enemy appeared. Even so, in reply to a message Frederick radioed out—"Nothing cooking"—both the Navy and the Army Air Corps protested that their vigilant reconnaissance revealed "the Japs can not have got away."* So, for two days Frederick and his men scoured Kiska and, in spite of wading through, and sleeping on, knee-high spongy tundra that left them aching and miserable, a new spirit pervaded his soldiers. Their leader, walking sixty miles around the island to check on his men, had showed his stamina and capability; and they now felt they well knew the quality of their commander, and had learned something else, too; with no females behind any trees the standard issue of condoms was still useful. Slipped over the muzzles of rifles, the condoms kept out the mud and moisture.

*But in fact, from the north end of the island the Japanese had skedaddled two days earlier on ships masked by a near constant heavy mist and banks of fog.

Late day on 18 August, Frederick boarded a standby headquarters ship, where awaiting him was a radiogram from the Navy Pacific Fleet Headquarters at Pearl Harbor:

HIGHEST AUTHORITY DIRECTS YOU RETURN THE SPECIAL SERVICE FORCE TO SAN FRANCISCO WITHOUT DELAY. (signed) ADMIRAL NIMITZ.

"They don't want us running around up here," commented Frederick to his intelligence officer, Col. Robert Burhans. "I will bet that Churchill," he continued, jokingly, "asked General Marshall 'Where is the SSF?' and when General Marshall said 'Kiska,' the Prime Minister probably said 'What's it doing up there? We need it in Europe.'"

And in truth, Frederick's guess was not far off the mark. At the time, Allied leaders were convened at a conference in Quebec, Canada, and Churchill had inquired into the whereabouts of the Canadian-American force. Told that it was in Kiska, and that now being contemplated was to send the unit of elite troopers into Burma, Churchill, keenly following all news of the Force, was not pleased. Reported a correspondent covering the conference for the *Denver Post* newspaper:

"The Prime Minister, in a masterpiece of Churchillian rhetoric, responded, 'Into those steamy, humid jungles those troops shall not be sent.'"

Among the U.S. delegation, faces reddened in embarrassment over the proposed "misuse" of the Force and, to right the issue, the Americans quickly agreed with the British that the Force should, instead, be offered to Eisenhower for use in the Mediterranean.

Meanwhile Frederick, catching a landing craft back to Kiska, was roaming about, to instruct his scattered elements to prepare to embark to Adak Island for reassembling. He then asked his assistant adjutant, Lieutenant Colonel Richard Whitney, to accompany him to Adak to greet the ship bringing in his troops—and what ensued sheds light on why Bob Frederick's troops grew to love him.

"As was often the case," said "Dick" Whitney, later, "Bob wore no insignia of rank on his uniform, and upon reaching Adak, we walked out on a long pier where a U.S. Army port company was at work. Seconds later a whistle blew for lunch, the port company vanished and, shortly after, Bob and I spotted the Victory ship we awaited heading our way. Standing alone on the pier, we concluded we were about to become a two man team to land this huge ship. So we spaced ourselves at a distance near metal stanchions we assumed would be used to secure it. Amid the hooting and hollering forcemen at the ship's rail were two civilian crewmen who tossed us coils of rope we pulled on, bringing in heavier loops of rope to go over the stanchions. One of the crewmen pointed to the stanchion I was to use, but as Bob went to throw his loop over the stanchion near him, the other crewman yelled through a megaphone, 'Not that one, you dumb son of a bitch, that one over there!'

Obeying quietly and quickly, Bob relished our landing the ocean going monster by ourselves, and it obviously amused his troops. This was typical of him, inviting such a situation by wearing no rank and enjoying every minute of it, and the fact those he led shared in the enjoyment. Which, for the troops, added to the stature of him in his position of command."

But a more important reason, also, had made Frederick feel good. Though the invasion on Kiska had turned into a fruitless attack, he had been given a superb chance to test his force, and it had suffered no casualties. (Unlike a unit that landed later, shot at dark shadows, and killed 17 of its own.) Subjected to the suicidal risk of a night landing in rubber boats on rocky shores—where hails of enemy gun fire were expected—his troops had shown exceptional courage, coordination, and discipline.

In apparent accord, General Corlett, the Army's overall chief of the campaign, got off a letter to Washington in which he generously praised Frederick's force:

"It is especially desired," he ended his letter with, "to commend Colonel Robert T. Frederick for his splendid leadership. Frederick has built a force that will be of the greatest value in any difficult battle situation."

The legend of the FSSF and its leader was launched.

Arriving in San Francisco on 1 September, Frederick granted half his brigade a ten day furlough on the west coast, with the other half to be given leave from Fort Ethan Allen, Vermont, where his force was to regroup. After working around the clock to figure out who would go on leave from these two places, Ken Wickham cornered Frederick and said, "There are two people whose leave I have not decided on, first of all yours. Where are you going to take leave?"

"I'm not," Frederick replied.

Wickham: "Well, all right for that one. How about Wickham?"

Frederick: "You don't get any either. You are to fly to Vermont to be there with me when the troop trains arrive."

Recalled Wickham, "And with that, he and I had sent off to Fort Ethan Allen to resume training the Force, and get it re-equipped for whatever destination lay ahead."

One month later, Frederick worked in a trip to Washington to see his family. Ruth Frederick had volunteered to be an air raid warden, and with the first wail of air raid sirens at night, as people turned off electric lights or covered windows with blackout shades—to keep what enemy may be approaching from seeing the lay of the land—Ruth strapped on her white warden's helmet, grabbed a flashlight, and went out in the dark to guide anyone stranded outside to the basement of the Fredericks' rented house. Stocked with bottles of water, cots, and piles of gauze and bandages, it had been designated the neighborhood air raid shelter.

But during his brief visit, Frederick determined that his family needed a large dog to protect Ruth as she patrolled the neighborhood, and at home as strangers waited out the alert in the basement. While he still could he would ensure his wife and daughters were safe. So the next week Ruth telephoned him in Vermont to say she had acquired a year old Doberman Pinscher named Donner. In a few months time the dog would be renamed Donner-the-Terrible; but for now, it eased Frederick's concern. He had just received orders stating his unit was to ship out from Newport News, Virgnia, on 27 October and, processed through North Africa, go into combat in Italy.

Consequently, flying on ahead to Morocco with an advance party Frederick, meeting the ship bringing in his force, directed his troop commanders get the men onto trains to take them east to an assembly area in Oran, Algeria. The next day he was mystified to hear a great many of his men were asking for new mattress covers, which they used as sheets inside their sleeping bags. And not until that evening did he learn why, when he saw mattress covers walking around Oran.

"The covers cost soldiers a dollar twenty each," he was to later say, "and although I had confined everyone to camp, many had snuck out to sell the covers for two hundred francs [four U.S. dollars] to the Algerians who, cutting out holes for heads and arms, had spiffy new burnooses."

His unit's M.P.s were kept busy rounding up all who had found the chance to profit—and some to spend it on wine and women—hugely tempting. But Frederick brushed off the behavior of the AWOLS as a "desire for some fun before going into battle." This was the force he wanted—rough and rambunctious. He was confident whatever job assigned it, it would do it well; that the composite heart of the force— the men's bravado, closeknittedness, and pride as highly skilled troopers would be, in military lingo, "a combat effectiveness multiplier." But it would take their baptism under fire in Italy before the high brass realized the power the Allies had in the elite bi-national unit Frederick had formed.

Back in early September of that year (1943), the top Allied commanders had projected knocking Italy out of the war within weeks, for on 3 September Italy had surrendered, leaving the Germans to fight alone for Italian soil; and six days later, American and British troops had stormed onto the southern shores of Italy. At his headquarters in Algiers, Eisenhower had talked of "being in Rome by the end of October."

But now it was mid-November, and the Allies were still over 100 miles from the Eternal City. The senior German general in Italy, Albert Kesselring, had persuaded his boss Hitler to hold a defensive line south of Rome and, given more troops and artillery, Kesselring had strung a chain of fortifications across Italy's midsection. Called the Winter Position, the chain was dominated by a fifty mile wide labyrinth of mountains atop which the Germans had dug in, well supplied. The U.S. Fifth Army, clawing its way up the west side of Italy—through hill masses, narrow valleys, and rivers swollen with rain—had reached the Winter Position on 12 October, and ground to a halt after twelve days of hurling itself against a seemingly impregnable mountain, Monte la Difensa.

Monte La Difensa, 3,120 feet high, loomed over the Allies' gateway to Rome, the Liri Valley, and sat shoulder to shoulder with another key German stronghold, Monte la Remetanea.

Up on the mountains, through the eyes of binoculars the Germans had watched the Fifth Army's approach, and poured deadly fire down on the exhausted Allied troops—while Kesselring enjoyed the opera in Rome and drank toasts with his staff; and the head of Fifth Army, Lieutenant General Mark W. Clark, waited in anguish for reinforcements. And though clearly Eisenhower was not guided by any sort of foresight that unconventional tactics would be needed, he had, fortunately, assigned to Clark the use of Frederick's special force.

Leaving Oran on 16 November, and unloaded at Naples, Italy, Frederick's unit was trucked to Santa Maria (25 miles from the front) and quartered in partially destroyed Italian barracks "out of the rain," wrote one content soldier in his diary. "It is raining all the time, all is mud." Frederick, putting his headquarters in one of the damaged barracks, now allowed his men to leave camp; but was curious about "why we want to go into Santa Maria," wrote the soldier. "For the wine? Females? He is almost motherly, as he keeps sending out his personal reconnaissance car to gather us up and bring us back."

As his troops began toning up, Frederick set off by jeep to Fifth Army Headquarters, five miles away at Caserta, to meet with General Clark. He had known him briefly earlier in their careers, when at the War Department in late 1941, Clark had been involved in planning and training the expanding U.S. Army, and Frederick worked in the War Plans Division. Since, Clark had risen rapidly in rank, being at forty-seven young for a three star general. A tall, rawboned man, "he had an arrogant air," later said one high ranked officer, "that was really very irritating." Plus, causing more than a little resentment among some generals under him, he was a publicity hound; wherever he went, Clark took along his personal photographers.

Frederick, however, had considered him a congenial person, who now had distinguished himself as head of the largest international force under American command in the first invasion into Hitler-held Europe. There was no question he had liked Clark; that he respected him for his competency; and would put his all into helping to ensure that Clark achieved a victorious advance to Rome.

At least, that was Frederick's sentiment as he drove to Caserta. Six months later his feelings changed—and vastly so.

One component of the U.S. Fifth Army was II Corps, to which Frederick's outfit was now attached. A plan to again try to break through the German's Winter Position was in the works, to be launched by II Corps on 3 December, and at Caserta, Frederick was informed that his force was to spearhead the attack and capture the so far invincible Monte la Difensa, and its sister Monte la Remetanea, while British troops moved on Monte Camino, southwest of his unit. Not until these peaks had been seized could Fifth Army advance upon other German defenses in the Liri Valley.

In incessant rain, Frederick flew in a Piper Cub over the targets; climbed several mountain paths at night to find the best assault routes and, with his troop commanders, reconnoitered the muddy low ground. The following day, as he stood under an oak tree considering his options for an attack, the Germans lobbed in heavy shells nearby. The tree shook, sending down a hail of acorns on Frederick and, next to him, Lieutenant Roll. (One and the same who had suggested using two small boats at Kiska, that had resulted in part of Frederick's staff floating out to sea.)

"Look at all the oak tree nuts the Germans gave us," Roll said.

Frederick looked at him squarely. "They are called acorns. Now, shush, I am trying to make plans."

Roll was from Norway; being fluent in both German and Norwegian, he had joined Frederick's force as assistant Intelligence Officer. He saw humor in most anything, and was an occasional bromide for some of the headaches facing Frederick. "To do what?" asked Roll. "Throw the oak nuts back at the Germans?"

Frederick smiled. Then, with a tone of certainty in his voice, said, "No. But those Germans won't get to play King of the Mountain much longer."

Back at Caserta, he outlined to Fifth Army planners his tactical decisions, which were both logical *and* innovative. "To attain surprise," he began, "we'll use the back door of Difensa at night."

Cigarette smoke fogged the air, war weary voices grew wearier, and the war shrunk to that one spot in Italy as planners questioned him about his decisions. He had chosen an assault route thought impossible to climb—straight up the sheerest face of la Difensa. When flying over the area he had noticed most of the Germans' weapons were aimed in the opposite direction on the premise that no one, especially troops laden with gear, could climb the sheer side.

Afterward, as the high staff of Fifth Army reviewed Frederick's plan, the consensus was that it would take him a minimum of three days to capture la Difensa, and in the process, his force would be nearly exterminated. Well out of earshot of the skeptics' froth Frederick, meanwhile, briefed his key commanders, and made assignments for the battle ahead. The 2nd Regiment would lead the assault; 1st Regiment would be held in reserve; and 3rd Regiment was to place one element as backup for the 2nd, while the rest of the 3rd was to assist the Force Service Battalion in resupplying the troops on the mountain. Frederick had set D-day for 2 December.

At dusk on 1 December, trucked part way, his assault troops then moved ten miles on foot in gloom and rain to the base of la Difensa, and in the dark made the grueling climb to the scrub pine halfway up the mountain. Throughout 2 December they lay secreted in the pines as the reserve troops got into position in well hidden ravines near the mountain's base. Frederick had spent the early morning putting out messages to his regimental leaders and checking the readiness status at supply points; and from there going to the ravines where his reserve troops waited, he walked among the clusters of men, pausing often to ask a soldier, "Did you remember to put on your sweater? It will be cold up there."; or to tell others, "Make sure you keep your feet dry. Change your socks at regular intervals."

A low murmur spread among the men.

"I kept wondering," said one trooper later, "why isn't our Colonel on the radio phone finding out more about the situation? Here we are about to go into action, and he's wasting time babying us. 'What's with him?' I asked a sergeant near me. He answered, 'Don't you know? That's his way of saying goodbye, and that he really cares about us.' Well, after that, nothing could've stopped me from struggling up the mountain to show him I'd fight for him."

By runner, at 4:00 PM Frederick sent word to his assault troops to prepare to move out, but to use no firearms until 6:00 AM the next day (3 December), "unless definitely pinned down by the Germans." It would be knives and bayonets until then; surprising the enemy was essential in his plan. A half hour later, nodding to his advance party, made up of "Pat" O'Neill—the hand-to-hand combat expert—and Finn Roll and three scouts, Frederick, saying, "Let's go," started up la Difensa.

As evening settled in, a diversionary barrage of Fifth Army artillery was poured onto the high Nazi defense while the secreted 2nd Regiment inched upward. At 10:30 PM it fell silent again—as the 2nd reached the 2,000 foot level, where ahead rose a 1,000 foot cliff. A selected few continued on, feeling for handholds, their muscles aching, as weighted down with coils of rope they worked their way up the cliff; and at the top secured one end of each rope, which they let drop down near where Frederick, crouched on a ledge not much wider than one man, had established his field command post (CP). Bunched together on the narrow boulder ledge, Frederick waited motionless with his group.

At 1:00 AM on 3 December he gave the signal to advance. Shinnying up the rope climbs, two hours later his assault troops reached the top of the cliff, and while downhill his reserve troops remained glued to the mountain, those above began sneaking up another 350 feet of a rocky slope leading to the peak. The assault was to begin at 6:00 AM, but as they maneuvered into position, a rockfall alerted the enemy.

In a heartbeat the battle for the mountain was on.

Blinding flashes from flares lit the area, followed by a frenetic stream of bullets bursting out from German pillboxes. Looking up, Frederick hoped a thick fog shrouding the peak gave his men adequate cover. He knew surprise had been achieved by his shock troops; knew the Germans were hampered by many of their heavy weapons aimed elsewhere; and he was confident his unit leaders, briefed thoroughly, knew precisely what to do. Still, not hesitating, he climbed up the rope scramble and crept to the crest, where the fight was heating up in the saucer-like top of the mountain.

"He believed leaders should lead," said one former forceman later, speaking as both a witness and subject of Frederick's tenet. "On the mountain, an enemy shell had come close to the officer commanding my unit, when ordering me to follow him he made a beeline backward, fleeing in such a hurry he lost his .45. Frederick spotted him, and went racing around a rocky projection, grabbed his arm, and swinging him around yelled, 'What are you doing! Get back over the crest and take command!' But by the time this officer wormed his way back to the top Frederick was already filling in for him.

Afterward, Frederick put me through a stiff interrogation, and though my moving backward had been involuntary, I was sure I was headed into hot water. But at the time, I didn't know Frederick was as observant as he was tough. Instead, twenty-four hours later he made me a second lieutenant!"

Exploding grenades, shouted directions, the cries of the wounded, machine guns hammering away—the cacophony of combat increased as the Germans, collecting their wits, savagely fought back. But while the battle raged on, sections of Frederick's troops, maneuvering to German strong points, wiped them out as others closed in on the enemy's flanks and rear. With the first light of dawn the fog parted briefly, revealing Germans approaching with their hands in the air, and more of them streaming down the ridge toward Monte la Remetanea. Frederick, his face smeared with dirt, his eyes bleary with fatigue, hunched over a radio phone and relayed to the foot of the mountain a short message to be forwarded on to II Corps: "La Difensa is ours."

It was 6:40 AM. In just two hours of actual combat, a part of his force had seized the mountain that had repelled Fifth Army for twelve days, and that high staff had predicted would take three days minimum to accomplish. Yet Frederick felt no elation. All his professional strengths had been in play when he had planned the attack: independence, responsible command, boldness, and innovation. And though the result satisfying, it was also horrid, due to the cost in dead and maimed men— Frederick allowed himself to feel discomforted over the twisted morality of war, but for a moment only. A German counterattack was probable, and his troops' ammunition supply on the mountain peak had grown low.

Holding up any further advance, he waved to the troops to find cover between rocks and in deserted German pillboxes; he then radioed below for packers to start bringing up supplies, which entailed a trip of at least six hours, with each round of ammo, case of rations, five gallon can of water, and stretchers and stacks of blankets carried on a man's back. Meanwhile, lead was flying in, from snipers in hidden positions and Germany artillery on every neighboring peak, including Monte Camino that, in a simultaneous attack, the British had failed to nab.

"With bullets raking the air," as later described "Pat" O'Neill, "Frederick moved from unit to unit, sending out patrols and placing men in outposts, to gradually widen the piece of territory we held. His casual indifference to enemy fire is hard to explain, for there were times when barrages of mortar sent us all scurrying for cover, only to come back and find him sitting in the same position and place we had vacated in a hurry."

Doubtlessly, Frederick was trying to calm and inspire his men, but he transcended the normal rules of risk taking. And if, perhaps, he was sustained by a quasi belief in destiny, it was obvious that influences of his parents' religions kept him from being a full blown fatalist. Several accounts exist where his men saw him kneeled down, praying at the side of a wounded soldier.

Soon, and without letup, enemy fire was equally harassing the men on the summit and the supply troops making the tortuous climb to reach them. Then more bad news—beside that the British still had not seized Monte Camino—reached Frederick at dusk. His units in reserve now attempting to move up to the top were also getting clobbered by every type of shell the Germans had. Hurrying down a steep slope to be with these men, though unable to contribute anything, Frederick hoped to allay any panic.

"I will never forget him walking by my position and telling me to keep my head down, while he was in full view of the enemy," remembered one survivor, Fred Pike. "I then saw him sit down and, dirty and grimy, his water bottle split in two by a bullet, he took it like the rest of us."

At midnight, getting some reserve elements up to attack positions Frederick returned to the summit, where his problems were mounting. Trying to be omniscient as he made plans for his next move and unforeseen contingencies, the weather presented a new dimension. On top of freezing rain, an icy wind had picked up fiercely; and with no shelter, few rations, and insufficient blankets, the frailty of his troops was increasing. Adding to this was a new sound of warfare. It began with a scream and ended in a heavy concussion. The Germans had begun to fire at la Difensa six barrel rocket guns called *Nebelwerfers*. Miles away in the mud and muck of the valley floor one war correspondent, Ernie Pyle, was writing that "even at a distance the sound is bloodcurdling."

Cut off from the rest of the world, the top of la Difensa had become a cold and lonely island. Going without sleep for a second night, Frederick subsisted on instant coffee as he kept moving around, making contact with each group of his men.

"He was everywhere," later commented James Underwood. "That night I was so weary, I didn't care if I lived or died. All of us felt that way. Only Frederick could have pulled off our will to stay alive—he was the inspiration to keep going."

And keep going they would.

To other units in the region the FSSF was already a legend in its own time—the taking of Monte la Difensa had been a masterpiece of maneuver and resolution. And it would go on to build an even more brilliant history, its leader, meanwhile, unintentionally gaining a reputation of his own.

8

"This Terrible Business"

"There is nothing further away than the next hill."
An old infantry saying

With his first tactical victory, Bob Frederick itched to keep up the momentum, yet early 4 December he postponed attacking Monte la Remetanea. His fighters were wet to the skin and blue with cold; the rain and biting low temperatures had turned the ground into an unstable, slimy trap for boots, bodies, and dropped weapons; and adequate resupplying would take another twelve hours.

Relieving or reinforcing his troops was not possible, as Fifth Army, holding on to its front at the time, had no spare units. Of particular concern to Frederick was his men's morale, and at 7:00 AM he contacted his executive officer, Adams, at the base of la Difensa.

"I don't care how you get them," he told Adams, "but I want six cases of whiskey up here by day's end. And several gross of condoms."*

Adams forwarded the message to the Force supply officer at Santa Maria, Colonel Orval J. Baldwin, who gave it his personal attention by driving to the Fifth Army Supply Depot, where he was met by instant disbelief.

*Which, besides covering their gun muzzles, his troops were finding doubly nifty—as a way to keep their packs of cigarettes dry.

"Condoms and whiskey, huh?" queried the Depot Chief. "What the hell has the First Special Service Force found on that mountain?"

So Baldwin pleaded he telephone General Clark's office; whereat, told to fill any request from Frederick, the Depot Chief complied, but not without squinting suspiciously at Baldwin. Frederick, consolidating his fighters, spent the day clearing the mountain of snipers; and getting the wounded and prisoners moved downhill as supplies trickled in—and the supply columns made the fiery trip back down la Difensa, six men to a stretcher. At twilight, some of the packers returned bearing the whisky, which Frederick personally oversaw that, "to warm them up, raise their spirits," got broken down two ounces per man. Wrote one soldier to home, "God bless our commander for the booze. It is a tremendous morale booster."

With the whiskey had come the first batch of mail, another morale factor. But for Frederick, the one note he received did nothing to gladden his heart. "Dear Sir," it began:

"Corporal ...... of your command on a recent furlough left my maid with child. I would like to know what steps you are taking to correct this offensive action."

Frederick handed the note to Finn Roll, saying to him, "Keep this. I need to first clear up other offensive action." Throughout the day he had kept pushing his command post toward Monte la Remetanea, in preparation for an assault on that mountain; and at dawn the following morning (5 December), he ordered the attack begin at midday.

The ensuing fight was one of the most savage in the war. Using a battalion to hold la Difensa, Frederick unleashed one regiment to nab two German fortified hills in the saddle between the mountains. Howling and baying to relieve pent-up emotions—as much as to scare the enemy—the forcemen, charging straight at the Germans, made a frontal attack. As this howling wave moved in close with fixed bayonets and grenades, the enemy, many of whose own tossed grenades were picked up and thrown back at them, fought bitterly—but had little opportunity to give themselves up. Their only chance was to run. By late evening, with casualties high on both sides, the last resistors in this throng of Hitler's panzer grenadiers had taken to their heels downhill.

Frederick had snuck forward with two scouts to observe the attack when an explosion of incoming mortar had sent a large rock slamming into his spine. As he and his group continued into the hills a wounded soldier returning from an outpost reported a badly injured man was lying at an outpost further ahead. Frederick, ignoring enemy fire, set out alone, and locating the man, and giving him aid, tried to lift him to get him to safety. But not able to due to his bruised spine (and later found, one badly chipped shoulder blade), instead, he sat leaning over the soldier, defending and shielding him from bullets, until the main body of fighters had passed by them, "and several of us walking wounded, heading back," recalled one forceman, "could carry the man to the aid station."

"It's just one of numerous times," he went on, "in which, though Frederick struck people as emotionless, his compassion was exposed as being boundless."

That night, nursing his back as runners brought him reports from his subordinates, Frederick slowly paced to and fro. His biggest worry was over the men holding the saddle; would the Germans counterattack? Deciding to give them no time for this, at 11:00 PM he ordered the regiment in the saddle to assault la Remetanea at dawn. But by a stroke of good luck, during the night the Germans deduced it wise to retreat; thus, before the end of the next morning, with little opposition his force captured the mountain, and some of his troops were even chasing Germans down into the valley. Sitting on a foodstuff crate on a slope of the mountain, Frederick used a plank of wood for a desk as he summarized the situation in a message to be dispatched to Fifth Army's headquarters. As it is a good synopsis, it bears repeating:

"(Dec 6–1200 hours). We have troops to our left boundary at [the saddle], and have consolidated for defense of the area south of la Difensa. Our attack west against [la Remetanea] has progressed beyond the crest .... we are receiving much machine-gun and mortar fire from several directions—from southwest of la Difensa, from west foothills of Mont Maggiore, from north slopes of Monte Camino. We are endeavoring to place artillery on troublesome areas, but it is difficult due to low visibility....

I shall push the attack west on past [la Remetanea] as far as condition of men will permit. Men are getting in bad shape from fatigue, exposure, and cold.

German snipers are giving us hell, and it is extremely difficult to catch them. They are hidden all over the area and shoot bursts at any target.

Please press relief of troops from this position, as every additional day here means two days necessary for recuperation before next mission. They are willing and eager, but becoming exhausted.

Communications are heartbreaking. Mortar fire [knocks] out lines faster than we can repair them. Every time we transmit by radio, enemy drops mortar on locations.

In my opinion, unless British take Camino before dark today it should be promptly attacked by us from the north. The locations we hold are going to be uncomfortable as long as enemy holds north slope of Camino."

The rest of the day, while sending out anti-sniper patrols, Frederick moved around checking the positions of his men. He had arrived at an area where forcemen recently killed were being placed by a path to be taken downhill, when a German firing from between two boulders killed two more forcemen. As soldiers shot in the direction the bullets came from, the German stood up, dropping his weapon.

Frederick was tired, but his reactions were on a hair-trigger. "Let me have your rifle," he said to one soldier and, taking aim, he shot the German dead. It was not Frederick's finest moment; he had fired at an unarmed enemy, a blatant violation of the Laws of War.

While the echo of the shot rolled through the boulders, handing the rifle back he said, "No one is going to kill my men and get away with it—not if I can help it."

Ten pairs of grimy hands began clapping, and it lasted a minute as ten unshaven, dirty faces looked on at him in admiration.

"I was there," later said Eugene A. Forward, "and I can tell you Frederick had a strong sense of what we needed. One guy the German had killed had a red cross on his helmet, and I don't care what rule our colonel broke, that damn Kraut knew that he was murdering an unarmed medic."

Sometime around midnight, the welcome news the British finally had captured Monte Camino reached Frederick. The next day, tying in his troops with the British front, in the process a group of fifty Germans was spotted hiding in a rocky crevasse and, in the process of taking seven of them prisoner, and killing twenty-five—with the rest running for their lives—it was learned they were Hermann Göring Division personnel sent in for a counterattack.

Now, nothing remained for Frederick and his weary men to do but wait to be relieved. Though weeks of fighting on other mountains lay ahead, by seizing la Difensa and Remetanea, Frederick and his force had opened a door to the entire German Winter Position. Fifth Army could now heft itself from the sludge and, unlike back in November, when war in Italy had atrophied, advance a few hills closer to Rome.

U.S. newspapers sensationally printed "CLARK'S FIFTH ARMY HITS ENEMY HARD! NAZIS TAKE BEATING IN ITALY!" There was no mention of Frederick and his night-stalking supercommandos. Fearing the Germans would send additional troops to combat them, a tight lid of security prohibited publicity of the unique North American unit.

For six bloody days, enduring awful privations—drinking muddy rain water from shell holes, eating few and cold rations, sleeping on rocks, and exposed constantly to a climatic chaos of wind, ice, rain, fog, and to the enemy's deadly intent to wipe them off the mountain—on 9 December, when Frederick and his men climbed down the steep slopes of la Difensa, "they all looked alike," recalls one G.I. who stood at the base.

"Their faces were grey, expressionless, and their clothes caked with mud and blood. I was told that Frederick said he would not leave the top until the last man was down; and he didn't, and he looked as beat as the rest of them."

Hot showers and food, clean clothes, time to relax; given eleven days to recuperate at Santa Maria, the forcemen could also watch movies and listen to a USO band. In his room Frederick could hear strains of the band music, and he wrote in a letter to Ruth:

"They just played the song 'Make Believe.' Right now that is what I am doing, imagining this countryside in springtime with a warm sun shining on the vineyards, the olive groves, and the medieval hillside homes that look as if behind their walls lay interesting remnants of history."

At moments like this Frederick found relief in thinking of his surroundings as something other than killing fields and tracts for tactical maneuvering. Anyone who has not been a battle commander cannot comprehend the enormity of the conscious burden of sending others into deadly duels; and for Frederick, sensitive to any suffering, behind his usual mask of equanimity he must have felt emotional torment to have pain and death at his footsteps night and day. He ended with:

"I have been rather busy, not until now realizing Christmas is approaching, and I have nothing to send to you and the girls. But I will make it up to you when this terrible business is over."

At a memorial service held for forcemen killed (73 in all), General Clark congratulated the unit for "acquitting itself well in action," and added in his plans "are other heights to be taken." Following him, Frederick praised his men and recommended, to unanimous approval, that money from War Bonds the Force had bought prior to going to Kiska be used to build a memorial in Montana for those fallen.*

Three days later, he was instructed that as Fifth Army began to push through the valley, the FSSF, by crossing several miles of rugged mountains to the north, was to capture the flanking high ground. The first target was Monte Sammucro.

With rain pouring down as usual, on 23 December, while his troops moved into attack positions, Frederick headed up Sammucro with his advance staff to view the whole situation. From there he discovered the other II Corps units in the area were not yet in position, making it exigent

---

*Today the handsome, marble monument stands in Memorial Park off the main street, Last Chance Gulch, in Helena, Montana.

that he postpone the attack twenty-four hours. Through the night and all of 24 December, as the Germans fired everything they had at the mountain, chilling snow and gale winds whipped over the foxholes his soldiers—shivering and praying that rations would reach them—had dug on the slopes. When darkness fell Christmas eve, one sergeant, Carl Ward, decided, "It would be a lousy Christmas without something to eat." Crawling across the snow to bum a can of rations, he climbed into the next foxhole, "to wake the kids up. The Germans started peppering us with *Nebelwerfer* rockets, and getting a little panicky I stumbled around, and shook every blanket before I realized all of the kids were dead. I got out and crawled back when I saw a guy light a match. I called him every name in the book. When I got through he said, 'Come over here, son.'"

It was Frederick, kneeling over a badly wounded soldier.

"I am sorry about lighting that match, but this boy wants a smoke," he said. "Would you help me carry him down the mountain?"

En route, they dropped the wounded boy when a mortar hit nearby. Picking him back up, Frederick apologized; whereon, with evident forbearance and spunk, the soldier replied, "Hell, Sir. When they come that close you gotta duck."

Frederick had returned up the slope and sent word to II Corps' commander, Major General Geoffrey Keyes, "All is ready" when, knowing his men were uncomfortable but their spirits good, before dawn Christmas day, to capitalize on their stealth and night fighting, he directed they "take off." Enemy fire tore at them from all directions, yet as savage hand-to-hand fighting mounted, once again, by their speed and ferociousness they overwhelmed the Germans. That night, having secured outposts on Sammucro, bearing its dead and wounded Frederick's force slowly climbed down the mountain.

Meanwhile, clad in pajamas and a bathrobe, Winston Churchill had spent a part of Christmas day at a conference he had called in Tunis, North Africa. Churchill had caught pneumonia when heading home from a summit meeting with Roosevelt in Cairo and, choosing to convalesce in warm, sunny Tunis, he had summoned high ranking admirals and generals, among them Eisenhower, to his conference.*

Unlike many American leaders who chafed, prematurely, to go after the Germans in northern Europe, Churchill had always argued the Allies first should march as victors in Italy, "as it would be folly to invade France with Rome still in German hands." But where once troubled by Fifth Army's slow progress up the boot of Italy, he was now agitated that the Fifth was bogged down in a protracted struggle in the mountains, and wanted to know what gains the Fifth had made toward breaking through to Rome.

It fell to Eisenhower to brief him, and tallying the few advances made by Fifth Army, Eisenhower mentioned "the key" that had opened the door to the German winter bastion was when "the First Special Service Force scaled up undetected and captured Monte la Difensa."

Churchill, leaning forward in his chair, his bathrobe stretching taut over his broad back, asked, "Who is the commander of that Special Force?"

"Colonel Frederick," answered Eisenhower. "The same officer who was assigned to form up the Plough Project."

Churchill settled back in his chair, and though he felt poorly, his mind was alert, and his voice robust as, looking around at his audience of top brass he pronounced, "If we had a dozen men like him we would have smashed Hitler in nineteen forty-two."

No doubt, waves of disagreement entered the thoughts of at least some present. But in fact, at almost the same time, Fifty Army planners were thrashing out an operation that relied heavily on Frederick's skills as tactician and leader. It transmuted on 1 January 1944 into a field order to Frederick; his brigade was to make the preliminary move in the final offensive in II Corp's sector, then capture Monte Majo, at 4,000 feet the highest peak in the zone, and all accompanying major heights further barring the Fifth Army drive north.

As the new year began in winterly fury, knifing deep into trackless ridges and peaks, Frederick's troops reached their first major objective,

---

*Though Eisenhower attended, his job as Mediterranean Commander had ended: the week before he had been named by Roosevelt to be Supreme Commander of Allied Forces gearing up to cross the English Channel into France, and he was to soon leave for England. (His replacement was the British general Henry M. Wilson, see p 109.)

Monte Radicosa, on 4 January; whereupon Frederick called on one regiment to make the attack. The defending Nazis, however—finding themselves outflanked—chose to withdraw. On top of the mountain at midday Frederick had ordered the area cleared of German mines when he received a message that two high ranked officers from Washington were waiting at Fifth Army Headquarters to speak to him. With wind-blown icy snow lashing the mountain he made the precipitous climb down, and six hours and a number of uncomfortable miles later, reached Fifth's headquarters.

Introduced to the visitors, he was instantly asked by one of them, "Are you receiving magazines in sufficient amounts to be distributed to all Fifth Army units?"

Tempted to respond "Are you nuts?," but then thinking better of it, Frederick kept still.

Only to hear the second of the visitors say, "We also want to know have you acquired adequate amounts of recreational equipment at all the facilities you set up?"

Now, realizing they assumed the name of his force to mean he was in charge of Special Services—the branch providing entertainment and recreation to troops, Frederick replied "with a few choice words," and telling them he had to get back to the war, "left quickly before they questioned me whether troops preferred dancers, comedians, or singers," he recalled, later. "I thought of a lot of good answers to give them on my back [to Radicosa], but it was too far to return, and besides, they probably had not yet recovered from my earlier emphatic remarks."

In one way he had been lucky. While he climbed back to the mountain top, a punishing barrage of enemy artillery slammed into the ground by his command post. But due to his arduous trip he was downhill thirty yards when it came in. Shrapnel went flying, one piece scratching his right eye and slicing a hunk of tissue off his eyelid. But the consequences could have been much worse.

With his eye bandaged, that evening he planned his next tactical moves. By patrolling in daylight, and attacking at night, his fighters had rapidly closed on the last objectives, Monte Vischiataro and towering Monte Majo. But the temperature was near zero, and not just enemy bullets, but frostbite and trenchfoot sapped the strength of his force. To continue advancing on a broad front the unit needed a transfusion of new troops. Of course, cognizant of this from Frederick's messages, II Corps' commander, General Keyes, acted quickly. Frederick had decided to make simultaneous attacks on Vischiataro and Majo; and so early on the 6th Keyes assigned to his command two battalions in reserve, an engineer company (to remove mines), and one division's entire artillery to act as support; which combined with the Force composed what Keyes called "Task Force B."

Organizing his brigade into two columns, that night Frederick sent one column sweeping toward Majo, and the other to attack Vischiataro. Orchestrating the columns' movement so they supported one another from over-watching positions, and using the attached battalions to come in after to occupy taken ground, he was prowling along a trail when he was again wounded, not severely, when enemy mortar blasted apart a boulder, and shards of it impaled his right hand. Sponging up the blood with his handkerchief he kept going, and there soon ensued a scene that starkly revealed Frederick at work.

The troops from one column had fought their way through the first line of the enemy's outposts, "to find," as described by a number of soldiers later, "Frederick sitting there waiting for us, and calmly watching us come."

Meticulous about his officers leading their men, with one scout Frederick had infiltrated the enemy position prior to the attack, "to make sure they were, indeed, in front of their troops," he explained when asked about this later. But what about the risks he took? "Can you think of a better way," he answered, "to evaluate those officers in command?"

The following dawn Monte Majo was seized. Cutting back and forth along the ridge, his troops had wiped out every enemy gun emplacement, and captured numerous German guns and ammunition supplies. Thus, over the next three days, as the Germans tried to retake the peak in twenty-seven counterattacks, each time they were felled by their own weapons. The enemy on Vischiataro was harder to dislodge, but to resolve this Frederick instructed one regiment strike westward to seize a nameless height higher than Vischiataro, and from there descend on the target. Then, with two scouts and Lieutenant Roll, he set out to establish a new forward command post. Huffing and puffing behind them up a steep mountain path were a war correspondent, Clark Lee, and *Life* magazine photographer Robert Capa, who had received permission from Fifth Army to tag along.

Reaching a small village "that was under the noses," wrote Clark Lee in an article:

"...of German machine guns and snipers on a hill a few hundred feet away, Colonel Frederick chose one room of a farmhouse for his CP. The resident Italian mentioned there were chickens about, and while the scouts rounded up the fowl and persuaded the man's sister to cook them, Frederick relayed orders to one company to take the hill. Right when it was nabbed the chickens were cooked, but the Colonel got only a few bites between phone calls—essential to keeping things going."

At which point, from a captured German, Frederick determined the enemy planned to try to reoccupy the real estate it had just lost. Lee continued:

"The colonel turned to Lt. Finn Roll. 'Come on, Finn, get your gun.'

'Yes, sir, where are we going?'

'Up hill 650.'

It was nearly eight o'clock when we walked out into the night, which had turned bitter cold, with swirls of snow and rain. We walked in single file to the patrol's push-off point.

Then the Colonel saw Capa and myself. 'What are you doing here?'

'Going with you.'

'No. There's an order against correspondents getting ahead of our lines.'

'Hell, we're ahead of them now, aren't we?'

'The point is you might trip over a mine and give the rest of us away.'

With that the Colonel and his party took off up the hill."*

---

*Of course, given the strict veil of secrecy shrouding Frederick's unit, any article or photograph was delayed for publication until it had become "old news."

About to begin the last task for the elite unit in the mountains., to keep pressure on the Nazis, Frederick now used one attached battalion for an attack as he sent his troops in a westerly direction—to wipe out the remaining enemy positions. On 13 January "Task Force B" was disbanded, and four days later Frederick's outfit relieved. What was left of it.

After twenty-three days fighting on the peaks, out of 1,800 Force combat troops Frederick now had a little over 400 men (more than half the casualties were due to exposure to the cold); on the other hand, the enemy had been "constantly astonished," to quote captured Nazis, by the speed and fierceness of Frederick's ace commandos. And thanks in no small measure to his unit securing the right flank, Fifth Army could punch further into the valley toward Rome. Meanwhile, the Force had ten days to recuperate and re-equip at its home base in Santa Maria.

There, Frederick found waiting for him a letter from Ruth. As may be recalled, he had pressed her to get a watchdog, and she had acquired a Doberman, "Donner." She now informed her husband:

"We had to get rid of Donner. He pinned three different neighbors to a wall by jumping up and, with teeth bared, holding his open mouth on their necks. I gave him to the Marine Corps to be trained for use as a War Dog in the Pacific."

Ruth's letter was dated 12 December. As it was now mid-January 1944, Frederick naturally assumed that had been the end of Ruth's dog troubles. Alas, it had not. In the interim, glancing out a window one day, Ruth had seen an olive drab truck pull up to the curb, four hefty Marines get out, place a wooden crate on the sidewalk, and drive off. Approaching the crate with caution she had found stapled onto the top a note that read: "THE MARINES HAVE FINALLY MET AN ENEMY THEY CAN'T BEAT."

The certifiably demented Doberman had been rejected. By the time Frederick had received Ruth's letter she had bought a muzzle for Donner and, pleading with a taxi driver to accept the unusual passenger, taken the dog to a veterinarian to be sent wherever souls of unhinged canines go. But unaware of this, her husband promptly wrote back to her, "I am certain the Marine Corps is greatly appreciative."

For the next three mornings he visited the casualties from his force at Fifth Army's field hospital. And one nurse, Lieutenant June Wandry, noting that he chatted at length with his men, would write to her family, "We have a mix of wounded, medical patients, and battle fatigued soldiers—all tug at our hearts. Col. R.T. Frederick, the commander of a special service force, comes to visit his men. They seem to be like family. He is a very caring person; usually only lieutenants or captains visit the troops."

The most seriously wounded forcemen, however, had been evacuated to a hospital in Naples. But, due to secrecy about Frederick's unit, the hospital director was baffled by the Canadian dog tags on some of the men who, he had decided, should be sent to England, for others to figure out what to do with them. The result was that dozens of court-martial orders began arriving at Frederick's office—as one after another forceman went AWOL in Naples.

Recalled one of the soldiers, Stuart Hunt, "After hitchhiking to Santa Maria, I was instantly told to report to Frederick. He asked me, 'Do you know why you are here?,' and picked up some papers. 'These are for a field court-martial. Why did you go AWOL from the hospital?'"

Nervously, Hunt replied he had, "...been in a predicament, Sir. If I stayed at the hospital I'd be shipped to England, but if I snuck out I could rejoin the Force." To his amazement, and relief, Frederick laughed, "and saying 'I need people who can think for themselves,' tore up the court-martial papers. Which in one way," added Hunt, "explains why us forcemen so loved, and so respected him."

In this regard, as soon was apparent, the high echelon appreciated Frederick, too. He could be counted on to do a job well; was a brave and inspiring leader (though in the lexicon of some Fifth Army brass, "a crazy SOB" for often ranging ahead of front lines); and while he had maneuvered the diverse units of Task Force B around the battlefield, proved he was an expert tactician.

On 23 January he was brought a deciphered message from the Assistant Chief of Staff of the Army, Major General Thomas Handy:

HEARTY CONGRATULATIONS AND WISHES FOR CONTINUED SUCCESS ARE OFFERED BY YOUR OLD FRIENDS IN THE WAR DEPARTMENT AND MYSELF. GENERAL HANDY

Assuming Handy referred to the great work done by his brigade, Frederick set the missive aside. At the moment he was busy planning an upcoming attack on Monte Cairo, overlooking the Liri Valley. And not until six days later did the staff at Fifth Army Headquarters realize it had omitted revealing the true reason for Handy's congratulations: General Clark had nominated, and Washington quickly approved, that he be promoted.

"The Force is delighted by the news," noted Bob Burhans (Force Intelligence Officer), "Frederick surprised by it." But he, surely, also had to be delighted. Only two years before he had been a major, and now at thirty-six, was a brigadier general. In fact, the youngest general in the U.S. Army's ground forces.

Soon after a courier jeeped up to his headquarters with orders from Clark. Frederick was to forget attacking Monte Cairo and immediately move his force to Pozzuoli, a port city near Naples, to embark for the Allied held beachhead at Anzio, Italy. Frederick's reaction was mixed. To send the Force to the beachhead was a misuse and total waste of men highly skilled as skiers, parachutists, and mountain climbers—what was Clark thinking? Yet on the flip side it would be a relief for his troops from the tortuous weather and terrain in the mountains. And, by late that afternoon, rapidly packed up, Frederick and his force passed through the bleak volcanic landscape around Pozzuoli—which in Roman mythology is posited as being "the gateway to hell."

Unfortunately, therein lay more than a little degree of truth.

9

The "Devils"

Because Anzio sat on the coastline thirty miles south of Rome, an Allied invasion there had seemed favorable. For as II Corps hammered forward in hills and valleys on "Route 6," another component in Clark's Fifth Army, VI Corps, could bolt from Anzio on "Route 7," a more westerly road and, linking up with II Corps, in a two-fisted punch destroy the enemy south of Italy's capital city. Expecting the Germans to get, initially, only parts of units to Anzio, it had been critical that first VI Corps seize the Alban Hills twenty miles inland, to cut German road and rail lines before more Nazis arrived.

True, the invasion had surprised the Germans when, on 22 January, the equivalent of three Allied divisions landed at Anzio. In two days VI Corps, commanded by Major General John P. Lucas, held a frontline sixteen miles long, seven miles inland, and had got on shore 50,000 troops and 18,000 vehicles.* But instead of sending men galloping to the Alban Hills, Lucas—worrying that if he stretched his front too thin it would get chopped to pieces—chose to take a step at a time. He had consolidated troop positions, secured the port of Anzio, and ensured the maximum supplies were on the beachhead. And had soon, by failing to exploit the surprise, lost any choice of what to do.

*"We must have a great superiority of chauffeurs," sarcastically quipped Winston Churchill, when told these numbers.

For meanwhile, the top German in the Mediterranean, Kesselring, had sent troops in France, the Balkans, and north Italy racing toward Anzio. By the night of 31 January, as the landing crafts carrying General Frederick and his force headed under bright moonlight to Anzio, parts of eight German divisions were in place, five more enroute, and the German Fourteenth Army Headquarters had arrived to lead them. From positions high on the Alban Hills, and heights nearby and low-lying countryside, they had the Allies in their gun sights—and trapped on the coast.

Morale in the U.S. and British divisions had already begun to rot when Frederick and his outfit landed and bivouacked for the night on a treeless field east of Anzio. Watching them, Brigadier General Raymond McLain, who had gone ashore with the U.S. 45th Division earlier in the week, kept shaking his head.

"I was amazed," he said, afterward, "they would take a position so much in the open. It was a strange thing—they were on ground plainly visible to the enemy at all times."

Frederick soon departed to get instructions from Lucas at VI Corps headquarters, which was set up in wine cellars under a hill near Anzio. Waiting for him, Lucas, at age fifty-four, appeared older and worn down by the beachhead situation as, dispensing with formalities, he said bluntly, "Your force will operate under the Third Division."

"That is not what I was told," Frederick responded. Willing to quarrel if need be to maintain independence over how his outfit conducted war, prior to leaving for Anzio he had "extracted," as he now said, "a promise from Clark that the Force will fight as a separate unit, and not be attached to a division."

Lucas nodded; and with the conversation obviously lagging one of his staff took over. The Force, he told Frederick, was to hold the right hand sector of the beachhead to defend VI Corps' southern flank. Although Frederick, due to replacements and casualties returned from hospitals, now had roughly 1,230 fighters, it was clear on everyone's maps the sector his small brigade was to defend was over one fourth of the beachhead, twice the area assigned to any division. On top of that it was one of the flattest pieces of land in Italy. Formerly marshland turned into farms in a public works program by Italy's dictator, Benito Mussolini, it was drained by a huge ditch, the Mussolini Canal, that formed the right line of the sector. Here and there sat an occasional farmhouse, and right across the canal lay three miles of heavily mined lowland in the hands of the left wing of the Hermann Göring Division.

The next morning Frederick, using his two regiments with the most manpower to defend the line, placed the remaining regiment in reserve as his force moved into position. He then drove to a farmhouse that looked big enough to install communication equipment for his command post, and upstairs, had several rooms he and some of his staff could sleep in. No sooner did he okay the site when, roused by the sound of trucks, the Germans opened up with a stream of artillery fire from outposts near the canal.

Frederick, who rarely raised his voice, yelled, "That's intolerable!" It also sped up his need to let the enemy know what it was up against. Contacting his regimental commanders he ordered they dispatch patrols to start "kicking the Germans out of their front yard." Whether or not Generals Lucas and Clark expected him to assume a strictly defensive posture, if the Germans did, they were astonished as Frederick—to keep them off balance—began a routine of nightly sending out hard hitting patrols.

"Frederick must have dozed during the day," remembered Sergeant Jim Kurtzhal, "because every night he was out checking on the patrols, or he'd be on patrol himself way out in a mine field, or in the lonely territory of an enemy position."

In five days the Germans pulled their outposts a half mile back from the canal, creating a wide no man's land ("and who owned it," later described Frederick, "constantly disputed.") But just as telling an effect of the aggressiveness of his leadership and his troops was found on a German lieutenant; in his dairy, referring to the forcemen in camouflage blackface, he had written: "Black devil raid again last night. We never hear these devils when they come."

Unfortunately for that lieutenant, he'd been shot dead, thus deprived of ever knowing he had originated what historians, and even Hollywood later would use as a nickname for Frederick and his force—*The Devil's Brigade*.

In the meantime, none of this was lost on the beleaguered Allied units arrayed north of Frederick's force on the beachhead: the U.S. 3rd

Division and 45th Division; the British 1st and 56th Divisions; and several attached battalions. In each day's teletype message to these units from Frederick's headquarters was word of "more prisoners taken"; "another successful raid"; "the Germans pushed a bit further back," because of the offensive spirit of the young general and his ace commandos.

"They gave heart to everyone," a number of Allied commanders were to recall.

On the night of 15 February 1944 a tense hush hung over Anzio. Instead of the endless din of flashing and growling German guns, howl of shells, and ground shaking thunder of explosions, the only noise detectable coming from the enemy side was the rumble of tanks moving about. It was too quiet. Indeed, earlier in the day Lucas had learned the German Fourteenth Army was preparing to wipe out the beachhead. Then, to the alarm of VI Corps interrogators of prisoners, a talkative Nazi had spilled the beans that "something big is coming tomorrow." Frederick, summoned to VI Corps headquarters mid-afternoon, and told to "make plans in case it is necessary to fall back," had replied, "We would end up in the sea. We will stand and fight where we are." Hurrying back to his CP, Frederick drew men and officers from his Force headquarters and Service Battalion to man anti-tank guns and heavy machine guns, and by nightfall he had a secondary line of defense running the width of his sector.

At 4:30 AM the next day VI Corps artillery opened up, in hope of disrupting the enemy's preparations. But at 6:00 AM German guns began roaring back, and with smoke and dust clouding the cold air, wave after wave of *Wehrmacht* troops and tanks swept toward the Allies—and charged straight at Frederick's force and, to its left, the U.S. 3rd Division. But these were diversionary attacks. Just as Frederick was instructing Corps Headquarters "The attack has commenced," the main German assault smashed into the U.S. 45th Division; and soon the battle raged along the Allies' entire forward line. As Frederick directed a fight to keep the invaders out of his sector, the guns of his force and supporting artillery sent the enemy reeling back at day's end. But further up the beachhead the Germans had broken through the 45th's defense line; and by dawn on 17 February, had penetrated two miles deep, two miles wide. From the air, German planes strafed the front and dropped bombs, as tit-for-tat U.S. bombers, U.S. naval ships, and VI Corps' full arsenal blasted away at the enemy.

Still, the *Wehrmacht* kept advancing and, early the next morning, launched its supreme effort to shove the Allies into the cold, grey Tyrrhenian Sea. In a glum atmosphere at Lucas' headquarters, the top Allied commanders decided to now throw in what reserves were left and counterattack. So while Frederick continued clandestine warfare that his blackfaced commandos were skilled at (and a captured German operations report cited as "Colored troops engaged in bitter, close fighting at the Mussolini Canal"), before dawn on 19 February columns of American infantrymen and tanks surged toward where the enemy had penetrated. Confused and exhausted, Nazi troops began to surrender; and by dusk a frustrated German Fourteenth Army had pulled back.

With radios buzzing in activity as the Allies' chain of command relayed the situation, Frederick, feeling satisfied the Germans would give his men a breather, headed to his sleeping room to nap for an hour. But as for General Lucas, he was denied any sense of satisfaction; he had just heard from Mark Clark that he was being replaced as head of VI Corps by forty-nine year old Major General Lucian Truscott, commander of the 3rd Division. For had not Lucas' lack of aggression, and his failure to advance on the Alban Hills, helped the Germans? It was a case of needing a scapegoat to calm the ire of British leaders to whom reluctantly Clark bowed. For, ironically, it was Lucas' cautious buildup of supplies at Anzio that had boosted the Allies' resistance.

Frederick, of course, had met Truscott, and his first impression had been shaded by Truscott's "self-glorious get-up"—he had had on his usual attire of cavalry boots, leather jacket, and a shiny lacquered helmet with two huge stars on it—but "that only briefly," Frederick was quoted, "detracted from his positive attitude." Indeed, as Truscott assumed his new job confidence pervaded the beachhead defenders while they waited expectedly for the enemy to attack again. At around the same time, Adolph Hitler was in his lair at *Berchtesgaden* and, purple with rage, demanding that Kesselring make another effort to push the stubborn Allies off the beachhead.

So the Germans tried again starting on 28 February.

This time the full weight of their assault was hurled at Frederick's force and the 3rd Division. Late that day, Frederick began to get reports of enemy tank and troop movement, and notifying his field commanders to "stay alert," he ordered demolition patrols to after sundown infiltrate enemy ground and blow up roads, bridges, and culverts, and to set up an ambush in no-man's land. As a result, the following morning, leaving countless Germans dead, his troops, at a cost of two forcemen slightly wounded, brought in eleven prisoners. Adding to their bounty for future enjoyment, they had enlisted one prisoner to push a baby carriage full of potatoes, one to carry a large crate of live chickens, and one was burdened down by a bed and mattress on his back. Frederick did not need to be told his men were enterprising, but that night's haul, he later insisted, "highlighted their talents."

After four days of fierce fighting in driving rainfall the enemy merely had dented the 3rd's outer defense, while against Frederick's force, an official history states, "it made no progress at all." And may not have been too enthused to begin with. The raids executed by patrols that Frederick sent out nightly had terrorized the Germans.

A directive from the German high command, taken off a prisoner, read: "You are fighting an elite Canadian-American force. They are treacherous, unmerciful and clever. You cannot afford to relax."

And confessed another prisoner: "The best view in the Hermann Göring Division is that you [the Force] are a division, by the long frontage you hold, and by having three regiments."

Frederick felt grimly content. Having designated his small combat units "regiments" when forming the Force back in Montana, here was proof, his Intelligence Officer wrote later, "the enemy was deceived, as General Frederick had originally planned."

Now, at Anzio, the war settled into a siege. The trapped Allies dug in deeper in the muddy ground—a throwback to World War I trench warfare—to wait for drier weather, and more troops and equipment, before trying to break out. All the while the horror remained night and day as the German big guns on surrounding hills pounded the beachhead.

But life at Anzio was not all shot and shell, particularly in the sector held by Frederick's unit. By now Fifth Army was releasing news of his force, and though secrecy still prohibited stating its location, it had become a magnet for journalists lured by tales of what other units on the beachhead called "an outfit crazier than hell" and its "fearless leader."

Many Italian farm families had been evacuated prior to the air bombardments, and much of their livestock and land was being tended to by Frederick's soldiers. One man kept a goat in his foxhole; others milked a herd of cows, plowed fields, and gathered rabbits and chicken eggs to vary the diet of rations; and the Force Service Battalion had thrown together a chicken slaughter and cleaning plant.

"I don't try to do anything about it," Frederick told one correspondent. "I prefer they be occupied, rather than idle."

But he did issue a maxim in regard to items his men kept bringing in to improve their marshy dugouts.

"Scrounge, never steal. To scrounge is to take something the owner might give you if he knew the extremity of your need for it. To steal is to take something the owner might one day be more in need of than you in your present situation."

However, rather than differentiate, most took to explaining they had simply "acquired" the rugs, chairs, and bedding in their dug-outs. They had also rounded up horses, and held races and rodeos. Some of Frederick's early experiences on horseback had, as we know, been dismal, but he too succumbed, as evidence by photographs of him riding a steed among his troops. All of this took place in daylight, plainly visible to the Germans in observation posts on hills. Yet, perhaps envious—and likely afraid of retaliatory raids by Frederick—they only intermittently interrupted the fun by firing artillery.

Then, as darkness fell, life returned to the deadly business of kill or be killed, as Frederick's commandos stole out to stalk their prey. Stopping by Frederick's CP one evening as he waited for his men to go on a raid, a journalist later sent in a dispatch to the U.S.:

"The commander of a Special Service unit must set the tone and give direct leadership that, rare in modern warfare, [is] more in the atmosphere of an older, even Homeric period of battle, when men looked to their leader to be in the forefront of the fight. No one looked less like the great Achilles.... A slight pale face man, the visitor to his dug-out headquarters near the Mussolini Canal would wonder if this was, indeed, the legendary Frederick, the outstanding battle leader of popular repute—until he began to talk!

The General talked swiftly and to the point—he fired me with the vigor of his gestures and the common sense of his attitude to the American soldier at war. 'You have got to tell the G.I. the reason for a job before he will do it, and you have got to show him you can do it as well as he can. When I am up at the front, of course I am scared, but know I mustn't show it. I light a cigarette coolly as I can, and then the boys say, 'Hell, if he goes there, we can.'"

One thing the journalist was not made aware of was *why* Frederick appeared "pale face." The night before, he had very narrowly escaped death in his sleeping room, which had the minimal equipment—a cot, field desk, field safe and, in a leather case, his field phone. It had been cold and damp when two of his men, rounding up a small charcoal stove and coals to burn for heat, had presented them to him. Sitting at his desk around midnight, Frederick had been writing a letter to Ruth, and got to:

"The heinous sound of shelling has been constant, and I am feeling so tired toni..."

Ink from his pen scrawled down the page. Some time after, in his room across the hall, Ken Wickham heard Frederick's phone ring.

"Normally," he said, later, "calls came into the operations room downstairs, but someone was calling Frederick direct, which was quite unusual. I noticed he wasn't answering the phone, so assuming he had dozed off, I opened the door to his room and found him, his head down on his desk, overcome by carbon monoxide and near death. Had it been just a minute later, both I and the entire Force would have suffered the extreme loss of our general. Who had made the call never could be determined, and makes one wonder if, as those of deep religious faith believe, God does work in devious ways."

Rushed by ambulance to the Anzio field hospital, Frederick, coming to the following morning, said he could spare no more time away from his troops. One of his officers, William S. Story, who soon ran into him at his CP, remembers, "He was white as a sheet, and I said to him, 'You look like death warmed over.' I had no idea of what he had been through, or how accurate the ring of my comment, to which he replied, 'Thank you, I feel fine.'"

And Frederick was fine. Not for quite a while would the effects of carbon monoxide poisoning, not then recognized in medical circles, unmercifully begin to ravage his health. The little farmhouse serving as his CP and sleeping quarters was, in any case, never a safe sanctuary. Each time a German shell pierced the walls, a snowstorm of plaster and shards of wooden doors and window sills swirled about, chairs and tables vaulted around, radios leapt up, and the harassed men fell down and hugged the floor, or crouched at guns to spit fire back at the unseen tormentor. All within a second's time—quick, and deadly.

But not every fight at Anzio was lethal; a portion was waged with paper. The Allies would fire propaganda leaflets in air burst artillery shells at the Germans, inviting them to enjoy the hospitality of the beachhead defenders; and the Germans would fire back leaflets depicting grisly death, and suggestions that the Allies' girlfriends and wives back home were unfaithful. Some form of psychological bullying was a device Frederick had contemplated when plans had called for the First Special Service Force to sneak into Norway to blow up German held hydro-electric plants. But as his "saboteurs" would not have carried artillery to fire off leaflets, he had considered using stickers. And recently returning to that idea as a way to increase the enemy's edginess, he had consulted his intelligence officers about the design, then had requested the Psychological Warfare group at Anzio print up stickers that bore his unit's shoulder patch, the red spearhead—and next to it in German the message, *DAS DICKE ENDE KOMMT NOCHT!* (The worst is yet to come!)

Consequently, when his troopers made lightning raids on German strong points at night, they had begun leaving these "calling cards." A German going out a doorway and seeing a sticker on the door, as well as finding them on fenceposts and helmets of dead comrades, made the enemy nervous, and gave Frederick the advantage he had hoped to achieve.

For spring had arrived, bringing with it drier weather. Frederick had turned thirty-seven on 14 March, and received a birthday card his officers and men had printed up for him, and from Ruth a box containing wool socks and photographs of her and their daughters. Writing to thank her, he described a bucolic scene in the hellish fury of his environment:

"This is the first week of spring, and it is lovely. Farmers who once lived here left behind flocks of sheep, and there are many newborn lambs that stray from the ewes to quizzically watch the older lambs at play and, trying to imitate them, they look like tiny bales of cotton buffeted by a stiff breeze. Red poppies, white daises are in bloom, the sky a deep blue, each color brilliant, such a pleasant change."

He also, finally, found time to write to the Assistant Chief of Staff in Washington, General Handy, to thank him for his congratulatory message back in January, and to say:

"[T]he missions assigned us have not been easy ones, and there are few replacements for the men I lose. It is the spirit that enables this unit to push forward and accomplish almost impossible missions. It takes time for that spirit to develop, and without proper facilities men cannot get the training to bring them up to the level of those with whom I entered combat. I wish this unit could have been many times larger when it came overseas. A much larger unit composed of men having the daring, competence, and confidence in themselves and in their comrades that my men have could do vast, serious damage to the enemy.

I have learned much the last few months—some of it I wish I had not had to learn—and wiser if not much older, I will never forget the lessons I have learned."

This hardly seems the missive from a man being extolled as the "fierce" young general, and by Churchill "[with] a dozen men like him we could have smashed Hitler in 1942." But only if not knowing Frederick. Who, unlike swaggering, peacocky generals tooting their own horns, saw himself simply as a soldier doing the best that his military education yielded. But it did reveal he was thinking ahead, to if ever the

Army saw the value of having more elite special forces on its payroll; for which, he somewhat hinted, he would be an erudite leader.

Yet he was not all that sure he liked a high position. His rank made him a figurehead, and according to Wickham, "What once had been 'Bob, do you agree?' had become, if he was present, 'Ask the General if he agrees.' Yesterday's comrades no longer felt they had the right to hash things over with him in a clubhouse mode."

True, a general is forced to be alone, isolated from the normal conversation and comradeship in situations that call for closeness. And Frederick needed good talk as much as other men need food, and wanted company. So Wickham filled both slots, "...as many an evening, we chatted in his room before he began his night's work, and enjoyed a fellowship that exists on battlefields."

But Frederick had little leisure time. Having escalated action by mounting large scale daylight attacks against houses the Germans used for observation, gun emplacements, and shelter, he was proving the Force's tactical superiority. He had got on loan some tanks from VI Corps, and directed attacks south toward the coastline, where his raiders captured sixty-one Germans, killed nineteen, and destroyed the houses; and also ordered an attack north to the far side of no-man's land, where again, trained as demolitionists, his men, overwhelming the enemy, flattened a string of houses. Then, for all the month of April, while the other beachhead units maintained static defense, he continued to lash out, taking more enemy territory. Besides forcing the Germans to go on the defensive, he had another reason to feel good. VI Corps had sent a request: Could he spare some of his officers to lecture the other units on how to raid and patrol? But of even more benefit to the penned-up Allies was that with each attack Frederick ordered, his troops gained experience in tank infantry operations, which—yet unforeseen—would be vital when eventually the Allies broke out of Anzio.

Now it was May. Now over three months of living under the noses of the enemy, with no rear area to withdraw to as German shells and bombs hit everywhere, including the field hospital (killing medical personnel and patients). The sense of being forgotten was prevalent among all involved in what has since been called "an epic stand on a lonely beachhead," and "a protracted horror." But something new was in the air. Additional units had snuck ashore, and behind smoke screens tons of supplies had been unloaded at Anzio's port. Seventy miles south in the mountainous mid-section of Italy, the rest of the U.S. Fifth Army and the British Eighth Army had managed to push forward, and anticipating their linking up with the units at Anzio, Mark Clark and the British general senior to him, Harold Alexander, had formulated plans for a drive to Rome.*

At Anzio, meanwhile, General Truscott had prepared four schemes of his own for a breakout. Frederick was busy studying the details of these plans when Finn Roll appeared to report "a German prisoner says he expected capture by one of our 'colored' troops who go out after dark."

Frederick was holding a square four inch map of Italy, the kind easy to carry in a helmet between the liner and metal.

"Did he say anything," he asked Roll, "about a division headquarters? Anything that hints of a new directional order in the near future? Or change of gear, or stepped up movement of tanks?"

"General," Roll replied, "he didn't even know he was in Italy."

"Well, two miles from where he was nabbed there is a pocket of German 88s [rocket launchers]." Frederick had spotted it while roving into the enemy lines. "We better take it before dawn."

"Hell, tomorrow we can take all of this country," said Roll.

Frederick gave him a flinty look. "What do you mean?"

"According to your map," Roll measured it with his pinky finger, "Italy is only four inches long."

Frederick laughed, thankful to share a lighthearted moment with Roll. For he had recently got word that Roll's father, a member of Norway's underground resistance, had been murdered by the *Gestapo*;

---

*Not without, however, getting into a riff. Clark wanted his Fifth Army to have the honor (and publicity) of being first into Rome, and had threatened Alexander that he would have Fifth Army troops fire on the British Eighth Army if it tried to take part. With gentlemanly élan Alexander had quickly allowed as how Clark could have his way.

and sadly seeking out the young Intelligence Officer, whose company he always enjoyed, Frederick had watched his face while telling him the news. Roll's features had hardened immediately, as he uttered, "From now on every prisoner will be more harshly interrogated." (He would, in fact, keep throwing some off a second story balcony of an Anzio farmhouse until they were willing to talk.)

Frederick had written to Ruth that "informing him of his father's death was the hardest thing I have ever done." This from a man with the smell of death around him constantly, and for whom the threat of death required 24-hour-a-day vigilance. But as Roll would say later, "Looking back at my commander," he had seen "a cloud of grief in his eyes."

On 9 May, Frederick was told by Truscott to pull his force back, to prime it for the drive to Rome. So, formed up in long lines, in a scene unlike any in military manuals his troops headed down a road with squawking chickens, cows, horses, and "acquired" household goods. And while for twelve days they brushed up on assault tactics, Frederick and the other beachhead commanders poured over one of Truscott's plans selected for the breakout. It called for a thrust northeast to the town of Cisterna and, crossing "Route 7," a swing north to capture the towns of Cori, Artena, Valmontone, and to cut "Route 6" to block a German retreat just below Rome.

Spearheading the assault would be the U.S. 1st Armored Division on the left, the U.S. 3rd Infantry Division in the center, and on the right Frederick's American-Canadian brigade, which of late had received reinforcements—some survivors of Ranger battalions decimated by a German ambush at Anzio—some men carefully chosen from replacement pools, but most were Frederick's own troops returned from hospitals. This gave him 2,070 fighters, less than half of one of any division's regiment; yet, positioned right of the 3rd as they pushed northeast and curled north, his force was to have the widest front and longest route, its own right flank fully exposed to the enemy.

If Frederick gulped over this it was not apparent; he wrote in a memo to Truscott, "This command can successfully execute its role." But he did petition for two companies of tanks and tank destroyers for the initial attack (he got one each). Continuing to send patrols out "to keep the offensive in the troops, to gather information, and to fool the enemy into thinking we still hold our sector," on 21 May, now with the breakout two days off, Frederick forwarded to his patrolmen his congratulations "for a superb job"; and to all his men sent a long message that ended with: "The eyes of Canada and the United States are upon us. Let them see as in the past we move only forward."

Which hardly memorable, nonetheless "put everyone" recalled one trooper, "in high spirits and raring to push to Rome."

Frederick spent a sleepless night 22-23 May as he moved under the blanket of dark back up to the Mussolini Canal with his force to its jump-off position, and went over his plan of maneuver. He was depending on the speed and mobility of his troops as, using his strongest regiment of 670 men to make the first attack, the other regiments followed close behind to protect the right flank. At 3:30 AM he rang up one 3rd Division unit commander—and West Point classmate—Colonel Lionel McGarr.

"You better be planning on making it to Rome," he told McGarr, "because either we all get there or we all will be eating potato soup in a POW camp the rest of the war."

McGarr would remember later, putting down his radiophone receiver, he thought to himself, "But if anyone makes this dagger thrust to Rome work, it is going to be Bob, who has the guts."

The sun had begun to peek over hills to the east when, at 5:45 AM, all workable artillery guns on the beachhead blasted into action; and ripping apart the sky, Allied planes streaked over German forward positions, dropped bombs, and roared off in the alley of safe air between opponents. Crouched in holes in the ground Frederick's troops, tensely waiting, checked their weapons and ammunition, and tanks started slowly clanking to jump-off points. Then, on signal, at 6:30 the big guns fell silent—and the "Devil's Brigade" surged forward.

Racing through woods into fields of tall wheat, Frederick's lead regiment crossed its first objective, Route 7, at 10:30 AM. One half mile ahead was the day's last objective, a railroad embankment; but having moved and overrun the enemy so rapidly his force's left flank had now also become exposed. And suddenly no one could find Frederick.

"An immense wave of grief and consternation swept over us forcemen," later said Sergeant Kurtzhal. "But as we were beating a route through a wheat field, with nothing between us and the enemy, a jeep came sputtering down a road up ahead. On the hood sat the jeep driver holding a gun on nine Germans, and steering the jeep, our general was herding the petulant prisoners down the road. We all were relieved as hell, but miffed at Frederick. For though used to him going off alone, we couldn't fathom the breakout succeeding without him. How he nabbed those nine, I don't know—he sure didn't buy them at the A and P."

Actually, Frederick had jeeped ahead to check the situation. Had things gone according to his plans, his troops were to cross and hold the rail embankment by noon; but with both flanks exposed his force was now in danger of being cut off. As for the nine unlucky Germans, they had sheltered themselves in a little train station to eat some rations when, sneaking in the back way, Frederick hollered, "Hands up!"

The incident soon was a favorite of his troops trying to explain how their commander differed from other leaders. Which in years since becomes better described: "The best example," recalls one ex-soldier, "is when breaking out of Anzio, zooming along in fields, we glanced over at distant hills and roads and saw other troops moving in rows and getting mowed down; and we all thought 'Thank God our general gives us the leeway to get to our objective the safest way, not by the book.' That was the biggest difference—Frederick respected our abilities, valued us highly, and trusted us so genuinely."

But by mid-day Frederick's problems mounted. Not only was the 3rd Division still on the outskirts of Cisterna, two miles south of his force, the supporting tanks and TDs, coming under fire, had not kept pace either. Trying repeatedly by radio to spur them on, he got in a row with the commander of the tank destroyers "who keeps quoting some rule," he fumed afterward, "that TDs are to stay 4,000 feet in back of infantry troops." If Frederick felt frustrated it was surely not assuaged, as he then learned some of the tanks were hiding behind houses.

Meanwhile, he had to hold his regiments in place to allow the 3rd to catch up. Whereupon, the Germans used the pause to assemble troops and huge Tiger tanks, and at dusk they counterattacked. Calling on VI Corps artillery to help stem the enemy, Frederick now also, after much prodding, got the armor to move up—but its effect was picayune. Most of the tanks were hit and disabled, and shells fired by the TDs bounced off the big German Tiger tanks. With few options left, at 7:00 PM, as the macabre task of using the night to bring in casualties began, he ordered his battered forward troops to consolidate behind the rail embankment; he then drove to Corps headquarters to discuss the next plan of action with Truscott, who had been celebrating the day's successes with drinks, and was feeling "pretty good." Frederick was disgusted.

"Yes, German defenses had been pierced," he would later say, "but thirty-nine of my men had been killed, about twenty captured, the rest extremely fatigued, and the 3rd and 1st Divisions had had significant loses."*

Arriving back at his CP at 9:00 PM, Frederick no sooner got in the door than was told to return to Truscott's headquarters; new information had come in and plans changed. So, repeating the trip, at 1:00 AM the following day he had finished coordinating his plan of attack with the Corps and forwarded it to his field commanders; only to again be summoned by Truscott, as there had been another change. It was 4:00 AM before finally, thinking "Enough of this veering of plans," on the floor of his CP, Frederick managed to grab fifteen minutes of sleep.

That day (24 May), his troops swarmed toward Mont Arrestino, overlooking the town of Cori, and as Frederick directed them up trails on the mountain, he radioed to Ken Wickham that he needed rations and ammunition. It so happened a mule train under a young lieutenant had been requisitioned by his unit, and going forward to deliver the supplies, the train was heading back to the rear when Frederick again radioed Wickham that he needed a second load of ammunition "quick as the mules can get here. Turn them around, send them back," he ordered.

All of a sudden, on the same radio frequency the voice of a German officer speaking English interrupted.

"I have been listening to your conversations and enjoyed them all, and will soon see you all," he said, laughing.

"You bet," Frederick barked. "We'll soon have accommodations for you and all your friends in a POW cage."

---

*Indeed, the 3rd had 800 men dead, wounded, or missing, and in the 1st, 86 tanks and tank destroyers had been knocked out.

Then, unsure how much the eavesdropper could comprehend, he said to Wickham, "Gittum that thar stuff this-a-way on them thar critters right fast."

Recalled Wickham: "That I understood, but I was not as prepared for the lieutenant's reaction to having to make trip two. I thought he was going to mutiny as he screamed, 'My mules are tired! They will die of fatigue!'"

True, some mules keeled over. But Frederick got the supplies by noon as, seizing Mont Arrestino, his men braced to sweep Nazis out of the way on the heights north of Cori—while the approaching 3rd and 1st Divisions encircled the town. At sunset, Frederick traveled in the shadowy dimness back to VI Corps Headquarters, and now learned General Clark unexpectedly had switched direction of the offensive and ordered Truscott—visibly shaken by the switch—to wheel four of VI Corps' divisions (three that had been following behind, plus the 1st Division) westward on a more direct route to Rome. In the meantime, now at Anzio, II Corps, under General Keyes, was to move right and eventually link up with Frederick's force and the 3rd. Which meant for days the 3rd and Frederick's outfit, already worn out, would be fighting alone on to Valmontone, and would be in danger of having to go on the defensive to survive.

"It was one of the worst decision ever made," claimed one officer in the 3rd. As for Frederick, displaying tact a bit reluctantly, he later said, "Some details of that strategy were beyond my position, but it did strike me that it smacked of Clark being in a terrible big rush to get to Rome."

He certainly was. Obsessed with garnering glory and publicity for capturing Rome, Clark was racing against time. The invasion of Normandy, set for two weeks off, would definitely eclipse any news of action in Italy; plus, the British Eighth Army, though twenty-six miles to the east, was steadily churning closer to Rome on Route 6.

In regard to the enemy, Kesselring had sent down more reinforcements, and had ordered the Hermann Göring Panzer Division to move to Valmontone in strength.

Thus, soon Clark's strategy would look more like a blunder—a costly blunder.

10

"Where are these Troops?"

Once again Bob Frederick was presumed captured, or dead. Early on 26 May, moving his force en masse into Cori and finding no resistance—the enemy was seen straggling north in the distance—he executed his next plan, to march his troops over the high ground to Artena. At dusk, receiving word the lead column had reached the last hill before Artena, Frederick took off on foot with his aide, Captain McCall, to check the position.

On the way he encountered a soldier who had become separated from the lead group, and telling him to come along, as they were going up to his unit, the three walked around the side of one hill to view the opposite side. There, sixty feet away stood a group of thirty Germans. Frederick was thinking that, not yet spotted, they could make it to safety, when the soldier tagging along fired his machine gun, and instantly the Germans shot him.

Armed only with pistols Frederick and McCall looked at one another and, nodding in agreement, "ran like the devil," recalled Frederick, "for a quarter of a mile toward a wheat field," where thus concealed, they sunk down to catch their breath. But one forceman had spied the Germans, "and come racing up to us," described another trooper, "screaming out Frederick was surrounded and shots had been exchanged. In seconds we were tearing toward the hill, and would have kept running all the way to

Germany to save our general when he, fortunately, appeared—none the worse for the harrowing experience."*

The next day, continuing to wind its way toward Artena, as his force settled in on a nearby hillside Frederick established his CP in the town, where the 3rd Division had been busy cleaning out the enemy. As it grew dark, the sky lit up with amber streaks of tracer fire, and shots were heard close by; the Hermann Göring Panzer Division had arrived, determined to halt the Force and the 3rd from reaching Valmontone, just four miles away.

That night the Germans moved in a string of tanks in woods north of Artena and, at daylight, zeroing in, kept firing at the streets of the medieval town and at Frederick's CP which, set up in a centuries old palace built like a fortress, sat on a cliff. The day before Frederick had commented that it had "an excellent view of the valley beyond," but now, with every few seconds another cyclone of shells and explosions coming in, no one dared to look out. "And to walk the streets was quick death," recalled one soldier.

Frederick conferred with the 3rd's commander, Major General John W. O'Daniel, and, told the 3rd would maneuver simultaneously with his force to remove the tanks, sent his regiments fanning out. But against tanks shooting at point blank range the toll on his men was growing heavy; and of added concern, a local citizen was flashing signals to the German guns. In hope of ending that, Frederick ordered all townspeople evacuated. Yet it would be three days before the constant firing ceased when the culprit, hiding in an attic, was caught red handed signaling with a flashlight. In the interim, Frederick could do little but dispatch reconnaissance and demolition patrols. Further west, meanwhile, the bulk of VI Corps was making slow progress at the Alban Hills where, to Truscott, it appeared the Germans "have slammed shut the gate." And as Clark agitatedly now realized, instead of bolting to Rome on the most direct route, he had stumbled into a stalemate.

---

*As for the soldier who fired the opening shot, he later was found waiting by a path for the rest of the Force to advance, his wound carefully dressed by the Germans, who had chosen not to be burdened with a prisoner as they fled north.

But luckily part of Keyes' II Corps was resolutely plowing toward Valmontone; thus, on 29 May Frederick got the welcome news that Clark had ordered Keyes to send two divisions (the 85th and 88th) in left of the 3rd's zone. For with their combined artillery, the situation would surely improve.

As would briefly the enemy's when, slipping in a battle group at 1:00 AM on 30 May, the Hermann Görings tried to retake Artena. However, forewarned the enemy was piling up on the Artena-Valmontone road, Frederick quickly put two regiments on the defense line with the 3rd's troops to stop the German infantry while supporting artillery repulsed the tanks. By 5:00 AM the disenchanted enemy had withdrawn, and in twenty-four hours the three U.S. divisions and Frederick's maverick bi-national brigade prepared to push forward early on 1 June. Indubitably, while Frederick waited he had concerns that again his force, positioned on the right flank, would have to cover the longest distance with the widest front as II Corps curled northwestward toward Rome.

On the German side troops had begun creeping north to safety, and Kesselring had instructed rearguard units to use demolitions "with sadistic imaginativeness" to slow the Allies' advance. One result on 1 June occurred when Frederick sent in a regiment to take a small town; the enemy's collapse was rapid, but a factory, ammunition storage bins, and every bridge had been wired to blow up. Warning his men that "dead Germans may be booby trapped, trees ripe with fruit surrounded by mines; touch no food or water, enter no vacant building," as II Corps engineers were moving in to defuse the time charges, Frederick was brought a message by runner that his lead unit had reached Route 6. Concurrently, the 3rd Division had entered Valmontone, and to the west, Truscott's VI Corps succeeded in bursting through the Alban Hill mass. The race to Rome was about to begin.

Late that day Keyes summoned Frederick to his headquarters, and told him to organize two task forces, which Frederick took to mean, "Be ready should a need arise for mobile forces." But now at dawn on 3 June, Keyes telephoned to say he had placed "Task Force Howze," an armored group led by Colonel Hamilton Howze, under Frederick's command; and next from his headquarters came word Keyes had given

Frederick a front the entire width of II Corps, and that, moving Howze's group at night, and his own troops in daylight, Frederick's force was to spearhead II Corps' assault on Rome.

With "something akin to gold rush fever in the air," one officer would remember, Frederick—ignoring the order to alternately move Howze's group and his own men, "as it was silly," he was later to say—decided to have two regiments advance with some of the tanks, with one regiment kept in reserve. Then, taking off in a halftrack he had acquisitioned that had the same radio frequency as the tanks, he moved up Route 6 to lead from the front.

At dusk, on a hill outside Rome, Frederick and his combat officers sat "quietly talking," observed one trooper, "and gazing at the lights of the city, before slowly walking back to the bivouac area, whatever excitement they felt muted by the impact this would be the first enemy-dominated capital captured by the Americans."

Or was it what Frederick recalled: that Rome was to be invaded from the south for the first time since Belisarius had marched north in 536 AD.

As darkness fell, his force spearhead reached the town of Finochio, seven miles from Rome, where, setting up his CP, Frederick spent a frightening night. German self-propelled guns kept shelling the CP-cum-farmhouse, while from above, U.S. Air Corps planes, flying up Route 6, kept bombing the place. From one or the other Frederick was wounded a fourth time when shrapnel whizzed through the left collar of his shirt, ripping out a two inch gash at the base of his neck. Binding it with gauze and tape, he waited for new orders from Keyes, who at 1:10 AM fired the starting gun, as he radioed to Frederick "Secure bridges over the Tiber River above 68 Northing within the city of Rome."*

Having already committed two of his regiments that were nearing a suburb of Rome, Frederick designated two companies in his reserve regiment and twenty of Howze's tanks to do the bridge job. But because at night tank drivers could see little through the tiny slits in their tanks,

---

*On maps, 68 Northing referred to an area north of the Vatican city. Fearing the bridges would be destroyed as part of Kesselring's withdrawal plan, Clark had instructed Keyes to ensure they remained intact so Fifth Army could continue north in pursuit of Germans.

forming up in a field in Finochio, the bridge force had to wait until dawn broke. Frederick was standing in the field by his half-track when five jeeps loaded with newsmen, eager to be first to file the story Rome had fallen, appeared; and one journalist, Newbold Noyes, commented to him, "You don't look like a man whose command post has repeatedly been getting bombed and shelled tonight."

"No, I do not feel tired at all," answered Frederick. "This is like Christmas eve, when you don't want to go to bed. But it is a long gamble— I have no idea what opposition we will encounter. Probably," he joked, "I will have to hold a conference with Kesselring at the city limits to decide what to do."

Asked another: "When you got the order, did you say anything to your troops like 'Damn the torpedoes, full speed ahead,' or 'Don't give up the ship'?"

Frederick smiled. "No, I did not have time," he said. "Anyway, you don't have to say stuff like that to these boys."

By now it was 4:10 AM. Behind him the tanks, motors rumbling, had started to warm up, and Frederick's hardened commando fighters had begun moving into position.

Before the end of that long day of 4 June the newsmen would get their story that Rome had fallen.

Speeding along Route 6 with some of his troops clinging to decks of tanks at the front of the bridge force column, Frederick followed in his half-track with McCall, a scout, and two radio operators; making up the tail of the column were more tanks and men of his force on foot and in trucks. Meeting little opposition—the enemy readily surrendering to tanks bearing down on them—the column rolled past a big blue and white sign that said ROMA. As this marked the city limits, Frederick checked the time on his watch and asked McCall to send the message to Force headquarters "We entered Rome at 0620 hours." (Which would be significant later, when other units started claiming to be first into the Eternal City.)

Suddenly the lead tank was hit, then a second tank set afire by German anti-tank guns hiding behind a stone wall. Scuttling off the armor,

Frederick's troops took cover in ditches and behind houses, the tanks wheeled away in evasive action into fields, and a reconnaissance patrol edged forward through the curtain of enemy shells. At 7:00 AM the patrol reported that ahead were about 300 German troops, tanks, and a heavy concentration of guns in a deep roadblock.

Frederick had a serious dilemma on his hands; though only a short distance back was artillery attached to his force, to use it to blast loose the roadblock was anathema to him, for it would inflict massive civilian casualties as well. In a twisted sense, he was getting his conference with Kesselring *in absentia*, on whose orders a fanatical rearguard devised the delaying action holding up the bridge force.

Calling on aerial observation to give him a clear idea of German positions, at noon Frederick got the information and, convening his combat commanders at his ad hoc CP by the ROMA sign, as they studied their maps he outlined his plan. The reserve regiment would continue to deal with the roadblock while his two regiments assembling in suburbs to the east made a coordinated end run west into Rome with some of the tanks to get to the bridges over the Tiber River. Walking up Route 6, Frederick then stood on a low hill, waving his men forward; and was heading back to the ROMA sign when a jeep drove up, and from it descended II Corp's commander.

"General Frederick, what's holding you up?" he asked.

"The Germans, Sir," said Frederick matter-of-factly.

"How long will it take you to proceed across city limits?" asked Keyes.

"The rest of the day," or, as long as needed, Frederick was about to say, without risking my men unnecessarily.

But Keyes had interrupted. "That will not do. General Clark has to be in Rome at four o'clock to have his photograph taken."

Staring at him for a long moment, Frederick waited for some expression on Keyes' face to reveal he was jesting—before realizing, oh my God, he means it!

Sure enough, at about 4:00 Clark arrived with four of his officers and a phalanx of photographers and newsmen. The sizeable convoy rolled to a stop where Frederick was observing the fight going on at the roadblock; and accompanied by Keyes, Clark strode up and inquired, "What's holding up the First Special Service Force?"

Frederick, replying that due to civilians in the area he would not use artillery, on a map showed his superiors his plan of maneuver—all the while flashbulbs popping and newsreel crews filming. Clark, then requesting that Frederick pose with him at the ROMA sign, added, "Golly, Bob, I would like that sign for a souvenir. Will you get it for me?" What ensued (and, caught on film, seen many years later on a PBS television series on World War II), a grim-visaged Frederick, standing beside a smiling Mark Clark, told his half-track driver to get a hammer and to hoist himself onto a high fence to knock down the sign that was easily four feet by six feet long.

At that point a German sniper opened fire, sending the knot of Americans diving into a ditch for safety, which provided Frederick a satisfying excuse to blurt out to Clark, "That is what's holding up the First Special Service Force!" Obviously his entry into Rome to be delayed, Clark and his entourage soon departed. Immediately Frederick took off to move with his troops toward the bridges; and, like any good soldier, he would keep quiet over how he felt about Clark's mania for self publicity.

But his actions would speak loudly, as will be seen.

Rome was falling, and becoming a bed of confusion, as one minute Italians, seeing Frederick's tank infantry teams infiltrate the city, rushed from their houses in a celebratory mood and clogged the routes, the next minute dashing back inside as Germans hiding in the maze of alleys and streets fired on their pursuers. Street fighting is a slow, dirty job anywhere, but also impeding Frederick's troops were Romans who, sympathizing with Germany, eagerly tried leading them into traps.

Frederick, with his teams advancing on multiple routes, had no network of communication, and constantly moving around to direct commands to his men, at 6:00 PM ordered most of two regiments to bivouac and rest outside Rome, while one regiment fought on to the bridges. By twilight little organized resistance remained except for rearguards holding the bridges, so leaving his troops Frederick set out with a party of four to learn were the bridges intact? Wired to be blown up? Stopping at a bridge called San Angelo—where the rearguard promptly fled—with his aide McCall, Frederick was walking across to inspect it for demolitions when out of the darkening streets appeared a German force retreating from the south. Frederick yelled "Halt!," and the Germans responded with gunfire.

Instantly the night sky lit up with a flaming exchange of shots and, while beside him McCall fired a tommy gun, Frederick emptied the clip in his .45, then felt searing pain as a bullet tore into his right thigh, another into his right arm, and several more entered his thigh. Sinking to the ground, he crawled along on one knee ("leaving a trail of blood a foot wide behind him," remembered McCall) to the end of the bridge, where a face popped up before him "and scared the hell out of me," he said later.

It was the face of a U.S. soldier whose unit just had penetrated Rome and, who in his own words, "was an AWOL sergeant—with a general I thought was going to die. He was bleeding from his pants, from his shirt, but kept saying 'I'm okay, okay.'"

The clash ended with the Germans withdrawing, leaving behind five dead and six wounded comrades, and eleven with their hands in the air. Frederick's half-track driver also lay dead. Shortly, one platoon from his force arrived to secure the bridge, and Frederick was taken to an advance aid station to have his wounds cauterized and bound; but he refused when a medic pleaded he get in the ambulance and go to an established hospital south of Rome. "I don't have time," said Frederick, hobbling away to tend to details and to contact his men.

"I tried to imagine the awful pain he was in," one officer later recalled, "as he kept directing the action that night with those wounds in his thigh."

However great his pain, though, Frederick was as much suffering profound remorsefulness. Said McCall: "He cared deeply about his men, each and every one, and felt responsible his driver had been killed."

By 11:00 PM all eight key bridges over the Tiber River assigned to his force were seized, and Frederick headed outside Rome to a tent serving as an office for Fifth Army's Chief of Staff, Major General Al Gruenther. On the way, stopping to, with McCall's help, yank down off a pole a small version of the big blue and white ROMA sign Clark had asked for, with it under his arm he limped up to the desk of the Deputy Chief of

Staff Colonel Charles Saltzman, and said, "It occurred to me that General Clark may desire to add this sign to his souvenier collection."

But his not too subtle jab at Clark difted past Saltzman, who was busy noting: "Frederick was continuing on his nerves and whatever pain killer was in him. As I recall, he said he hadn't slept for sixty hours when I took him in to see Gruenther [to be 'Gruenther-ized' many called it, due to the grilling he put men through], all of whose questions Bob answered accurately and completely."

In that regard, as one of the Force Headquarters staff officers would recount later, "Frederick had the most phenomenal memory, and coupled with his instinct for always knowing when and where he was needed, which often had him up with troops at the front, little ever escaped him."

For what was left of the night of 4-5 June, at an elaborate building in the center of Rome Frederick rested in a room commandeered by the Force surgeon; and gathered around him were ten of his staff bearing notebooks and maps. Outside, pushing through throngs of happy Italians, meantime, was a soldier whose weapon was a pencil. Sergeant Bill Mauldin (later a well known editorial cartoonist of social and political issues) drew cartoons for the G.I.s' newspaper *Stars and Stripes*, in which he depicted the life of the enlisted man through the characters Willie and Joe—on occasion causing the ire of one or another general. He had been driving toward Rome when "catching up with a section of Frederick's organization," he was later to say, "I hauled twelve pissed off forcemen into the city. They were mad because they knew their outfit had been forced to rush to Rome, and knew comrades were killed and Frederick had been shot."

Reaching the city, Mauldin then: "sought out Frederick, and found him laying on a bed with bandages on his serious wounds. But it was not a hospital scene. He too was angry, angrier I was told than he'd been earlier, but was having a party. People were milling around, and some were passing a bottle of wine between them. He didn't say anything indiscrete, but it was blatant that party in his room was a snub at Clark. I can tell you Frederick dug what I did; he saw me thumbing my nose at some high echelon in my cartoons, and that night at least, he was thumbing his nose in the same direction."

Under a hot, bright sun, the next day at 8:00 AM Clark entered Rome. Most American units that had spent the night liberating the city had moved on in pursuit of Germans, but Frederick's Special Service Force was still fighting pockets of enemy and guarding the eight Tiber Bridges when Clark, summoning his corps commanders Keyes and Truscott to join him, strode up the steps of the city hall, and at the top rail, with newsmen crowded around, posed in every direction. He then briefly spoke. "This is a great day for the Fifth Army and for the French, British, and American troops in the Fifth who made this victory possible."

Which did not sit well with some of the newsmen, among them Eric Sevareid, who would write:

"It was not apparently a great day for the world, for the Allies, for all the suffering people.... It was a great day for the Fifth Army. Then Clark spread a map on the balustrade, and [he] proceeded to point out something or other. The cameras ground, the corps commanders, red with embarrassment, looked back and forth from us to the map."

And as Clark's staged self-promoting affair wound down and Sevareid descended the steps with his colleagues, one of them remarked to him, "On this historic occasion I feel like vomiting."

Throughout the day, cheering and parading Romans celebrated as columns of Allied tanks, jeeps, and trucks rolled into the city. In the meantime, Frederick's outfit began making its way back to the suburbs; II Corps had sent word the Force was relieved of further action; and except for one battalion left to guard all the bridges, that night the weary forcemen who spearheaded Rome's liberation fell thankfully into deep sleep.

"We were bruised, hurting, and sick after two weeks of high pressure fighting—breaking out of distant Anzio and days of atrocious pushing into Rome," said one.

And like their commander, the first big news to reach them upon awakening 6 June was that a second front had been opened, that Allied troops had landed in north France at Normandy.

Up to then, Italy was the main place the Allies could fight Germans on the ground. Yet that campaign, plagued by blunders, slow advances, and entrapment at Anzio already was being criticized. Was it worth the cost? The count in Fifth Army alone, so far, was 3,145 Americans killed, 13,740 wounded, and over 1,800 missing, including many of Frederick's highly trained soldiers. Already too, however, the achievements of Frederick's force due to its fierceness, flexiblity, and intrepidness were legend.

But then: "His force did have a reputation of being roughneck," recalls one retired general, "and any place there was a roughneck job, it got it. By and large, the conventional U.S. Army was scared to death of Frederick's brigade."

In Washington, Ruth Frederick was listening to a radio broadcast about the Normandy invasion when, at midday 6 June, a news reporter telephoned.

"Have you seen the article filed by the war correspondent Newbold Noyes about your husband leading the way into Rome?" he asked.

Saying she had not, the reporter read it to her; and Ruth responded, "I'm simply thrilled to death. I hear so little about him. The last letter I had was on May 22nd, then I read in a New York newspaper he had been awarded a Distinguished Service Cross [for 'bold leadership'], a Silver Star [for his action at la Difensa], and a Bronze Star [for 'sound and forceful leadership in ground operations']. But I'd not heard anything since. Thank you," she said, hanging up.

So of course she could not know her husband just had won a second DSC "for heroism" in Rome and, bringing his total of Purple Hearts to seven so far, on 3 and 4 June received three wounds. At around the same time in Italy (it being six hours later), that night, finally Frederick acquiesced to be treated at a hospital near Anzio, where it required a surgeon put 256 stitches in his thigh to hold together muscles and tissue. Yet he had been lucky. No bones had been shattered. Even so, his right leg would hamper him for the rest of his life and, sometimes, just walking would be a painful experience.

After nine hours at the hospital, telephoning his Force medical officer to say "Come get me," Frederick, sneaking out with a metal IV stand, a bottle of sulfur and an IV tube attached to him, headed to Lake Albano, south of Rome, where his North Americans were to rest for three weeks. Getting his men set up in tents alongside the lake, and some officers in houses, he chose a little house on a slope for himself that "was pleasant"; later remembered Wickham, "except it had no furniture."

Frederick said he could fix that. One mile from the lake's rim sat the Pope's summer villa, and Frederick had a letter from a Catholic bishop which he had carried through battle, and decided to now use. It had been given to him when forming his outfit in Montana, he encountered a group of nuns trying to get a stained glass window for their chapel, and he had arranged to have it manufactured. Grateful, the nuns had told the Bishop of Montana, who had written a letter in Latin that said: "Should Robert T. Frederick ever need help from the Church I ask my brothers please extend it to him."

So now he sent his aide off to the Vatican, where McCall, showing the letter to a secretary of one Cardinal in charge of civil affairs, was asked, "What does General Frederick need?"

"Furniture," reposited McCall. "We have this house, but it's empty"; to which the secretary replied, "If tomorrow you send trucks to the [Pope's] summer residence, the staff will solve the problem."

The upshot was, okaying use of one truck, Frederick got more than he needed, and all of it—chairs, tables, chests, beds, linens, glassware, and silver—inscribed with the Papal crest; and in a note to Ruth, he mentioned having "unique furnishings where I am staying." But he was not the only one to enjoy them. A while back Wickham had been wounded in his right hand, and as it was immobilized in a wad of bandages, and Frederick was a semi-invalid due to his leg, Frederick asked he stay at the house and set up a buddy system. Whereupon, Wickham would walk to the lake on Frederick's missions, and Frederick cut up Wickham's meat and put paste on his toothbrush.

By the front door stood the now unused metal IV stand which, on returning to the house one evening, Wickham saw now held an inverted bottle of whiskey, and connected to it a tube with a clamp at the end.

"That's my invention," Frederick said, grinning at his housemate. "It could be the catharsis for patients for whom morphine has become addictive, though as it takes an overt action to use the clamp, there is a chance a patient could drown in liquor if losing the ability to turn off the flow."

Wickham laughed, "but was as unsure," he said, later, "as many times previous, how much of this was Frederick's proverbial humor, how much seriousness, and how much an extension of his boredom with his imposed convalescence."

The proximity of the Pope's summer villa had, meanwhile, lured some forcemen to help themselves to its contents, one going as far as to adorn the entry to his tent with a gold statue belonging to Pope Pius XII. Told by the villa's indignant director items were disappearing, Frederick agreed with him "it oversteps the line of decency" but, unlike martinent generals who would subject men to child-like rebukes, he worked quietly, ordering a thorough inspection; and almost all items stolen were returned. Between swimming in the lake, lots of sleep, and liberal passes into Rome, his troops were coming around to their former selves when, on 23 June, directing they assemble near the lake, as they stood in formation he presented to several men awards they won in battle. His right leg strapped to a board for support, Frederick then slowly walked up to his microphone.

"One of a general's pleasant jobs," he said, "is to decorate soldiers with medals they richly earned, and," he paused a moment, then went on, "one of the toughest jobs is to tell an outfit he loves goodbye, which I am telling you now."

As if one man the Force let out a loud gasp.

"I will never," said one soldier years later, "forget the collective gasp that arose. Part of our force died that day...we were losing a man who we all loved."

Observing the scene was a correspondent from the *Washington Post*, Frederick Painton, who wrote in a story for his newspaper:

> Battle toughened soldiers had tears in their eyes. The men wanted to know where he was going, so as to transfer to be under him. He shook his head—he couldn't tell them. But he said he expected them to go on fighting not as Yanks or Canadians, but as North Americans, upholding the tradition of the best damned combat outfit in existence. He turned to smartly salute the only North American flag in existence, [and] the men openly now

wept as their proved leader, beloved by them, climbed into his staff car, and with one last proud look at his Force drove off.

Frederick's own sentiment at the time was, "I was leaving a force I had formed, and men to whom I owed much for their sacrifice and courage. So sure, I was teary-eyed."

Yet a message informing him he was reassigned had left him also "feeling elated"; for he was now to be the commander of the 36th Infantry Division (which had fought on the "Winter Line" and at Anzio, and been a part of II Corps' march on Rome). But not for long.

Six days later, while he was at his temporary office in Rome, he got another message that he had been re-assigned, his new job a "secret." He was to fly immediately to Algiers, North Africa, to meet with Deputy Supreme Allied Commander Lieutenant General Jacob L. Devers. Who, upon Frederick's arrival, explained to him plans for an Allied invasion in the south of France—to deal an uppercut blow to the Germans.

"Huge seaborne landing forces will hit France's southern beaches and, in what will be the largest airborne operation in the war, airborne troops," said Devers, "will go in to block the roads and other enemy accesses. And you," he continued, "are going to command the airborne troops."

"Where are these airborne troops?" asked Frederick.

"So far," replied Devers, "you're the only one."

11

A "Most Remarkable" Exploit

They say in this war we are fighting for all
Those good things in life, and for freedom,
But the crazy galoot in the silk parachute
Won't live long enough, as to need them.

So ends a poem about a paratrooper's lament. And if anyone had reason not to serve as a paratrooper, it was certainly Bob Frederick. He had jumped but once from an airplane back in Montana and, as may be remembered, taken only ten minutes of instruction. Yet he was now to formulate and lead "the largest airborne operation in the war."

Among his concerns, weighing heaviest was that Devers had said the invasion of south France was set for 15 August, and the airborne force to be activated 11 July—leaving Frederick barely five weeks to organize and train his airborne troops. What on earth, he at some point had to have wondered, were War Department planners thinking?

Actually, tucked away in a file at the National Archives is the record of a telephone conversation at the War Department that led to Frederick being picked for the task. On 23 June (1944), a General Hull had rung up another high ranked officer, and the following ensued:

HULL: We just got a message from General Devers in which he requests by earliest date an airborne commander. What can you do?

-: What we have to do would be strip the 13th Airborne.

HULL: Who's got it now?

-: General Chapman.

HULL: Oh, got any other?

-: No. We would have to smoke somebody up.

-: HULL: What do you think of this? Devers put Frederick in to take over the 36th Division. Frederick raised the First Special Service Force, you know. He has the battle experience, and some airborne training.

–: That might be a good solution.

Next, Hull had phoned George Marshall who—as Chief of Staff, no stranger to Frederick's skillful constructing of the Special Service Force, and his bold hard hitting attacks in combat—had sent a "TOP SECRET" missive to Devers, requesting he accept the "solution." Then Marshall did what he felt was merited, but what also definitely sweetened the new airborne commander's job of rapidly having to weld odds and ends of units together for the invasion in southern France. He upped him one rank.

Thus, at thirty-seven years old, a happily surprised Frederick was now the youngest major general in the U.S. Army.

The plan to invade south France (code-named DRAGOON) had for weeks had tons of criticism hurled at it. At his headquarters in London, however, Eisenhower had remained adamant; he needed the ports of Marseille and Toulon to funnel more supplies and divisions into France to start pushing the Germans back to their homeland. Yet, as the invasion date had hinged on availability of ships and landing craft, meanwhile England's roly-poly prime minister had been bombarding President Roosevelt and Marshall with cablegrams urging that they drop the plan, and instead invade the Balkans, before Russia's Red Armies got there. "Good God!" Churchill had exploded, in one message, "The Russians are spreading across Europe like a tide!"

And it was true. Soviet forces had invaded Poland and Lithuania, and were about to enter east Germany and Czechoslovakia. But despite Churchill arguing that not to invade the Balkans would lead, postwar, to communists dominating central Europe, DRAGOON—which some British and U.S. high officials called "Stalin's Plan"*—had stayed on the boards.

---

*Already envisioning his armies swarming into the Balkans, with cunning prescience Russia's dictator, Joseph Stalin, was strongly backing the invasion plan.

Adding to the controversy, Marshall had told the man who was to head the invasion, U.S. Seventh Army commander Lieutenant General Alexander Patch, to pick the units he wanted. Whereupon, Patch chose seven divisions, two corps headquarters, and the First Special Service Force, all from Clark's Fifth Army—bringing another seething disputant into the fray, as Clark acidly contended it crimped his "Fifth's victorious advance." But opposition was the lesser of problems: the entire invasion plan was now fast becoming the worst kept secret in the war.

For, as Frederick got busy establishing his headquarters at Lido de Roma airfield, twenty-three miles east of Rome, among French Resistance fighters sending out information from France about German positions and movement were double agents working for Hitler; and from the air German reconnaissance planes closely watching the Allies build up airstrips and amass equipment on the island of Corsica, off France's Mediterranean coast. But though Frederick was not unaware this left him little chance for a tactical surprise, he was preoccupied by a menu of complicated planning.

He needed to coordinate with the Air Corps for planes and gliders to ferry his troops to France. There had to be determined what were safe loads for gliders—a fairly new form of vertical warfare. Then there was the fact that areas available to train his troops were scattered all over and littered with German mines. And most ponderous, in the conglomerate of units being rounded up for his outfit, half had no combat training, half had no airborne training, and none had worked together.

On the other hand, Frederick was keenly aware he had been thrust into a job that magnified his abilities. Many generals would be overwhelmed if told to, in one month, cement into a cohesive force the sixteen disparate units on Frederick's list. (It read: "2nd Chemical Battalion; 460th Parachute Field Artillery Battalion; 517th Parachute Regiment; 596th Parachute Engineer Company; the British 2nd Parachute Brigade; one antitank company 442nd Regiment; Company 'D' 83rd Chemical Battalion; 509th Parachute Infantry Battalion; 463rd Parachute Field Artillery Battalion; 550th Glider Infantry Battalion; 551st Parachute Infantry Battalion; two platoons, 887th Engineer Company; 602nd Pack Howitzer Field Artillery Battalion; 512th Signal Company; 676th Medical

Collecting Company; and one detachment, 3rd Ordinance Maintenance Company.")

But there were tricky moments ahead.

One officer earmarked for Frederick's force was in North Africa when, "whisked to Italy, arriving at Lido de Roma airfield," he later said, "it was clear to me Frederick was favored as no other general in that Theater of War. He was permitted to select all his staff, and screened a huge number of records to get officers he considered most competent...quite unusual, as staff for most any outfit invariably was chosen for its commander by higher headquarters."

In addition, Frederick had asked for Ken Wickham, who, on leaving the Special Service Force (now led by Colonel Edwin A. Walker), eventually would be chief of staff of the makeshift airborne unit. For the time being, though, Frederick stuck him with the job of mollifying the thirty-six staff officers rushing in from around Europe and America.

"They'd never been in combat," said Wickham, later, "but were in a big hurry to get things done. One of them came in and, pounding on Frederick's desk, said 'General, we must quickly get some decisions from you! We are going into combat!,' and Frederick answered, 'When I am ready to make up my mind, I will do so.' It was a technique he often used, to decide not to make decisions, which had great validity, as they kept pressing him to act fast, and he kept waiting until he got all the facts he needed."

One detail Frederick dealt with swiftly, however, was the name of his outfit, which had been tagged "Provisional Seventh Army Airborne Division." Ringing up Patch at the Seventh's headquarters in Naples, he told him that, as his amalgamation of units totaling 9,732 men "has no insignia of its own, to give my troops a unifying identity, I want the name changed."

"To what?" asked Patch.

"First Airborne Task Force [FABTF]," responded Frederick.

As Patch readily agreed, an appreciative Frederick added, "This is a good time to say twenty years ago, when you were an instructor of Military Science at Staunton Military Academy, I was one of your students. So you see, you influenced my thinking."

"Or more likely," Patch, chuckling, replied, "you just had an aptitude for the subject."

Which raises the unanswerable age-old question: What makes a good leader? Education? Environment? Genetics? A combination? Certainly environment and education are factors only if within a person is the ability to absorb that exposure. A case in point could even be that Frederick, in spite of long hours spent as a boy on lessons and on practicing, produced nothing but a horrendous squeal as he sawed his bow across his cello.

But, whatever the answer, Major General Bob Frederick now needed another man's expertise. Seventh Army had produced a vague plan that had paratroopers dropping all over the south of France. Lapsing into a mood of disgust he grumbled, "I cannot accept it," and sent one of his unit leaders, Colonel William Yarborough, racing off to Patch's headquarters to revise the plan, so his paratroopers would land on just three zones fifteen miles inland near the small town of Le Muy—which strategically was a giant. It was there the main roads and rails used by the Germans intersected.

Still, other snags were piling up as his FABTF began training. Patch had reported "utmost difficulty" getting supplies for men not previously paratroopers. A shipment from the U.S. of 600,000 pounds of cargo and parachutes to carry it failed to arrive. The Air Corps could not find enough gliders to train glider-borne troops. Nor could anyone find detailed maps and photographs of the Argens Valley. Likewise, there was a glaring shortage of parachute repackers to refold chutes, necessitating that, instead of holding realistic rehearsals, Frederick used two men to represent his force in practice drops while his troops stood waiting on the ground to assemble on mock drop zones.

Working seven days a week until 2:00 AM, Frederick spent a few hours, off alone, to conjure up what to expect on landing in France. Intelligence reports showed three German battalions, one assault gun unit, and a German officer school with 1,000 candidates in Le Muy. Six miles north was the German LXII Corps headquarters in the town of Draguignan, 12 miles away two German divisions closing in, and 20 miles off waited the German 148th Infantry Division on full alert. In fortified buildings and hilltops they were familiar with exits, corners, and the terraced character of the valley, and had 200 artillery pieces, minefields and, planted in the ground, row upon row of "asparagus stalks," twelve foot tall wooden poles spiked on the top to impale paratroopers and rip the wings and bellies off gliders. As surprise was paramount, Frederick decided his force would start to strike from the sky in the dark of night, before the seaborne Allied units waded ashore. But for half a day, at least, his troops would be working alone without heavy artillery and transportation, and the enemy, once aware of its combat supremacy over airdropped troops, were bound to react, he figuratively imagined, with fanatical opposition.

Frederick's own risks would be great: much more so than most generals undertook in the war. He planned to jump with the first wave of parachutists, and make a beeline or fight his way to his CP, a farmhouse in the village of Le Mitan, two miles from Le Muy he had chosen by using a photograph of the area taken from an airplane. In the blurry print the farmhouse looked habitable.

By 9 August, 407 gliders to ferry some of his troops had arrived, unassembled. As crews rushed to put together the wood and canvas crafts, like a last minute blessing the equipment bundles of ammo, weapons' parts, medical supplies, and chutes to carry them appeared from the U.S. Only one thing now snarled up Frederick's complex planning; a lack of vehicles to convey his troops to ten airfields spread out 150 miles on Italy's coastline.

With D-day racing toward him he insisted his staff "Go out and find anything with wheels!" The result was, "In a slow four day process," a trooper recalled later, "and a menagerie of jeeps, horse drawn wagons, and trucks and cars of every size and vintage, the General got his 10,000 men to the departure fields. Then D-day minus one, as we waited in a hot, hot sun to embark, he had tents set up to provide us shade and arrange we get bread and jelly, delicious pastries, and cold fruit juices."

Always before, Frederick walked among his troops prior to battle, stopping to ask them, "What is your hometown?," "Did you remember to fill your canteen?," or simply say, "I wish you well, son." But to be at ten airstrips was humanly impossible, and the tents and snacks, as he hoped, imparted to his men he was, even so, thinking of them. That night the air was sultry when, on runways bathed by floodlights, at 00:30 AM

(15 August) teams of Pathfinders took off. They were to jump into the Argens Valley to mark drop zones (DZs) with portable lights, to guide pilots bringing in Frederick's main lift of 5,700 paratroopers. But unbeknownst to anyone on the runways, the valley in the south of France was shrouded by fog.

At 1:30 AM the main lift departed in 396 lumbering C-47s, the air roaring with the drone as the huge sky train flew in a V-on-V formation over the Mediterranean. In a plane at the front, Frederick sat studying his map, wind whizzing in the open cargo door making conversation difficult. Somewhere below were 1,200 allied ships slipping through the dark waters; to deceive the Germans, the armada had first headed toward Genoa, Italy, only to now, altering course, aim for the French Riviera.

Other hoaxes were going on too. Far west of the invasion sites, Allied planes were releasing 500 dummy paratroopers rigged with explosives that, on hitting ground, sounded like gunfire; and other planes were dropping wide strips of tin foil which, on German radar, resembled a mass of aircraft. Even earlier, Frederick's old outfit of commandos, the FSSF, had climbed from ships in the Mediterranean into rubber boats, paddled to two small islands off the Riviera, and were now busy scaling the islands' cliffs to silence German guns that might disrupt the seaborne landings.

By 3:30 AM the Pathfinder teams were in the Argens Valley, the planes carrying them having circled round and round as pilots tried to discern something through the fog below. Jumping blind, over half the teams were nowhere near the DZs they were to light up, and would remain lost for most of the morning. So began the second D-day in France (Normandy being the first)—or as the French author Jacques Robichon wrote later, "a day of flames and blood."

Frederick stood at the door of his C-47, his flashlight in hand, and his .45 on his hip. Behind him were his aide McCall, six of his staff, and a French soldier named Schevenels, who knew the Argens Valley layout. At 4:40 AM the green GO light flashed on, and shouting "Go" Frederick leapt out. Plunging down into a fog bank "with" he admitted later, "a case of jitters," he landed against a rock wall, blood gushing from his right leg where protruding rock had cleaved open the mending ten inch scar on his thigh. (With his history of wounds, this being his eighth, indisputedly Frederick was the most wounded general in World War II, and perhaps in all of modern times.)

By the blue beam of his flashlight he tried to orient himself. West was a hill one unit should have landed on, and far north, a town resembling where he had chosen to put his CP. Cutting a cord from his parachute, he tied it as a tourniquet on his thigh, and starting out alone saw "what in the dark looked like a German due to the shape of his helmet." Circling behind him, Frederick threw an arm around his throat "to break his neck, when he sputtered 'Jesus Christ!' in an English accent. He was from the British Brigade and, losing his rifle in the jump, said he was sticking with me, as I had a .45." Soon McCall, whispering the password "Lafayette," joined them, and with his band of two, Frederick took off on what became a two hour speed march to locate his CP.

On the way, he pushed open the door of a cottage where lamplight filtered out. Inside was a German captain about to devour a meal who, yelping in surprise, put his hands in the air. Frederick gestured he move to a corner, and that they were hungry, and as the German watched wide-eyed, his captors attacked his plate of eggs and tomatoes. The fog had begun to lift when, finally—the German walking briskly in front of their guns—at 7:00 AM they found the farmhouse-cum-CP. In it were seven Germans equally startled to see these blackfaced invaders in jumpsuits. With no troops on hand, Frederick ordered all eight to squeeze into a little chicken coop across the road, where the befuddled Nazis were left to glumly stare from their wood and wire cage at one unarmed British soldier standing guard.

By now, as none of his staff had shown up, Frederick's darkest suspicion was confirmed. Lacking ground lights, and to get above the fog, pilots had flown not at the designated 700 feet, but had dropped each stick of paratroopers from 1,800 feet. Some were twenty-six miles from their DZs, while others were far south on the coast at St. Tropez, a town so well defended, Seventh Army planners had ruled it out as a landing site even for seaborne units. And as for the French soldier, Schevenels, who was to have guided Frederick to the farmhouse, he was playing dead after finding himself surrounded by Germans in a distant field.

With no radio, and thus no liaison, Frederick told McCall, "We have been up all night, and can do nothing now but get some rest." Lying on the floor, Frederick listened to the far off martial thunder of U.S. Naval ships softening up the coastline. At 8:00 AM seaborne units would come on shore, followed at 9:10 by C-47s bringing in Frederick's gliderborne anti-tank gunners, mortar, and jeeps. In the meantime, he was counting on the psychological advantage of troops he had on the ground—of knowing where they were to go; whereas the Germans had no idea the direction they would take—as the air grew thick with smoke from gunfire.

Frederick would have had a nightmare on his hands if his troops had been of a different caliber. But determined to nullify the enemy, they were cutting telephone lines, blowing up German ammunition dumps, and setting up roadblocks, singly or in small groups; and some had made contact with French Resistance fighters. One of whom, "Andre," had been told to "take what paratroopers I found to General Frederick," as he was to later say.

"But in the fog I couldn't tell them from the Germans and shot a few of them. But I did lead two Americans to Les Arcs, a town I only then learned wasn't even one of the targets."

Adding to the chaos, the equipment bundles of automatic weapon parts and ammunition dropped with the paratroopers were also strewn about in orchards, thickets, and hilltops, and over seventy percent were never found. Yet the air assault had succeeded in being a complete tactical surprise, and it was not until 8:00 AM that, alarmed and confused, the Germans gathered their wits to begin to ferociously fight back.

But as now some of his staff arrived at his CP with radiophones and reports trickled in, Frederick kept redesigning his orders as his troops forged into makeshift units and, ambushing German patrols, advanced to towns they were to take. Then, on schedule, the armada of gliders filled the sky. Fifty miles long, it stretched out over the Mediterranean Sea, the gliders riding higher than the C-47s towing them to avoid the propwash until above *terra incognito* and, released, they soared down to landing zones bristling with "asparagus stalks" (that French Resistance groups were to have removed, but had not got around to). Hitting the poles, crushed frontally and wings shorn off, hundreds of gliders littered the landing fields in piles of wreckage. Frederick waited with lively apprehension before told most of the guns and jeeps in the gliders were salvaged, and his gliderborne men heading to their missions; and only then turning to other reports coming in, he was buoyed up to hear at St. Tropez his troops were leveling the last German stronghold; and, again, when at 11:00 AM his force now occupied four towns (La Motte, Le Mitan, Castron, and Les Serres), and controlled every road leading to the coast.

But it would be dusk before his remaining 4,400 troops arrived, some by parachute, some in gliders. Meanwhile, he was holding a thin liquid front over twenty miles long due to the misdrops, and German units were pouring in from all directions.

That night, while on the Riviera beaches supplies that would move north with the Allies were being unloaded off ships, several of Frederick's troops made contact with a seaborne unit. For eighteen hours his force, isolated inland, had been fighting alone; and only one of his plans was not effected. He had assigned the British brigade to seize Le Muy, but taking a bridge outside the town, the brigade attached itself to this real estate and failed to advance. Frederick had rushed to the bridge and, not concealing his frustration, curtly asked the brigade leader, a Brigadier Pritchett, "Why don't you go in and take that town?"

"There are Germans there," replied Pritchett. "An attack would be costly." But if trying to conserve men (and England was running low on soldiers), he'd met another enemy, as rushing back to his CP, Frederick put out an order the brigade was to be shipped off to Italy. By the end of D-day, other elements of his force were creeping toward Le Muy, and toward the German LXII Corps headquarters at Draguignan. Inside the headquarters the corps district commander, *Generalmajor* Ludwig Bieringer, was trying in vain to telephone his units, but with all the lines cut by Frederick's troops, he was literally talking to himself.

Then, after sunrise on D-day +1, something occurred that gave the airborne troops greater insight into their commander, who up to then had seemed remote.

"When the Germans felt they could no longer defend Le Muy," said Colonel William Bryant (the FABTF's Intelligence Officer) later, "they sent out an emissary who told Frederick if he would stop firing they would surrender. Frederick told the emissary he was going to increase the firing, and to inform his commander 'he better figure out his own way to give up as soon as he can.'"

Without further ado the Germans surrendered; and with the same cool decisiveness Frederick said, "We will now attack Draguignan."

By sundown on D+1, his task force held seven towns, had taken 1,350 prisoners, and had decimated enemy defenses in a region far beyond U.S. Army planners' wildest dreams. "It was the most successful airborne operation in Europe," one official army historian wrote. But it was U.S. VI Corps commander Lucian Truscott who paid the FABTF's leader the highest compliment: "Frederick's feat in organizing and training this composite force and perfecting the operation in a period of less than five weeks is the most remarkable exploit of the war."

At midnight Frederick sat at a table reading the casualty lists, his head bowed. He had lost 434 men killed or captured, and another 294 had been wounded. Sitting across from him was the haughty—and monicaled—*Generalmajor* Bieringer, who through an interpreter said, stiffly, "I request you allow my orderly accompany me with two suitcases of my uniforms." He was referring to when, early the next morning, Frederick would escort him to a prisoner of war cage.

Glancing up at him, Frederick resumed reading the casualty lists, under his breath muttering "The hell I will."

In four days, U.S. Seventh Army's seaborne units were sweeping through the captured town, and Frederick had been told "to protect" the Seventh's entire right flank as it pushed northward to link up with troops from Normandy. To the enemy it appeared this would be their last stand before the Allies swarmed into their homeland, and fighting stubbornly, two German divisions took up positions on the rugged French-Italian border running from Switzerland to the Mediterranean Sea. Frederick had just learned that his old outfit of brutally efficient commandos was now a part of his task force, to replace the British brigade he had sent back to Italy, "and his eyes were shining," recalled one of his staff, "as he said, 'The First Special Services Force is again under my command.'" But that heartfelt emotion was the only joy of the hour for Frederick.

To "protect" the Allies' right rear he had begun a supply-starved campaign against the very real possibility of a German counterattack from Italy. Airborne and special forces are equipped only with light weapons, little transportation and, always, are short of food. And it was under these conditions that he had deployed his troops north to Grasse, east to Cannes and Nice, and on toward the Franco-Italian border: "where German troops," later recalled Captain Geoffrey Jones, who led covert operations with the French Resistance, "outnumbered Frederick's three to one.

Plus he faced the pitfalls of liberating and controlling the Riviera's complicated one million people," added Jones. "But to Bob Frederick, 'protect' meant attack, and he was a great improviser."

Calling on artillery from U.S. ships offshore to pound inland targets Frederick also, unblinkingly, directed his men"to have your way into any vehicle," and soon trucks, even a tanker of fuel, were flitting around, on which hastily had been painted large white stars, or in huge letters "Don't shoot!" to identify them as now being American property. Meanwhile, within the indigenous populace trapped between German and American fire as Frederick aggressively pursued the enemy, there were brewing varied reactions to the prospect of being freed from German occupation. In towns where homes were shelled into rubble and families starving, the advancing G.I.s seemed a godsend, but there was also every political persuasion—socialist, communist, fascist, Free French Resistance, and pro-Nazi Vichy French—for whom liberation meant a chance for revenge. Then there was the flotsam of expatriates, mainly from England and the U.S., expecting special treatment. And there was Monaco. Neutral in war, its gambling tables still operating, the tiny principality was a haven for spies working for Hitler.

Like most soldiers, Frederick's education in civil affairs was limited. But while he kept pushing the enemy eastward, he needed to build calm cooperation in the population, in which "suddenly wanting to ally with America," he was to say, with much lament, "there are a number of stinking rats."

And not all of them easy to catch.

By 30 August 30 his force occupied Nice, Cannes, and Grasse, and with units fighting on the mountainous border as well, Frederick held a front stretching sixty miles east. But the troops in the mountains were spread out with spaces between them where German forces could sneak undetected. So, moving his headquarters to the Alhambra Hotel in Nice to be nearer an airfield, he made repeated flights over the border in a single engine L-5 piloted by Sergeant Eugene Woods.

"We often flew in horrible weather," said Woods, later. "But I doubt a hurricane could have kept Frederick on the ground. He was not just a gentleman, he was a gentle man, and while any good leader evokes loyalty from troops, what set him apart was his troops knew he was always loyal to them."

By jeep, plane, and radio Frederick, his tactical plans sound, knew in detail where his men were as they kept the enemy on the run—though outgunned by German weapons. The constant rattle of rifle fire, cough of machine guns, and thunder of artillery echoed in the mountains and wafted into Nice, where in a clashing landscape, heading in for two days rest, grim-faced, sleep-deprived G.I.s in grubby battle gear passed their grinning, cleaned up buddies heading back to combat after a hot bath, decent food, and two nights of French girls and champagne.

On 4 September *Time* magazine printed Frederick's picture, and below it a long article about him and the First Special Service Force. And in U.S. newspapers under titles like "Beyond Riviera, A Roaring Death," people read something about the action in southern France. But usually on page five. It had already become a forgotten front, the big news being Allied forces up north had crossed the Seine River and marched through Paris. For those at the homefront with a loved one in the south of France, the scant news magnified their worrying—Was he all right? Still alive? However, Ruth Frederick was to soon find out firsthand, though the reason was bittersweet.

Dr. Marcus White Frederick, the general's father...

...and his mother, Pauline McCurdy Frederick (circa 1905).

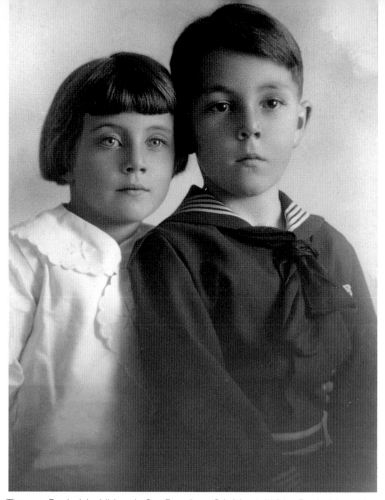

The two Frederick children in San Francisco, CA. Marcia White Frederick and her older brother, six year old Robert Tryon.

Frederick, back row left, when a senior at Staunton Military Academy.

THIS IS AN UNFINISHED PROOF SUB-
MITTED FOR APPROVAL ONLY

PROOFS REMAIN THE PROPERTY OF
WHITE STUDIO AND WILL BE CHARGED
FOR IF NOT RETURNED

A very serious looking Cadet Frederick his first year at West Point, 1925.

His beautiful bride, Ruth Adelaide Harloe, on their wedding day, 9 June 1928.

2nd Lt. Frederick on duty as Adjutant of the Civilian Conservation Corps, Oregon District.

Frederick prepared for his one training jump as a paratrooper.

A color guard carries the American and Canadian flags at Fort William Henry Harrison, MT, where Frederick formed the elite and only North American force.

At Fort Harrison, Lt. Col. Frederick, fourth from left, awarding jump wings to American and Canadian volunteers as training of the First Special Service Force began.

The flag of the First Special Service Force, the stiletto Frederick designed represented on the white shield.

Wearing face camouflage, Frederick (right) immediately after leading the night assault on Kiska in the Aleutians on 15 August 1943.

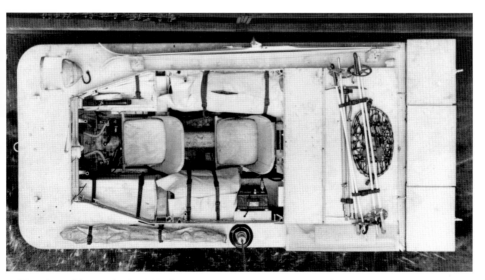

Top view of the tracked vehicle Frederick oversaw development of for use by his commandos.

A sand table model of Monte la Difensa showing the steep side, left of center, scaled by Frederick and his troops the night of 2-3 December 1943.

4 January 1944, Frederick (far left) leads an advance party toward Casserna as the First Special Service Force continues its assaults following the capture of Monte la Difensa.

Frederick caught on film, a bandage over his wounded eye, as he sets off to secretively patrol Mount Majo.

On the Anzio beachhead, one view from the First Special Service Force sector of the wide no man's land and hills held by the Germans.

Mark Clark strikes a pose on the beachhead after awarding to Frederick (facing) a second Distinguished Service Cross for his bravery and leadership.

Frederick, just informed of his promotion to brigadier general, salutes Generals Lucian Truscott and Mark Clark as they depart his CP at Anzio.

On the outskirts of Rome, Frederick shows (from left) Generals Geoffrey Keyes, Donald Bauer, and Clark the routes he will use to move his commandos into the city. Note: hanging from Frederick's left hip, his special force's stiletto.

FINALMENTE
Gli Anglo-Americani a Roma...

...Inquadrati
tra le baionette Tedesche.

"FINALLY," said this poster printed by Italians, as Allied forces breaking out from Anzio reached Rome.

Three of the 464 gliders, the one on the right wrecked, that ferrying in men and equipment for Frederick's First Airborne Task Force, landed in fields littered with anti-glider poles.

Frederick receiving the flag of Le Muy, France, following liberation of the town by his airborne force on 17 August 1944.

Leaning against a windowsill to rest his wounded leg, Frederick interrogates the German general Ludwig Bieringer, captured near Draguignan, France, on 16 August 1944.

With one of his unit leaders, Frederick (on right) consults a situation map early December 1944 as he begins pushing the 45th Infantry Division into Germany.

Along with hundreds of prisoners, in the forefront seven German generals nabbed by Frederick's troops as he moved the 45th through Bamburg, Germany, 14 April 1944.

Men of the 45th advancing toward Dachau, alongside railroad tracks leading to the Nazi Concentration Camp.

Frederick, in overseas cap, discusses the situation inside Dachau with his men and a member of the

General Wade H. Haislip, XV Corps commander, awards Frederick a bronze star for capturing Nuremberg, Germany.

Official U.S. Army photograph of Bob Frederick taken the week he returned to the States from Munich.

Frederick when commander of U.S. forces in occupied Austria, with his Soviet counterpart and nemesis, General Igor Abakomov, as they enter a conference hall to discuss Russian transgressions in Vienna.

While CO of Fort Ord and the 6th Division, Frederick flew to Fort Benning to visit his daughter Jane and, on left, her husband Captain George Fee, who was to soon ship out to the war in Korea.

Frederick in dress blues at his daughter Anne's wedding reception.

On a mountainside in Utah, Frederick observing filming of "The Devil's Brigade" with actor William Holden, who portrayed him in the movie.

Following the showing of "The Devil's Brigade" in one city, Frederick prepares to autograph items for a crowd of fans.

Frederick and his wife Ruth on vacation at Blue Lake with a clan of grandchildren.

One of two U.S. memorials to Frederick, the Frederick Physical Fitness Center, at Fort Bragg.

In Canada, at the main entry to Canadian Forces Base Petawawa, this memorial to Frederick was erected in 1988.

Ruth's father had died suddenly in August, and Frederick now had arranged to fly to Washington to comfort her, leaving in charge of his task force his senior headquarters officer, Colonel Bryant Evans. On 20 September Ruth heard footsteps on the porch of their rented house, went to investigate, and to her surprise saw her husband. She noticed a change in him. He looked, in spite of his wounds, still in topnotch physical shape, but was tense, and occasionally pacing the floor, he told one of many newsmen—who acting on the rumor he was in town flocked to the house—that he found "civilization a trifling wearing." But between trips to the Pentagon and getting reacquainted with his daughters, his visit seemed much too brief when, after five days, he departed for France.

In his absence Evans had scrounged up nine choice automobiles for the staff, and reserved for Frederick a low-slung convertible that he proudly drove to headquarters to show his boss. Frederick took one look at it and turned to Evans, saying, "Well, I tell you what. If you don't mind too greatly, I will make my own choice." What he picked was a Cadillac limousine taken from the Germans "that was very comfortable." later Ken Wickham was to relay. "And I was lucky enough to get to ride in it with him all the way into Paris." But this was not to be for some time.

For in the Riviera's mess of political enemies, hostilities now were coalescing into murderous vendettas, particularly between Nazi sympathizers and French Resistance fighters; meanwhile, the craven were rapidly setting up black markets. With a vacuum of government control Frederick, left to his own devices, found it took infinite patience, plus mental jujitsu, to sort out who to turn over to French police for punishment. Among those most deserving was the Minister of State of Monaco, Monsieur Roblot. Relying on reports brought to him by his intelligence officers, Frederick read one day that Roblot had collaborated with the Nazis, and now had hired guards to protect German spies hiding in Monaco. That night, with three jeeploads of military police Frederick went to Roblot's villa and, stationing the MPs around the grounds, rang the door bell.

"I thought we had him cornered in a hole like a badger," later Frederick said. "But he snuck out a secret tunnel and ran off to Marseille, which suited me fine. It was one less person we had to see went to trial, in our effort to stop the widespread civil unrest."

Of no assistance was Monaco's reigning royalty, Prince Louis II (grandfather of the recent Prince Rainier), who though angrily anti-German, was toothless in dealing with the conflict in his realm. Frederick had put neutral Monaco off limits to his troops, and was hoping to avoid even a pretense of himself interacting with its inhabitants. But he was interested to know the depth of food shortages there, and thus yielded on receiving an invitation that read:

"My dear general, Would you please me in coming to my house any day next week you would choose for lunch at 12:45 and bring with you a man talking French, as I am the only one here speaking english[sic]. Prince Louis of Monaco."

Taking along an officer from the Special Service Force who was fluent in French, and greeted by a fanfare of blaring trumpets, Frederick was ushered into a dining hall, and while lunch was served he tried to pin down the major problems confronting his host. But instead in a realm swarming with malodious crooks, the Prince, minus power and a pulpit, talked only of a plan he had to gain both. Would Frederick, he asked, notify Washington that he (Louis II) desired to make Monaco "the territory of America?" And would he please convey to President Roosevelt he would cooperate in every way for "a facile transference of government"— the Prince, of course, to serve as governor of the new territory.

Due to his well bred upbringing Frederick maintained a congenial manner and, betraying none of his true emotions, departed courteously, to, only upon entering his headquarters, double up with laughter as he told his staff, "We almost got the U.S. a forty-ninth state!"

But most days heralded in grave situations: unlawful killings of traitors; demonstrations by communists; and witch hunts for fascists. And always a stream of people jockeying to get the American commander's attention. "My office sounds like the Tower of Babel," Frederick remarked during one session he spent with Polish and Italian refugees, Russian and Romanian expatriates, and exiled Turks and Arabs.

While he met with each group his expression was passive, a look that his staff knew meant he was weighing every word, dissecting every inference; for to give military aid in a region of weak civil authority, one misstep on his part could set off a blaze of hatred for the liberators.

"But what he did," reported Captain Jones later, "was successfully convert the Riviera from a German beachhead to an area of civil obedience." One key was food.

Anchored at Marseille was the flagship of the admiral who had led the D-day naval operation, H.K. Hewitt. So ringing him up, Frederick requested that two shiploads of food slated for the Allied units up north be sidetracked to the harbor at Nice. Having marshaled the shiploads, and going to the harbor to oversee them being unloaded, he was incensed to find a British officer on the docks loudly proclaiming the food came from England, in an attempt to offset Britain's poor showing in combat at Le Muy.

Barking at him, "Clear out. You have no relationship to these supplies," Frederick personally saw to it the food was distributed to representatives of each population group. French newspapers called him "Le Sauveur" (The Savior); and as one reporter wrote: "He has such young eyes, his uniform so simple, he looks more like a lieutenant than a general, and if he did not have this dark moustache across his smiling and kind face, one might say he was just out of West Point!"

Yet still burdened with combat operations—enemy resistance was deteriorating , but his troops were daily attacked by 88s, tanks, and railroad guns—Frederick despaired, in private, that now adding to his men's hardships snow had begun falling early in the mountains and hills. "Have five feet of it," radioed one of his unit leaders. "Need winter clothing pronto." With the clothes went a requisitioned civilian snow plow to clear paths. But the plow could make no headway and, with the weather worsening, Frederick now had to enlist French ski patrols to evacuate his wounded men.

Soon to follow, one of the fiercest attacks was launched from German fortresses on the mountains when, having decimated the German 148th Division, his task force now faced its replacement, the 34th Division. But as it turned out, the enemy's big show of fire power was rearguard action, to cover the 34th as it hastily withdrew into Italy.

About the same time, Frederick got word that southern France no longer was part of the Mediterranean Theater of War, but in Eisenhower's European Theater. It was the harbinger of many new situations: on top of one already. Back in late August, Frederick had pointed out to General Devers (the Mediterranean Deputy Commander) that with most Seventh Army supplies being channeled north, his First Airborne Task Force had dire shortages; and told that to ease the problem the FABTF would be detached from the Seventh, ever since with less than 10,000 men Frederick had been commanding, in essence, an independent army off on its own.

Which by 30 October solidly held the Franco-Italian border. Coming to an end was what Italy's dictator, Mussolini, in 1940 called "a stab in the neighbor's back" when with 32 divisions he invaded southern France.* And now too, Frederick was notified his task force would soon be deactivated, his airborne troops to join units up north—and the First Special Service Force to be disbanded, the Canadians to go to England, with the Americans to sail to Norway to provide coastal defense. The reason given for disbanding the unique North American force was it took a complex administrative effort whenever the War Department made a proposal for its use, as in turn it required getting the Canadian government's approval. But Frederick knew the true significance of this news. The fight against Hitler's regime had grown huge and, with the Allies now advancing on a front 500 miles long, planners at Eisenhower's headquarters saw the need only for large conventional forces, the days of a small assault unit's employment ended.

Yet it disturbed Frederick that, welded to tradition, the U.S. Army in the future might ignore the value of commandos, of how their stealth, swift strikes, and cold courage could be used. Of course he was also speculating over his own future, when next he received a telegram from Devers, who had just been named Commander, Sixth Army Group (composed of the U.S. Seventh Army and French First Army).

---

*Not that Italy got very far. Its units had such a lack of drive, it was said "They seem to be marching in place"; and Hitler had had to send troops in his *Werhmacht* army racing south to bail out Mussolini.

TO CG, FABTF, PERSONAL
PRESENT PLAN IS THAT UPON REASSIGNMENT OF
UNITS OF YOUR TASK FORCE, YOU WILL BE DETAINED
WITH SIXTH ARMY GROUP. ASSUMING YOUR
EVENTUAL ASSIGNMENT TO COMMAND AN INFANTRY
DIVISION, WHAT STAFF OFFICERS NOW WITH THE
FIRST AIRBORNE TASK FORCE WILL YOU DESIRE TO
TAKE WITH YOU?

Frederick's outgoing cable to Devers was brief: "Staff officers I desire in probable future command are Col. Kenneth Wickham and Lt. Col. Emil P. Eschenberg [his operations officer]."

Frederick made friends easily, and kept them, as much due to his lack of hubris, as to his truthful and considerate treatment of them. Having known Eschenberg since creating the First Special Service Force, and Wickham since posted in Hawaii, both men would stick like glue to him for seven more years as faithful subordinates.

On 22 November, his airborne force unceremoniously deactivated, Frederick went to where the Special Service Force had assembled, to say goodbye to these troops in what—as an international experiment— he had built into a force famous for its spectacular fighting skills.* The following dawn, taking off in his "liberated" Cadillac with Wickham, by dusk he had reached Sixth Army Group Headquarters in the town of Vittel, in northern France, to await his new assignment. Late that night Devers, a large man with a bland face but quick smile, greeted him warmly, then proceeded to describe, "French units were to attack a big concentration of Germans at Bordeaux [which had a port the Allies needed to bring in supplies]. But as they failed to," said Devers, "I have ordered they attack early in December, and for now you are to act as my liaison, and stay at French Army headquarters in Cognac to make sure they do."

*At a later formal ceremony, as the sad notes of Taps were lofted overhead, the red Force flag with a black dagger on a white shield was wound to its staff and a black case slipped over it. This was the only North American flag, and is now displayed in a glass case at the Special Forces Command building at Fort Bragg, NC, where each night the case is gently taken down and laid on its back to prevent the toll of gravity from damaging the rare flag.

Going to the hotel where he was billeted, Frederick looked at a map, and summoning Wickham, grinned at his friend. "I remember him saying" later Wickham related, "that wherever Cognac was, the shortest route must be through Paris, as neither of us had seen that city."

In reality Paris was 200 miles out of the way, and was sealed off to everyone without orders to be there. So, telling Wickham to write out the orders for them, after two days spent sightseeing in Paris and driving leisurely through the French countryside they had been in Cognac an hour when a telegram was delivered to Frederick by a courier in hot pursuit. It read:

CONGRATULATIONS, FROM DEVERS. YOU ARE TO ASSUME COMMAND OF THE 45TH INF. DIV. DEC 4 LATEST.

This was a milestone. On average division commanders were thirteen or more years older than Frederick: many had fought in World War I. But he had shown that he could outfox the nastiest enemy; and as he began the long drive back across France to where the 45th was grinding its way toward the German border in Alsace he had to have realized, and perhaps relished, he was now the youngest ground forces division commander in the U.S. Army.

12

Chasing "Bastards"

As Frederick was well acquainted, the 45th Infantry Division had an outstanding battle record. It had plowed across Sicily, fought at Anzio, and made an amphibious landing in the southern France invasion. From there, as part of Seventh Army it had swept forward, and was now clashing with some of the German armies' finest units on the edge of the Vosges Mountains, in northeast France, where its former commander, General William Eagles, had been injured by a German mine.

That was hardly the first thing Hitler had messed up for the 45th. In the 1920s, when forming his National Socialist Party, Hitler chose a swastika for the party emblem, and at the time the 45th patch was a reversed swastika, an American Indian good luck symbol. But in short shrift sewn onto the patch was a thunderbird with outstretched wings (another Indian symbol); and ever since, its troops were known as Thunderbirds. Hard hitting and proud of it, they had been in combat 357 days when Frederick arrived. A division is the largest force on which a commander can impose his personality, and the Thunderbirds had liked Eagles, and were not enthralled Frederick was taking over. One of the first to see him was Bill Mauldin, who was hanging around the 45th in search of ideas for his cartoons, "when not by coincidence I found myself at 45th headquarters, to renew my association with Frederick, who I'd not seen since his Rome days."

Mauldin had got an earful of the troops' sentiments toward Frederick, the consensus being he "was a whippersnapper" and looked "like some goddam movie actor with that moustache." Rapping on the door to Frederick's office, Mauldin went in with "the intent of alerting him the troops weren't about to accept him," and discovered Frederick was anticipating a none too cordial welcome.

"It will take these men," he told Mauldin, "an inordinately long time to get used to me, partly because of my age, partly because I replaced a well thought of leader."

But when two weeks later Mauldin again made his way to the 45th sector he learned, "Frederick was very accepted, the guys now knowing his reputation to be every bit the truth—he was brave, aggressive, and smart."

In those two weeks, changes both on Hitler's ravaged landscape and on maps in Eisenhower's headquarters had put the Thunderbirds in the thick of things. The month before, Eisenhower had had to issue to General Patch—whose Seventh Army was then driving east over mountain and dale toward Germany—"No crossing of the Rhine River to be contemplated. Your army to turn north parallel to the Rhine." What had happened was Lieutenant General George C. Patton, commanding the Third Army, had pushed the Third forward in hope of being first to the Rhine, and got bogged down east of Paris. To close the gap between armies the Seventh, cinching up, had to swing north, and as its divisions moved their mammoth configurations of foot soldiers, vehicles, hospitals, service and supply units, and artillery, they were raked with fire. For meanwhile Hitler wrought a miracle. In spite of the Allies' bombs clobbering his country, German factories had produced tons of ammunition, and nearly all German males age seventeen to fifty had been pulled into his army.

Typical of late fall in northeast France the ground was layered with frost, but not hard enough to support heavy vehicles, when Frederick took over the 45th early on 4 December while the Germans, knowing the soft ground would slow U.S. tanks and put the burden on infantry troops, were trying to rub his division off the face of the earth. Fighting resolutely to reach the rolling farmland on the Alsatian Plain, the Thunderbirds were unaware they had inherited a commander whose dexterous tactics would have them, for the rest of the war, almost constantly in front-line combat.

Frederick read the battle reports, briefly studied a map of the sector and model of terrain, and wrote out an order specifying four towns needed to be taken. Then, going to the senior officers' mess that had a bare wooden table and granite-ware plates issued years before for field use, he walked into the kitchen and told the cooks, "I want this place bucked up immediately." By lunchtime, the mess sported a bolt of linen rolled out on the table and china dishes, and prompted one officer to loudly postulate, "My God! The cooks stole all this!"

But it was part of a timely technique Frederick often had used to enhance the support he got from his men. Regularly eating with his staff, he would invite in from the front a lieutenant or captain to be his guest at an informal dinner where conversation flowed easily; and the benefits were twofold. It gave Frederick a unique insight, as he asked his guest "What do you think of [some maneuver]? How do you view the entire operation?" The captain or lieutenant left with the sense a bond had developed between them and, returning to his unit, where word trickled down of where he had been, the men under him felt they too enjoyed an unusual bond with the general.

And the linen and dishes?

"When a man expends the energy and time to come off the line to see me a couple of hours," Frederick said at one point, "he deserves the most pleasant conditions available."

That night of 4-5 December, the muted rumblings of the division preparing for battle mixed with the drumming of sleet carried by a freezing wind. From midnight to 1:00 AM Frederick rested on a cot as he reviewed his tactics for taking the towns—and tried divining what the close by enemy was up to. The attack would be initiated at 4:00 AM. Out on the jump-off points his troops shivered and waited, those with an appetite for sleep curled up in sleeping bags they cut the bottoms off of, their feet protruding to give them instant mobility. At 3:00 AM an apparition appeared out of the dark, and slowly moved past the dim hooded lights illuminating the area. It was someone wearing an overseas cap instead of a helmet, and a shirt open at the collar.

Staring hard, one soldier turned to the fellow next to him and whispered, "Who is that—he's got to be nuts," and got back the reply, "Pass the word. It looks like two stars on his collar."

Frederick walked quietly along the jump-off points, talking with each company commander, and ensuring their support and artillery were ready. Recalled one officer: "He didn't shake and rattle in the cold, and as he passed by the men you could see them stop shivering as they thought, 'If the General isn't freezing, why am I?' It was a terrific morale booster."

To which Wickham added: "Frederick believed he should never be warm when his men were cold, but at times, on leaving the line he'd be nearly frozen to death, and not even several pots of hot coffee could thaw him out back at headquarters, where he did his rattling and shaking."

Playing no favorites, the weather that night made life equally miserable for the enemy, as they glumly shifted defenses to adjust for the 45th poised to attack. To the Germans the region of Alsace was already sour grapes; it had been annexed to Germany in 1871, but France had won it back (peacefully) in the post World War I Versailles Treaty. Even so, many towns retained German names.

Before sunrise, lunging over a frigid battlefield with the hell and fury of artillery helping pave the way, Frederick's troops made contact with four enemy strong points he wanted, towns called Mertzwiller, Riechshoffen, Niederbronn Les Bains, and Gundershoffen. It put his 45th in control of a vital route east into Germany; and to exploit this, he ordered one regiment climb left to the wood line of the Vosges Mountains to block passes to the Alsatian Plain from the west. Once the Germans woke to the fact they were isolated out on the Plain they withdrew north, their obstinate rear lines throwing out barrages of ammunition at the pursuing Thunderbirds.

On 9 December photographs of the region taken from an Air Corps recon aircraft were delivered to Frederick. They were exceptionally clear considering the weather, but were, Frederick pointed out to the Air Corps officer who brought them, "useless."

The officer looked stricken. "Why?" he asked, plaintively.

"They show me nothing."

"Sir, in every one of them you can see the German front line."

Frederick shook his head. "What you are seeing in every one of these pictures is our rear area."

His division's speed of advance enabled Frederick to establish a rest center within seventy hours, in the now 45th held town of Neiderbronn Les Bains. Here men slept on beds a few hours, got a change of clothes, a haircut, and a bath and warm meal, the war seeming far away. But the respite was brief. Up ahead lay the Maginot Line, a strategically important objective—with a cankered reputation. The Maginot Line, a wide string of fortifications on the French border, had been built by France in the 1930s as an impenetrable barrier; yet by skirting its north end, German forces had flowed into France anyway, and were using the fortifications to fend off Allied attempts to reach Germany. To those fleeing the 45th it was a convenient bastion as, clumping into concrete pillboxes and hillside entrenchments, they aimed their tanks and artillery south—with the barrels protruding like long snouts from camouflaging bushes—and planted a front lawn of roadblocks and minefields.

Frederick employed what he felt now most valuable, to sneak up on the enemy's flanks with wider flanks that carried more power, while at the same time keeping the center of his front strong to attack from the south and southwest. As patrols carved out routes through the mines, though pinned down frequently by storms of German bullets, the Thunderbirds then blasted their way past barriers, scotching the enemy's hope of holding out. Once more the Germans headed north, shifting their weight into rugged hill country while stubborn rear guards remained in cities on the Maginot Line to fight delaying actions.

The first city in the path of Frederick's 45th was Wingen. He ordered contingents of one regiment to take the city. But the Germans, rallying, took it back with G.I.s still inside. Again the 45th attacked, encircling the enemy, so now there were German soldiers held by the Thunderbirds imprisoned by surrounding Germans surrounded by Thunderbirds. It was one of those confounding events of war, and as Frederick rushed in his jeep to the regimental CP, using the jeep radio to keep in touch, he received the message, "Have casualties on both sides, but few medical supplies." Returning to his headquarters he relayed the developments in a call to Patch's Seventh Army headquarters, about fifty miles west in Luneville.

Within the hour, someone from Patch's office called back, asking had "any progress been made?"

"Tell Patch we are working away at things," replied Frederick.

Thirty minutes later, Patch's office called again with the same question; and again, every thirty minutes for the next three hours— bringing Frederick to a boiling point. Relieving his radiophone man of the receiver, with unusual vitriol he shouted at the caller, "If you will stay the hell off the phone, we can get something done!"

Out of the hub of Wingen a jeep had emerged with one German and one Thunderbird, who waving flags of truce as they passed their respective growling enemy lines had driven to Frederick's headquarters, to get his go-ahead to carry back medical supplies. But many issues first needed to be settled, such as: How much of each medical item was to be parceled out to each side? What kind of accommodations were to be made available to shelter the wounded? And, greatly important, every unit had to be notified "to hold its fire and make *doubly sure*," Frederick intoned, "the Germans *understand* this."

Once the rescue party got underway, Frederick found the wait interminably long as his watch ticked off twenty-four hours of fettered hostility on the battlefield. He had moved to an observation point and was kneeling by a field radio when finally, word came from the heart of Wingen all wounded were treated. "Thank God," sighed Frederick, his voice catching, then growing louder, "All right, we are coming in."

Plunging through Wingen, his 45th entered Germany on 15 December—the first Seventh Army unit to fight on Nazi soil. The next day overrunning two border towns, his division reached the vaunted West Wall (in the Allies' lingo the Siegfried Line), extending from Belgium to Switzerland to protect Germany from enemy incursions. Confused by Frederick's flanking tactics, German troops had raced behind the West Wall's five rows of concrete obstructions and into its fortifications bristling with guns. On the high ground, peering defensively south they had a good view of the Thunderbirds forging ahead, while Frederick, manipulating the advance of his men over flat open fields, had a perspective that was anything but advantageous.

Even without an amassed enemy the obstacles were horrendous. The weather had grown colder; near constant rain soaked through clothes to skin already blue and painfully numb; and the terrain was an undulating series of wide ditches and rivers swollen with frigid water. And of as much gravity for Frederick was that in this, the land of Nazi government, the civilian population teemed with spies trotting to the West Wall defenders with vital information.

Ordering mortar, artillery, and tank destroyer fire be poured on the enemy—who returned it ferociously, but the results unsuccessful—he signaled his troops move within rifle range and, waging a deadly close battle 17-18 December, the following morning they broke through the outer West Wall defenses. It was Frederick's fifteenth day as their commander, and the Thunderbirds were no longer thinking he was a "whippersnapper." By now, despite "his extremely youthful appearance," (then Colonel) Raymond McLain remarked later "and often I had to smile when hearing it, the men were referring to him and rather fondly so as 'the old man.'"

As ill luck would have it, the Germans were against abandoning the West Wall, and at times could only be routed out when a Thunderbird's lobbed grenade made it through an air ventilator. But it was Hitler's words, not a liking for close warfare, kindling their staying power. As Germany's protective breastplate, the West Wall was "to be held," ordained Hitler, "to the last man." For just beyond it lay the sacrosanct banks of the Rhine River.

Not that Frederick had ignored the dictum that all Seventh Army units "move north," and "no crossing of the Rhine" contemplated. If one looks at the Alsace area of France on a map, it resembles a nose poking into Germany; and by pushing north, his division, starting out at the nostril, had ended up on the tip facing the Rhine, which at that point, lies close by the border. That it could become a situational imbroglio bothered Frederick. He was not about to stop his men; they had wormed their way into the West Wall, and were on the brink of opening a huge wedge in it. Yet, with discomfort he contemplated the negotiable question: For how long should he ask their flesh and souls endure the hardship, if a harness was to soon be thrown on the 45th's advance?

As if fate was listening in, the answer came abruptly the next day, 20 December. In the Ardennes region of Belgium, the German battle line had bulged west, and a tidal wave of Nazis broken through the Allied front. In a frenzied need to persuade them to stop Eisenhower had no choice but to send up additional strength from France.* So, Patton's Third Army was now pulled into Belgium, and from Patch's Seventh Army the 103rd Division, flanking Frederick's forces, moved further north. The upshot was, the communique Frederick received read "Spread out—your front must contain the 103rd's sector."

Behind blackout curtains at his headquarters, Frederick sat in silence as he digested the magnitude of the news. To cover the 103rd sector meant handing back to the enemy every position recently gained—and deploying his men dangerously thin over an area twice as long, and half as secure. With nothing in the way of options to destroy the Germans' advantage, he ordered a no-man's land of felled trees rigged with demolitions be laid across the front to slow them down.

It took the Germans four days to cross the sabotaged front, and as they attempted to slither back into France, Frederick's best defense was to try divining where they would attack, and when, and launch an attack immediately prior to foul up their timing and blunt their potential as they regrouped. Then, on 24 December, he got a warning call from General Patch "that excellent intelligence sources report the enemy," said Patch, gloomily, "is building up for an offensive in your sector, and imperative all your defense precautions be taken."

In the rest of the world France was getting little notice, the action in Belgium far more captivating a news item. Not that it was good news: censors blotted out most details, but things were not going well for the Allies in what was hoped to be Hitler's last grandstanding act. Yet, though Hitler now was snubbing some of his advisors (and his thinking erratic), he was about to again surprise the Allies. He had recognized he needed more strength at the West Wall to save Germany, and had sent in crack SS troops who, at that very moment, had arrived at the West Wall in Frederick's sector. For inspirational reading they had battle sheets

---

*Both Eisenhower and his staff had been so engrossed in planning what the Allies could do to the enemy, they neglected to consider what the enemy may do to the Allies; and later, Eisenhower accepted the blame, justifiably, for not having enough divisions in the Ardennes.

reminding them "The opportunity of this winter comes only once, for whoever wins this winter, wins the war!"

Frederick dispatched a message back to Patch on Christmas day: "Am having trouble procuring ammunition—my supply lowering."

Nothing is more a morale factor for troops than a good ammunition situation. Yet in Washington, General Marshall had just announced the stockpile of ammo in the U.S. "is exhausted"; and such was the reply Patch relayed back to the 45th's young leader, adding "Use ammunition sparingly."

December 25th had dawned with a snowstorm, nature's *coup de main* to the Thunderbirds huddling cheerlessly in foxholes. Some struggled with numbed fingers to open a package or letter from home; others had only memories to suggest it was Christmas day. Frederick, by now, had acquired a sleeping van (an ordinance truck converted to hold a bunk and a desk), a common piece of equipment for division leaders; and had earlier written to Ruth Frederick of his joy at "having a place to bed down, provided the motor has not konked out." Mentally tired by the excesses of war, the worry and inhumanity of it, he sat in his van looking at a photograph of his wife and daughters, and wept.

"His family," later his aide McCall said, "could never have known how much he loved them, but those around him knew. He seemed to think about them constantly, as he was always talking about them."

But Frederick's purge of emotions was brief. Wading through snow drifts to a requisitioned shack serving as headquarters, he spent most of Christmas waiting for a favorable weather report. With a snowstorm grounding reconnaissance planes, he had no way of getting information on the size of enemy forces holed up at the West Wall. And while no one hazarded a guess that the climate was also keeping Hitler's great offensive from starting, for the next six days the fight became one of surviving a killing -14°F temperature.

At midnight, 31 December, a blast of German artillery brushed a wall of Frederick's headquarters and demolished an adjacent outhouse. A close call, with Frederick and his staff gathered at headquarters, the shelling nonetheless evoked humor. Outside was a vast hole "that certainly exceeds," noted one officer, peering out, "the proper depth and length for a latrine." Laughing, Frederick responded, "Maybe we should notify top brass our facility has been revamped, and we can now accommodate Hannibal's elephants."

On the serious side, the slightly misaimed barrage signaled the onset of Hitler's new operation, code-named NORDWIND. Hitler expected this offensive to strangle the Allies' efforts on the Franco-German border; he expected it to then draw a batch of Allied forces out of Belgium back into France; and thus, by stretching the Allies' strength, NORDWIND, he dreamed, ultimately would bring victory to Germany.

However, Eisenhower's cerebrations were on a different track. He viewed it crucial to keep beefed-up forces in Belgium; and let Seventh Army to the south make do with what overworked troops it had to stop the enemy from surging deep into France. But more than the immediacy in Belgium slanted Eisenhower's thinking. Fascinated by the strategy of a "broad front" of divisions moving simultaneously into Germany, as this could not be effected until the enemy was pushed out of Belgium he now ordered the forces in France to consolidate their strung-out fronts by retreating.

"It will be disappointing to give up ground," Eisenhower said, in so much an understatement it heightened others' awareness that he had never fought on a battlefield.*

On 1 January 1945 the order cascaded down to Frederick to "fall back, dig in, and pin down the enemy." Initially appalled, he told Wickham "It is getting hard to know who most wants to keep us from reaching the Rhine, Ike or the Krauts"; to, in a way, put off showing his many concerns. Any commander who has to make a planned withdrawal worries that as his units move backward the enemy will strike; and in Frederick's sector the rugged terrain and broad, winding banks of the Rhine gave the enemy a perfect setting for flanking attacks. Waiting until dark to pull his units back, the next morning he rang up Seventh Army's headquarters and rapped out: "Tell Patch we are in the process of taking the Maginot Line,

---

*And later raised the question: with Seventh Army diverted both in November and December from advancing into Germany—which gave Hitler time to regroup his armies for NORWIND—how many costly months was war in Europe prolonged due to Eisenhower's "broad front strategy?"

again. Tell him I am disinclined to sit still. Tell him I want to probe far east in wide arcing moves, to nab high ground so I am looking in the Germans' ear drums."

To get a response to any proposal, a commander usually then went directly to his superior. But Frederick had a method which was like going through the pantry to get to the banquet. Waiting two hours before driving to a superior's headquarters, walking in the back door he chatted with secretaries, then junior officers, working his way up until he had engaged a superior's top aides in conversation—which ordinarily gave him an edge. But this time there was no room for persuasion.

"Forget trying to take high ground," Patch said, cradling his head in his hands, his tone depressed. "Just take what you need for observation to keep the enemy from trotting too far into France."

So, now, stuck in a static situation Frederick ordered his men to emerge from holding positions, strike furiously, and return to their positions to merge again—each strike like a knife piercing the enemies' initiative and forcing them to go on the defense. "The violent, fleeting, and sudden raids," some historians later wrote, "were one of Frederick's best tactical talents." The Germans were meanwhile trying to grab all the hills, to use as springboards for a breakthrough; and one 45th combat leader, Colonel Marion Crouse, never forgot the device Frederick used to get him to climb hill after hill in draconian fights with the enemy. Crouse was to attack with his battalion when he was summoned by Frederick to headquarters, where a situation map reached from the floor to the ceiling.

"There," Frederick said, pointing to a spot at the top of the map. "That is your objective."

"Good Lord, what are you doing to me, General!" gasped Crouse. "My position is at the bottom of the map."

"What if I make your objective here," Frederick indicated a spot near the bottom, "two hundred yards forward? Where will you go?"

"Two hundred yards forward."

"What if it is here, five hundred yards out front?"

"I'll go five hundred yards," Crouse answered.

"Oh, for Pete's sake, Crouse! Now are you beginning to see why," asked Frederick, "I put your objective so far out?"

Later Crouse received a bottle of Scotch from Frederick, who gave them to unit leaders, no matter the unit size, for doing an outstanding job. Though a small gesture on Frederick's part (a general's Scotch supply was unlimited), it was appreciated recognition; and as Crouse proudly recalled, "By the war's end, I had won four bottles."

On 11 January the collision of U.S. and German forces in NORDWIND changed when, in the dark of night, enemy artillery pounded the 45th, followed by a stampede of the better parts of three Nazi divisions enforced with the SS 6th Mountain Division. As Frederick rapidly shifted defenses the Germans paused; whereupon hurling itself against them his division, though battered, forced them to withdraw. But the day's conflict promised a horrific future.

Dug-in on hills and mountains in Alsace, the Germans had every advantage, and from forests thick with pine trees—their shields—threw out round after round of fire, as Frederick moved his units slowly forward in an inverted V, the apex aimed for hills south of Mouterhouse. In one bitter fight, a battalion of his men was cut off by savage SS units. "Give us everything you have, we're coming out," they radioed, and Frederick ordered all available weapons be fired in the air to distract the enemy. But only two Thunderbirds made it back to the 45th lines.*

That night, troubled over the fate of that battalion, Frederick vented in a letter to Ruth: "Tell the people you say whine about the rationing of meat they are despicable. That they are even thinking about fattening their larders, while here hungry and exhausted men fight valiantly, sickens me."

In every way January, and much of February, were months of extremes. The heartbreak and suffering in Alsace was constant; the screech of German rocket bombs and racket of heavy artillery filling the air day and night, and the cold intense and snow so deep the wounded, often unreachable, lay freezing, their cries of "Medic" drowned out by roaring guns. And always the grievous fact that SS units fought in fur-lined parkas and boots. Whereas Frederick's force: well—the War Department had

---

*When, during the following April, Frederick's 45th overran a POW camp in Germany, inside were many from the battalion who had been treated well, their wounds cared for, and their dead given proper burials by the SS who, one Thunderbird later stated, "proved to be humans after all."

been slow to even consider training divisions for all-weather combat, and winter clothing was not a priority. And finally when, in mid-January, new-issue jackets arrived, Frederick stared at them in disbelief; they had no hoods that could be attached. Between exposure to cold, battle fatigue, and casualties, his number of infantrymen had steadily dwindled when on 20 February he was notified that the 42nd Division would take over the 45th's front, and Frederick was to move his division to Luneville to shape up replacement troops, and to fill out ration and equipment supplies.

With his units billeted around Luneville, Frederick was settling into a small house where he could catch up on sleep, just as an Army Press Corps man arrived saying he wanted "an interview," because he knew the 45th commander had: "been awarded with a Distinguished Service Medal, and two Distinguished Service Crosses, one for your very brave and heroic action on a bridge in Rome."

Frederick's innate modesty prohibited his enjoying the moment. "If you feel you must mention that," he replied, "stop making me sound like Horatius at the Bridge."

Horatius was a Roman in the 6th century B.C. who kept an enemy's army from using a bridge over the Tiber River in Rome. But the Press Corps man, taking notes, only furthered the legend of Frederick by writing in an article: "The young General's actions make the Horatius story seem quite slow moving!"

A day later another visitor, a French general, stopped by to decorate Frederick with his second Legion of Honor with *Croix de Guerre* with Palm award. Meanwhile, in the U.S., not infrequently the press mentioned "the famous 45th"; which by early March was geared up, its morale soaring, when Frederick learned he was to breach enemy defenses east of the Blies River, break through the West Wall, and seize the key German city of Homburg.

So, now again moving his whole fighting mass north, in the dead of night on 14 March Frederick reconnoitered the banks of the Blies for crossing sites, wrote up orders for the attack, and at 1:00 AM the next day sent his division crashing toward the bowels of Germany.

Using assault boats stored in Luneville since the prior November (when Eisenhower aborted Seventh Army's crossing the Rhine), pulling the boats in carts to the river's edge, his front line of troops paddled swiftly to the far side. While they cleared paths through mine fields engineers threw an eighty-four foot bridge over the water and the 45th swarmed across, the confused Germans falling back. But by noon heavy shelling rained down as, pushing inland, Frederick's division took fourteen fiercely defended towns and, once more, attacked the West Wall. Because NORWIND had vastly increased ammunition shortages, Frederick had 40 percent of a normal supply and, to compensate, moved his three regiments abreast. Seventy hours later a call on a West Wall switchboard came in from a distant Nazi leader who exhorted all telephones be destroyed and everyone to withdraw; but there were no Germans to hear it—only curious Thunderbirds. The rapidity of the advance Frederick led had the enemy on the run and, with the minor delay of rounding up 2,055 prisoners, his troops were now poised to take Homburg when, crouched in a shallow ravine one soldier, Jim Parks, saw Frederick run past along a blacktop road, draw his .45, and head into a patch of woods.

"Be careful, Sir!" Parks yelled. "This here's the front line!"

"I know, son," Frederick shot back, "But we cannot let the Nazi bastards get away."

As Parks said later, "After pondering Frederick's reply, the guy next to me, who was a new replacement, gushed 'Boy, that there's a *real* General!' And I, of course, enjoyed boasting, 'Oh, we got us a general who is always like a banner out front."*

Allied fighter bombers had, meanwhile, pounded Homburg, and when the Thunderbirds attacked on 20 March, few buildings still stood, every civic leader had fled, fires raged unchecked, and everywhere lay human corpses and dead animals. As Frederick picked his way through the rubble the following morning he dispatched to the Air Corps' tactical commander, General G. Barcus: "We have freed forced laborers of the Nazi state streaming in who, along with recovered Allied POWs need food and housing, but it is difficult to even find places for our CPs."

---

*That this was of some concern to his field officers is evident in a number of messages they sent to the 45th Intelligence Section, in which they stated "having routinely seen General Frederick unescorted in an area of enemy fire, I recommend he be furnished a bodyguard." Which Frederick routinely, in turn, refused to have.

Whether or not he wanted to add "You overdid it," he ended with, "In my view, this is distressedly a total scorched earth."

Yet out of it had straggled large disorganized columns of enemy troops and vehicles; but instead of giving chase, Frederick pushed his division east-northeast. By now winter's white crust had melted, and the 45th's strings of men, trucks, tanks, and artillery moved at a gallop while, bouncing along on the seat of his jeep, Frederick studied a map of the city of Worms. He had just been told his force had been selected to from north of Worms spearhead—with the 3rd Division—Seventh Army's crossing of the last barrier to the German heartland, the Rhine River.

Called the Rhineland Campaign, it was not without some egos acting up. Immediately George S. Patton decided "not to coordinate [his] Third Army plans with [Patch's] Seventh...but attack as soon as possible"; and as Frederick's 45th was rolling toward Worms on 22 March, from a zone further north Patton slipped a unit across the Rhine, where it met a scrawny skeleton of Germany's Seventh Army. To the south, however, now nervously alert for more Allied assaults at the river there waited the stronger German First Army.

By 25 March Frederick had chosen landing sites across the Rhine that would enable him to cut the Autobahn, to snip this easy passageway for the enemy. At 2:00 AM the next night he walked quietly on the river's edge through brush bursting with new spring growth; it was not necessary to see the Germans 1,000 feet away to know that they were peering from behind tall willows, crouched at weapons. Frederick had received no accurate diagnosis of their strength—but trying, by osmosis, to get into their heads, he felt they too did not exactly know their strength, and after an effort of determined resistance, would soften.

At 2:30 AM blue lights flicked on in back of shacks nearby, and in hushed rows rising, his troops ran bent over to storm boats. The roar of boat motors brought murderous fire from German machine guns and 88s—the water churned by shells; the moonlight picking out dim forms— as wave after wave of Thunderbirds crossed over, leapt ashore, and fanned out. Almost half of the boats were lost, some when making a second run with troops, who then had to swim to the far shore, as meanwhile the 45th's tanks free-floated across.

At dawn Frederick had a bridgehead to the east, the first for the Seventh Army. And by noon, his troops had overrun the crust of resistance. Dashing from one spearhead front to the other Frederick, keeping his three regiments abreast, called on the Air Corps for an umbrella of protection as they rapidly advanced.

"It became," Frederick was to later say, "a magnificent display of cooperation and of timing. Every twenty minutes a flight of eight planes hovered above us, then proceeded to its prearranged bombing mission as another eight planes checked in overhead."

In all, eighty of these sorties were executed on Frederick's orders as the Thunderbirds swept across and over fields rimming the Autobahn, and pounded ahead to high ground, enlarging the bridgehead by nightfall to thirty-six square miles.

By now, well beyond his assigned objective, Frederick hurriedly moved his CP into a pickle factory.

"And that was really very funny," remembered (then Brigadier General) Paul Adams, "because Nazi Germany was against Jews, but the factory was making only Kosher pickles, and they were so good, the crews from our 45th messes spent all night looting most of the pickles."

However, Frederick had bigger concerns. Ahead were a dozen towns, the Main River, and a German "fortress," the city of Aschaffenburg. He had read enough history to know there was a strong corollary between the distance one got into enemy land and the intensity of civilian reprisals uninhibited by rules of warfare.

What could he, or should he, expect?

As he began maneuvering his regiments through the dozen towns, they encountered white flags and passive faces; and by a stroke of good luck, found a railroad bridge over the Main River intact. Frederick sped across it in his jeep, scattering what few Germans were attempting to blow up the bridge. Then, while engineers threw down planks and the 45th crossed over, he got his answer. Just south of Aschaffenburg was an organized mass of weapons manned by fanatical civilians, side-by-side with German troops.

They put up hysterical opposition as Frederick, to initiate the siege of the city, ordered it be gradually encircled. His troops then pushed in and met even fiercer civilian opposition, motivated, somewhat, by the commander of Aschaffenburg's defense, Major von Lambert. He had issued to both civilians and his over 3,000 Nazi troops a decree "Everyone to fight to the last," and erected grisly reminders not to give up. Dangling from streetlights and buildings were a number of Lambert's own officers, on their limp bodies pinned signs that read "Cowards and traitors hang!"

As the 45th punched in deeper, with a thousand decisions to make from dawn to dawn Frederick, orchestrating his infantrymen, tanks, and artillery, called on one chemical battalion to fire off rounds of explosives and phosphorous shells. In the ensuing inferno, his troops moved house-to-house, room-to-room, slugging it out with bayonets, while civilians on rooftops hurled hand grenades at them—and German reinforcements steadily arrived.

To bring all pressure he could, on day four Frederick directed all 45th tanks and artillery level firepower at the city; whereupon Lambert sent out a note: "If an American will come to my headquarters, I will be willing to negotiate the terms of surrender."

Frederick wrote in reply: "There is absolutely nothing to be negotiated. You can keep defending to the last man, or it will be a total surrender."

Forty hours later, finally, now reduced to wreckage, Aschaffenburg surrendered. It was 3 April—the siege had consumed six days.

During the fury of the battle Frederick had headed down a road toward one unit's front when he saw numerous small children wandering about alone. The most telling index of what he felt is in a letter to Ruth.

> To encounter civilian combatants is difficult, to view them as enemy more so, but that their actions result in perhaps orphaned, helpless youngsters is heartbreaking.

And would have a lasting effect on him.

In two weeks his division had traveled 114 miles, smashed West Wall defenses, made three river crossings, and captured over 10,000 prisoners, all in record time. Now nothing could dam its push deep into enemy land. Germany was nearly devoid of reserves, and its tanks and artillery were in defensive positions—which Frederick utilized by rolling his armor ahead, forcing the Germans to extricate their tanks from one area to another, while he now began to wheel the 45th in a wide arc southward.

Back on 1 April, an order had reached his CP that—to fulfill strategy originating in Eisenhower's headquarters—in a combined attack with the U.S. 3rd, Frederick's division was to seize Bamburg. Then being the pacesetter for Seventh Army, the aggressive 45th leader to next drive his hard-hitting 45th sixty-five miles further south to Nuremberg, and ninety-two miles beyond to Munich.

Eisenhower had no plans to move his armies to Germany's capital city, but to let the Russians, who were closing in on Berlin from the east, take it. Which, besides creating in U.S. and British leaders a band of critics, brought forth a burst of fury from Winston Churchill, who had (as earlier mentioned) warned that having to deal with communists in control of major cities postwar would lead to problems. Now rumbling "Berlin remains of high strategic importance," Churchill added his unrestrained opinion, "Eisenhower is hopelessly naive!"

And as much, it seemed, misguided. Unperturbed that the Soviets were about to also take Austria's capital, Vienna, as Supreme Commander Eisenhower had got the idea that he must prevent German forces from consolidating in the southern German-Austrian area, because—it was rumored, not substantiated by fact—it was there Hitler and his top leaders planned to make a last stand.

For that reason Frederick was directing his force south on muddy springtime roads when it captured many German generals and other high ranked officers blundering around looking for someone to surrender to. However one general, Franz, was the top prize; he commanded the division that ferociously had fought the 45th in Alsace, France. But all German forces in the 45th zone were now crumbling and, to tire them out, Frederick was leapfrogging his force forward, with two regiments attacking in daylight, the third regiment attacking all night clear across the front.

By now too his troops knew Frederick's routine by rote. At dawn he was out at their forward positions or on patrol out in front; at 10:00 AM, back at his CP, he evaluated battle reports, napped an hour, and returned to the front before writing up orders for the next day; then from 9:00 PM to midnight he called every company and battalion headquarters and talked with every sergeant on duty, which kept him informed in great detail. And while he showed no physical or mental fatigue despite averaging less than five hours sleep at night, it was his field leaders who felt the brunt of his schedule as they phoned in to report, "My CP is at....town. I'm done for the day."

"No, you are not," Frederick told them. "Now that it is spring and we have at least one more hour of sunshine, I am moving my CP to where you are, so you have to find another one for yourself."

Which, tending to keep his troops pushing rapidly forward, positively wore out the Germans. Proceeding to Bamburg, Frederick sent his units east and south to cut escape routes, while the 3rd Division moved in from the north. In two days (on 13 April) Bamburg was secured, and Frederick barreling toward Nuremberg, when soldiers on the road called out to him, "Roosevelt died!" Never having a permanent address, Frederick was not ever able to vote, but favored Republicans, and felt a brief concern whether the new Democratic president, Harry S. Truman— who had been vice-president only 82 days—was up to handling the war.*

Shortly after, over his jeep radio came word that George Patton had claimed *he* had captured Aschaffenburg. Frederick hated dishonesty and, having met Patton several times, had come away thinking, He will say anything to inflate his importance; and now if ever accused of stepping out of character Frederick, seldom using a profanity, blistered, "That SOB of a windbag of self-promotion is a damn liar."

That same day Soviet troops entered Vienna, and both this and Truman becoming President was to later affect Frederick's career in ways he could not foresee. What he did know, from messages filtering in, and the usual scurrying around to get a coherent picture, the resistance at Nuremberg was as fanatical as at Aschaffenburg.

In the scheme to take Nuremberg two divisions, the 3rd and 42nd, were to attack from the west, while the 45th, taking the longest route, hit the southern portion. But getting there in record speed one day ahead of time, Frederick was vigorously patrolling the direction his troops would move when he decided to attack from the east, southeast, and south, to

*Truman, in the meantime, was himself vastly concerned regarding this, as Roosevelt had kept him in the dark about all things military.

form a three prong pincer. Carrying in his head an inventory of his units' depth, breadth, and supplies, early 17 April he began the assault, and controlling the battle flow by his orders, by noon the 45th was wrathfully advancing inside the city when the 3rd and 42nd struck from the west. Enemy artillery blasted the Thunderbirds as, pushing in, they beat back two counterattacks and, by midnight had 4,869 prisoners. But the fight had only begun. For two days *Gestapo* and SS units threw out all sorts of fire as street by street the attackers slowly progressed.

Frederick had stopped to confer with officers "in my battalion," later said one trooper, Ed Palmer, "and I could do nothing but stare. To us grunts he was the greatest father figure we could have. I stood within ten feet of him and, looking deep in his eyes, I saw compassion, consideration, daring, and an inner strength of determination."

Indeed, determination. Figuring the Germans were well past their last hurrah Frederick, to bolster that, had now committed all his regiments to round-the-clock attacks. On 20 April Nuremberg fell—and in the city where Nazi leaders once shouted "Germany will rule the world!" it was the din of the 45th rolling through filling the air.

Already having mapped a route to his next objective, the Danube River, Frederick designed his orders to be more a pursuit of routed enemy than an offensive, as battling across Bavaria, plowing through towns and fields, where isolated German units put up sharp fights, his troops reached the Danube before sunrise 26 April, and came to a halt. The enemy had blown up all the bridges—and the river was a wide expanse of rapidly flowing muddy water.

If Frederick cherished any hope of making a quick crossing, it faded when a footbridge, thrown across, washed away in the swift current. Further delayed while engineers constructed a pontoon bridge for vehicles, and a treadway bridge for armor, and rounded up motorized assault boats, it was late night when, by extensive shuttling, his men had a bridgehead twelve miles wide. By then, their youthful commander had a new mission. General Patch had relayed that, being far out ahead of other Seventh Army divisions, the 45th was in the best position to on its way to Munich, pause to take Dachau Concentration Camp.

To keep the pace fast to prevent effective counterattacks, Frederick mobilized his troops for the last leg of the southward advance and, as they rode down the Autobahn on the 45th's tanks, tank destroyers, and bulldozers (and anything else with wheels), he diverted one regiment to liberate Dachau, ordering, "Let no one in, or out." On 28 April the regiment's lead elements crept past brooding dark woods rimming railroad tracks that led to a gate at the camp. Inside were 32,000 prisoners and 560 SS guards.

Meanwhile, Frederick was drawing up plans to attack Munich, the bastion of Nazism. The 3rd and 42nd Divisions were to approach from the south and west, respectively, leaving him a narrow front to move his forces from the north, once Dachau was sealed off. The fight at the camp took four hours; as the Thunderbirds—crying or raging, some vomiting—rounded up the SS guards. Pressing against wire fences, half-starved inmates emitted raspy howls of joy, while those who had undergone medical experiments lay on racks, not able to move; and everywhere was an overpowering stench of hundreds of dead stacked like twigs in open rail cars.

Frederick arrived at Dachau at midday to discuss the conditions with part of his staff and one camp doctor. The inmates were Italian, Yugoslav, Greek, French, and Russian; and before sorted out and sent to their homelands had to be fed, deloused, clothed; and a field hospital brought in to treat the ill. Frederick thought he had arranged every detail to only now realize he also must allot troops to quickly gather up inmates who snuck out in the chaos of the fight, before they spread diseases to the population. When he left, the drivers for his staffs' cars snapped to, "and, saying 'At ease,' he visited with us for half an hour," remembered (then corporal) Emil Hessel.

"That's the way he was, always talking with the G.I.s. He asked if we had any problem he could help us with, and of course we all said we wanted to go home. He then asked about our hometowns, and by the time he departed, he had us in such good spirits we were thinking we preferred not to be sent home, unless he was going home too."

At a briefing that evening, Wickham asked, "What is at Dachau?"

Frederick didn't respond.

"Well, what did you see?" persisted Wickham.

Frederick remained silent. Despite the mental games that like most soldiers he played, to cope with the violence of combat, to describe

Dachau required risking an emotional overload, as no moral imperative existed for the inhumanity committed at the camp.

Fortunately, many other things were on his mind. Through excited reports coming in, he knew that fierce delaying action by the German 2nd Mountain and SS 17th and 25th Divisions was stalling one of his units; that another had run into intense sniper fire, and to continue was having to lay down smoke screens; that the regimental elements now advancing from Dachau had encountered and were busy seizing a second concentration camp at Moosbach, that held 8,000 political prisoners.

But as with most unknowns that no commander can control, Frederick had allowed for setbacks while steadily pushing his division south. By 30 April he had his infantrymen on launching sites, and the 45th artillery on the outskirts when, at 5:30 AM, he signaled the storming of Munich to begin.*

Munich would collapse in thirty hours. In the meantime, with small arms fire whizzing by him Frederick drove erratically through the city in his jeep, on a course dictated by his need to check the action. He had just got from Patch a message that, one: the 45th sector had been widened, and Frederick to clear out the enemy in over half the city; and two, while the rest of the U.S. Seventh Army spread a dragnet over southern Germany, the 45th was to take over Munich, the surrounding counties, and all prisoners the Seventh rounded up.

But by 1 May, as his men garrisoned off Munich, already thousands of seething prisoners, and anxiety-ridden displaced persons, had poured in, causing Frederick to aloud ponder, plaintively, "Where are we supposed to put them all?" He had instructed camps be rapidly set up in the suburbs, and to use German Army warehouses for rations for these people and local farmers to feed the area's citizens, when next, in marched to surrender the commander of a Hungarian division with his staff, 7,400 troops, and 3,000 horses. To get rid of the latter Frederick sent a note to every mayor in Bavaria "to come get the horses to use to pull plows in spring planting." But of the many challenges that would for weeks ahead engulf him, the administration of Munich was the most staggering.

---

*At 3:30 that afternoon Hitler, with Soviet troops closing in on his bunker in Berlin, committed suicide.

The city was without water, telephones, or electricity, and to get it to function was imperative. Yet, with breathtaking myopia, Eisenhower had now put out an order forbidding "fraternization with Germans," and that "no Nazi is to hold any position of responsibility." On reading this Frederick fumed with unmuffled exasperation, "That is impossible!" And no more realistic than expecting a wagon to function without wheels.

As a commander of an occupying force, Frederick was committed to stabilize the city and its inhabitants; and that required Germans who knew how to run electric, water, and communication stations, knew where equipment was to clear out sewers, and who could fill postal and other government jobs. And most in some way were connected to the Nazi party. So, assembling his staff for a meeting, Frederick tore up the order, and holding aloft one piece said, with laconic clarity, "You need to adhere to this part of it only."

On it were the words "any position."

On 7 May an announcement funneled out from Eisenhower's office reached Frederick: Germany's armed forces had surrendered unconditionally (officially 8 May to be the date of victory, when at midnight all shooting was to cease). A weary relief swept over Frederick. But beside managing Dachau, housekeeping Munich, caring for the prisoners, the displaced, and thousands more roaming the 45th sector looking for lost relatives, with the perplexing task of handling both occupation and peace looming large, he felt no sense of joy.

Two days later, outside a handsome house that Wickham chose he use for a CP, Frederick watched one of many memorable dramas in Germany's wholesale surrender. A huge part of the German air force was streaming in from the Russian front and Czechoslovakia, to land at nearby Furstenfeldbruk airfield, the planes swooping low and rolling over as in an astounding aerial show, the pilots gave a final salute to their machines. Frederick stood riveted—until the logistics of it hit home: all those pilots had to be added to the already taxed 45th POW enclosures bursting with close to 124,000 prisoners. Then, little time elapsed before another incoming group diverted him. From their safe offices in Washington the watchdogs of military behavior—sent by the Army Inspector General to enforce no fraternizing with ex-enemy—were surging over captured areas where sixty-one U.S. divisions had put on their brakes; and one team, accompanied by newsmen, now came to Munich. Ushering them into the house, Frederick was instantly annoyed, as they fired off questions with naive dimwittedness about controlling the aftermath of a deadly affair.

His mouth drawn to a taught line, he spelled out, "To restore this city, we need German engineers to run utilities, German physicians for health care, Germans with agricultural experience to irrigate the land to get it to produce more food, Germans to help keep civil order, and Germans to start up the economy."

"That doesn't explain," charged the lead inspector, "why do you allow your men to date German girls? I witnessed that coming here."

"Rubbish!" Frederick rumbled. "I had the Provost Marshall bring to me men suspected of that, and I asked them if the girls were German, and they said, 'No, displaced girls from Poland,' and that it is easy to differentiate because German girls wear silk undergarments, and the Poles wear burlap."

The inspectors left Munich rather sheepishly. "And had they asked one more question," said Frederick afterward, "they would have left on stretchers."

About a week later a one line letter from Ruth arrived. Having read in an east coast newspaper an abridged account of her husband's statements she asked, "How do you know what underwear girls have on?"

Another letter to reach him was from one of his officers, Raymond F. Huft (who was to later be the Adjutant General of Louisiana). Huft had been wounded, and from a hospital had written:

"I guess every general likes to hear what his men think of him, and I can say that all the guys in the 45th will go through hell and high water with you, because they know you will always be at the front of the fight. I also want to let you know I will again be in fighting shape soon, so I can join you to get our share of the Japs."

Neither man, like most all Americans, had an inkling of some new weapon being tested in the U.S.—something that scientists secretly working on referred to as atomic power. So it was no surprise to Frederick to next receive a dispatch to expect to, in midsummer, move his division across two oceans and invade Japan.

Meanwhile, to observe Memorial Day the 45th troops assembled in a large square (called Koenigplatz) where gigantic Nazi rallies had been held. Standing on a makeshift platform, to avoid any semblance to Hitler's loud charades that had brought roars of Heil!, Frederick turned down the volume of the microphone and spoke of the "significance," as in "the very heart of a conquered nation, we pay tribute to our comrades who fell facing an enemy whose object was the destruction of ideals Americans hold dear.

These men," he continued, "were our friends. With them we shared our dangers, our successes, and our hopes. We cannot bring them back, but can do our part to ensure the endurance of those ideals for which they died. Today at the halfway point of the war, some of us will go to other theaters, some remain here, and still others return home. I hope wherever we go, we never forget our debt to our fallen comrades, but carry on their fight, even after the last armistice is signed. Only by doing so, unceasingly, can we fulfill our obligations to our brothers in arms who lie in foreign soil."

Then stepping off the platform, "Frederick said to me," relayed Wickham later, "'Oh God, how I hate war,' his eyes filled with tears."

Whether Frederick intended it, in hindsight, his words "even after the last armistice is signed" are a clue to his profound resolve to fight for freedom, anytime; which was to later bring him a heap of trouble. But for now, the only "trouble" on his mind was a pride of fifteen U.S. congressmen who, parading around to get in on the act, had visited Dachau, and were due in Munich any moment.* At Dachau, they had asked Frederick's assistant division CO, Paul Adams, "Where are all the Meissen porcelain figurines?"

"What are you talking about?" Adams had answered.

"Meissen is made in Germany, so you must have a lot of it," said one congressman; another adding, "Where is it? We want some."

---

*England's forces called these unwelcome visits by unnecessary people "swanning," a word derived from a swan's habit of making short flights that cause a great commotion but have no serious purpose.

Frederick, deeply disgusted when Adams told him this, had devised a plan that would allow him to bring the politicians to their knees, literally. He was to entertain them in his CP-cum-residence; and calling in two of his men, directing they gather up German handguns, when they returned with two bushel baskets full, he dumped them in a pile on the living room floor. And now when the politicians arrived, in control of the situation and gaining immense cheer, he watched as they crawled around on their knees, scratching through the pile for souvenirs.

After they left, he noticed that so too had some sterling silver flatware. So contacting his Provost Marshall, Frederick asked him to catch up with the group, pat them down, and search their luggage. And if any sign of dishonesty in American politicos is needed, in all but the suitcases of one congressman, Everett M. Dirksen, was the pilfered silver found.

As a big reshuffling in Europe of U.S. Army units began in June, Frederick learned that his force would be shifted from the Seventh to Third Army, and its commander, Patton, to put his CP in Munich, with the 45th to move to towns near the POW camps. But before this transpired, troops from the Third were seen skulking around Munich, looking for a place for Patton's CP. When hearing of this Frederick bristled, "Tell them they are not welcome here. We are still Seventh Army, and until we have all of our facilities in the suburbs, the Third is not to set one foot in Munich!"

Which in no small way reflected his sentiment toward Patton, who he loathed—and had not forgiven for claiming he'd captured Aschaffenburg (when, in fact, some of his units had rolled through a part of it, and Frederick's division then fought a week long battle to seize the city). As for Frederick's cantankerousness, "Many in the Army shared his view," said one general, later, "that Patton was the antithesis of how an American leader should conduct himself."

And when soon the 45th moved out, Frederick gave his engineers a go-ahead to install on all main roads leading into Munich signs that read "Third Army Area" and, above this, "THROUGH COURTESY OF THE 45TH."

By July, all POWs had been sorted and were gone, the problems of dealing with Dachau over, and Frederick again got a dispatch designating the 45th "to proceed to the Pacific war." Some of his 18,000 troops had already departed for the U.S. to get re-equipped for the invasion of Japan, and he had arranged the remainder soon to be transported when, on 6 August, an atomic bomb was dropped on Hiroshima; then three days later a second atom bomb fell on Nagasaki. Suddenly there was no need for more men in the Pacific. The war was over—at long last.

Frederick had spent 551 days in combat, and had been decorated with twenty-eight U.S. and six foreign medals. It was seventeen years since he had graduated from West Point, and in that span of time he had risen at amazing speed in rank. There is the old adage that "a good leader can take others through any tide of events, but a better leader tries to change the tide to get the most advantageous results," and Frederick— by his physical energy, military skills, and personal courage—exemplified the "better leader." But, in his last letter from Munich to Ruth he wrote, "There is no telling what the future holds."

For he had turned thirty-eight in March, and beside middle-age generals who would also be returning stateside for peacetime employment there were older generals who had spent all the war years in the U.S. waiting for choice commands—though he did not yet know they had been doing so with the green blood of envy coursing through their veins.

13

Quasi Welcome

That August, the victors had begun to return to the U.S., and to jubilant celebrations, when Frederick traveled from Munich to Reims, France, for a highly secret talk with Eisenhower on postwar military defense. ("Ike" had been picked to replace George Marshall as Army Chief of Staff in November.) From France, flying on to Boston, Frederick greeted seven ships bringing in his 45th Division amid a cacophony of ear splitting cheers and bands blaring patriotic songs. A red carpet had been rolled out for him and, as he made his way along it toward one ship, those nearby in the crowd noticed he was limping, and badly so.

In Washington the next day, at Walter Reed Hospital he was fitted with a steel brace on his shot-up right leg; and while there, told he had an enlarged heart as a result of nearly suffocating when overcome by carbon monoxide at Anzio. But his health was not a question affecting his future; what was, was dozens of senior generals needed to be planted somewhere, and though he had more experience than many—as a commando, airborne, and infantry leader—both age and time clocked in were taken into consideration.

Then, while enjoying a quiet reunion with his family, a call from the Pentagon informed him that he was being offered the position of Quartermaster General. It was a job that would bind him to Washington in command of Supply troops and the huge logistical web of furnishing the Army with food, equipment, and supplies. He quickly declined, and missed a good opportunity to cultivate acquaintances in high places in Washington. Yet neither had he a desire for any of that, nor for any administrative regimes' hassles of politics and routine; he always had wanted to earn his credits by his deeds, not connections. Thus, while the Army dealt with a human avalanche of returning soldiers, temporarily posted at the War College in Washington, Frederick asked as a "former coast artilleryman" he be given command of the Coast Artillery School housed at Fort Monroe, in Virginia.

It was from the Coast Artillery School that, eight years before, he had graduated when a lieutenant. But in this time of big changes in the U.S. Army, though the school had a usual amount of students, another 200 officers were stuck there, awaiting new assignments; and in some of them festered resentment that Frederick, junior in age, had been successful. One brigadier general who had fought the war from a desk top was dining at the Officers' Club when, walking up to where Frederick's photograph hung on a wall with those of previous commanders, he turned it backwards.

"This was a sour moment," later Frederick said, "of reality."

But mercifully, those officers who let their envy demote them to public childishness were limited in number.

Meanwhile, newsmen were writing pantingly about him, "Frederick wears no ribbons on his chest to show he's won most the medals the country awards for valor!"—and called him "The versatile general...the fighting general!" Even the syndicated pictorial column *Ripley's Believe It or Not!* got in on it, trumpeting "This general was wounded eight times!" But otherwise, in the near normalcy of peace, like many who had survived the terror of combat, Frederick was reclaiming his equilibrium. And though some nights he paced the floor when "war nerves" set in, and his eyes welled up with tears at mention of his men killed in action, and sometimes, after sundown, he walked barefoot alone on the sand at Monroe to try to strengthen his right leg, he had the essential camaraderie of another veteran, Wickham, who he had brought in to be executive officer of the school.

At the start of 1946, Frederick heard the Pentagon planned to make Fort Monroe the U.S. Army ground forces headquarters, and the Coast Artillery School to go elsewhere. Asking, "To where?," he got back the reply, "You have full authority to move it anyplace." So making a mental list of coast artillery installations he chose with no hesitation Fort Winfield Scott. Which meant he now also commanded all harbor defenses for his hometown, San Francisco.

It is a measure of his familial ties that the first person he visited with his daughters in San Francisco was his boyhood governess, who had shown him the attention his parents never had. He then made use of a small yacht the Army kept nearby at Crissy Field to take his family around San Francisco Bay, and promptly steered the boat up onto a sandbar; where it sat for over three hours, its stern bobbing like a buoy—as the crew worked to free it, and Frederick conceded he still didn't know a darn thing about seamanship.

The downside of his commanding Fort Scott was a lack of demand on his time. The war had reorganized defense of the seas and air by proving aircraft and naval vessels capable of intercepting enemy airplanes and guarding coastal waters. And though Frederick argued coastal artillery should encompass rockets, missiles, and other new weaponry, air power was seen as now having the most viable role in guarding shorelines (and the Coast Artillery Corps soon to go the way of wooly mammoths when consolidated with the Field Artillery branch).

Not one new student came to the school at Fort Scott. To keep Wickham busy, his boss sent him all along the west coast to inspect installations where he had had to establish "caretaker" units to ensure that government property was cared for; while Frederick himself spent a part of some days meeting with the board of directors for the Golden Gate Bridge, which begins and ends on land then under the domain of whomever commanded Fort Scott. But discussing bond issues and safety and maintenance related to the bridge hardly was time consuming.

Luckily, Eisenhower had another job for him. Knowing from their days together at the War Department that Frederick was an effectual and astute speaker, Eisenhower asked that he go around the country promoting the idea of Universal Military Training before it was put to a public vote.

As Frederick wrote out the speech he would use, he chose for his opening remarks:

> It is true we emerge victorious from wars, but our victories have been costly, because too many of us not appreciating our rights and privileges will remain ours only as long as we shoulder our responsibility. Democracy is not a license, it is a responsibility, and by our negligence and failure to face this we have repeatedly risked the inheritance of freedom passed on to us by our forefathers and soldiers. One means before us to guarantee both our freedom and the manpower to resist foreign aggression is Universal Military Training, a thoroughly democratic program endorsed by our country's foremost churchmen, scientists, and educators.

But Americans were demanding the Army halve its number of men still in uniform, and in a quarrelsome mood that the military kept soldiers in Europe and Asia as occupation troops—or as Frederick put it, "National attention had swung from the fury of battle to the fury of peace."

Thus, Universal Military Training, though elevated on Eisenhower's agenda to a place of high priority, was shot off its pedestal by public opinion.

But Frederick was also going to the Army's top schools to, on orders from Jacob Devers, now Chief of Army Ground Forces, lecture on leadership; and to conferences in England, where problems of past bombing strategies were rehashed in hope of finding solutions. Frederick's lecture on leadership comprised all the qualities he deemed essential, which he broke down into the categories: Unselfishness and Loyalty; Perseverance of Purpose; Initiative; Resourcefulness and Imagination; Intelligence; Energy, Enthusiasm and Industry; Confidence in Decision Making; Common Sense and Judgement; Duty, Honor, and Responsibility; Endurance and Physical Fitness; Coolness and Courage; Self Control; Appearance and Dignity; and Example Setting. And always he ended with "Sense of Humor—the quality that makes one's point of view generously human."

His talk on leadership was so well received at the schools he was afterward detained for hours. As for those meetings in England, Devers had it in mind that Frederick would coach the Air Corps, which was to soon become a separate entity from the Army known as the U.S. Air Force. In the meantime an old war acquaintance, Mark Clark, had arrived late in 1946 to command Sixth Army at the Presidio of San Francisco. Frederick was not bothered by the proximity of their commands, but could not dismiss even those nearer in age and of equal rank to Clark found him, though very capable, hard to like, when he saw in Clark's quarters a big painting of the General—and it reminded him somewhere must also be hanging that big ROMA sign Clark had used up historic minutes to obtain for a souvenir.

After 15 months at Fort Scott, Frederick got word the Coast Artillery School would be disbanded, and he was to report 20 September (1947) to Maxwell Field, Alabama, as the Army's representative at the newly formed Air University; as now after decades of being a segment of the Army, the branch with planes and pilots came into its own. On the eve of Frederick's departure to Alabama a note was delivered to him that read:

> I pray you continue your flexibility of thought, together with your drive to come up with answers for security of the future. The Air University is not on nearly so sound a foundation as our school system, but they [sic] have a liberalism of thought which is beneficial, and from which should develop progressive ideas.
> Kindest personal regards,
> [signed] Jacob L. Devers

It was Frederick's job to advise the university commander, Major General Muir S. Fairchild, in academic matters related to Army Ground Forces, and to supervise all instruction on army techniques and tactics. The purpose was to shape a cooperative strategy between the two services—whose views did not converge. The Air Force contended bombers and fighter planes win wars, while the foot soldier mops up; the Army contended those planes just soften up an enemy's wallop, and field forces win wars. But now the United States was dealing with the peril of being a dominant power in war's aftermath. The former ally Russia had humongous occupation forces in Bulgaria, Yugoslavia, and Hungary, was threatening to take over Turkey, and backing communist guerillas swarming into Greece as the Soviet despot, Stalin, tried exerting his influence across Europe. It seemed a new conflict was imminent. So not only had U.S. inter-service defense now become a popular concept, it looked to Frederick to be "an urgent necessity."

Remembers one of his assistants at Maxwell: "He gave those fly boys a really rough time." Pulling no punches in speeches at both the Air Force War College and University, Frederick packed in all the facts he found about "the U.S. Air Corps in the war erroneously bombing and strafing areas in American hands, killing and wounding hundreds of men and destroying vehicles"; and on how "in the south of France and elsewhere airborne troops were dropped into sea waters and drowned, due to pilot error."

A hardened critic, he then told his audience, "You cannot learn from wishful thinking, you learn from lessons."

Of course, he made enemies at Maxwell; and it did not help that he lambasted Air Force officers for taking Wednesday afternoons off (which the Army did not condone). Yet they were heedful, almost enamored, when he lectured that: "Air power and the atom bomb are at present the pre-eminently destructive instruments, and the Russians know this, and it is unlikely we will find ourselves in a ground war except in instances of an accidental war brought on by a power-drunk Soviet satellite, a false move by an unwary diplomat, or the action of an incautious statesman lulled by communist propaganda.

But," he went on to warn, "on walking miles all around the Pentagon in search of the role the Army would play in future global wars, I got a lot of sympathy, for as stated in the final report of the War Department Plans and Program Board, 'there is complete lack of war and mobilization plans under which a balanced armed forces could be developed'—and nothing about the future of the Army."

Which was dangerous for the nation. Redolent of pre-war years, Congress was hacking away at the Army's strength; and the failure to maintain military readiness to lead, Frederick anguished, to more sacrifices by soldiers. For the world was teeming with displaced and disillusioned people, and in a mess economically *and* politically.

In late spring 1948 Frederick's sister, Marcia, who had divorced a businessman and had one son, died of cancer at thirty-nine, and her brother grief stricken by her early death. Flying to California to attend her funeral service, upon his return to Maxwell Field he was immediately notified he had been reassigned to duty overseas. General Geoffrey Keyes (who had led II Corps in Italy during the war) was now head of America's occupation group in Austria, and had requested Frederick to command U.S. Forces Austria (USFA) Headquarters in Vienna. Once a part of Hitler's plan for a greater Germany, Austria had been divided into zones controlled by Britain in the south, France in the west, the U.S. in upper Austria, and Russia in the big eastern area that included Vienna—a city now dissected into zones run by the four occupying powers. Besides commanding U.S. headquarters, Frederick was to represent America at all Four-Power Council meetings held bi-monthly in Vienna.

His heart fell. It meant again being separated from his family because Vienna, being in the Soviet zone, could quickly become a hot spot of inter-allied tension, and no dependents were allowed. So peregrinating to Washington, after a tearful goodby Ruth moved into the Westchester Apartments with their daughters, and Frederick headed to the Pentagon for a complex briefing on East-West relations.

From there he went to Westover Air Force Base in Massachusetts, and with propellers swirling a C-54 rolled down the runway and lifted off, carrying him to a ravaged Europe. Among reporters covering his leave taking, the most concise one wrote: "Frederick is a tough young general who has drawn an assignment that puts him face to face with Russians."

And into what was becoming known as the Cold War.

14

"All Sweetness and Light"

The lumbering transport plane put down at Tuln Air Base in the U.S. zone of Austria, where a waiting four-seater Stinson ferried Frederick over Soviet territory to Vienna's airstrip. There to greet him with a command car was Keyes' chief of staff, Brigadier General Thomas Hickey. The official papers Frederick carried with him amounted to lists of who held what job in Austria; everything else about the Allied occupation was by highest authority secret, and waited for him in his new office. But not even securely guarded reports thwarted his concern that what Americans were led to believe was a far cry form the truth about Allied "momentum" in restoring Europe, and after his Pentagon briefing Frederick was not cheered that to be forewarned was to be all the wiser. During his tiring fourteen hour flight he had written to Devers:

> The situation requires remembering politics and much soft-pedaling to appease the Russians are involved but I cannot say I will be able to keep silent if [the] State [Department] continues to be shortsighted.

Clashing on ideology was common to military men and politicians. The military was used to swift disciplined action; by contrast, the administration aspired to get its way in Europe by being flexible to Soviet demands, which to warriors like Frederick was the reverse of what experience had shown—that it took a firm stand to gain ground.

Climbing into the command car that had on its hood four small flags representing the occupying powers, as he rode along the war-torn streets Frederick saw malnourished children laying on sidewalks, pitiful clutches of humanity sitting on curbs staring vacantly into space, and bedraggled refugees pawing through garbage bins.

"What demands my immediate attention?" he asked Hickey.

Sensing his weariness Hickey replied, "Nothing. But every day somewhere in Vienna you can expect a nightmarish problem."

The car stopped at the Bristol Hotel, a once plush establishment since confiscated to house U.S. civilian and military members of the Allied commission. Dropping off his luggage, for seven hours Frederick accomplished little as, instantly going to his headquarters at 4 Peregingrasse, what should have been a brisk round of introductions turned into a full afternoon and evening of military personnel inveighing against the Russians.

Early the next day he planned to inspect the American zone and later confer with the civilian commission. But his driver, certain he had not heard right when Frederick said, "Pick me up at four," was sound asleep, and the command car in the motor pool. Frederick contemplated calling him, but as more like his nature, he set out on foot, and finding it cured a sluggish adjustment to Austrian time, vigorously returned to the Bristol at noon. Not likewise, however, his driver, who by now, discovering his error, was too intimidated to show up to take his boss to the commission buildings. So again walking miles of city blocks, it was dusk when Frederick once more returned to the hotel, just in time to meet with General Keyes.

Keyes had asked that he speak at the opening of a new service club, where the ceremony included a variety show put on by enlisted men; and the event waxed long past midnight when, before the gathered crowd, Frederick claimed he was pleased to be at the new recreational facility— but his face a contradictory signboard. Afterward Hickey whispered to him, "You looked like you were ready to belt someone."

"No," Frederick assured him, "just thinking at this rate I may never find time to unpack."

Meanwhile, the Soviets had been nipping at the heels of Allied relations with nonstop propaganda, which for Frederick shed light on what filled agendas at meetings of the four powers. The communist newspaper DER ABEND, printed in Austria, had run two articles that began with:

—The U.S. occupying power kidnaps those in rival intelligence. Young people finding employment in the U.S. group think it is because of their knowledge of languages. This is a pretext....they are forced to be spies
—Western powers do not intend to return radio stations to the Austrians, but to use the stations for war talk and attacks on Austria's neighbors.

At the same time, Frederick hastily read in compendious drafts of other news that hundreds of Yugoslavs, Romanians, and Hungarians fleeing communism had slipped illegally into the U.S. zone; Viennese courts had sentenced five Nazis to hang; and two transport planes were to soon depart Vienna to take 800 immigrants to Argentina and Brazil.* Then his third day in Austria brought a bittersweetness; it was the third anniversary of V-E Day. Involved in demands at headquarters, it was nightfall before, alone in his hotel suite, he resurrected how he had felt at the end of the war in Europe—that it was not relief, but sorrow. His eyes closed, he was immersed in a silent tribute to his men who paid with their lives when there was a brusque knock on the door. Revealing no one in the corridor, it had been to signal the clandestine delivery of a note on the threshold that read: "How long will you tolerate the impertinent Russians? Some bombs thrown on Moscow would be best! This is the wish of the entire Viennese population."

"What was most striking," Frederick said, later, "was not that it arrived on a day commemorating the end of a conflict, but in few words it conveyed the depth of desperation that existed throughout the defiled city."

*As surmised only later: Nazis arrested by the Allies who then escaped and disguised themselves were in the routine transportings to South America.

As for the U.S. complex, it was self sufficient, with its own mechanics, cooks, physicians, judge, and squads of soldiers who policed Vienna with their opposite numbers from the British, French, and Russian zones. But out on the streets, the restless wanderings of refugees magnified shortages of clothing, food, and shelter, plus with the steady influx of homeless came a rise in polio, syphilis, scarlet fever, tuberculosis, and theft of the Allies' property; and as all this meshed with running U.S. headquarters, Frederick's job consumed twenty hours a day. So to his staff, the last thing he needed to add to his orb of duties was a visit to his Soviet counterpart, Major General Igor Abakomov. But Frederick was dead set on "getting to know him" before their first council meeting, "to establish a direct line of communication." Reports showed other than at meetings, messages were relayed through subordinate channels, delaying solutions to crises, or muddling their intent in journeying up chains of command.

His visit was a disaster. Approaching Abakomov's headquarters, with Frederick were his interpreter-aide and two bodyguards he had relented to have for their collective bulk only after his chief of military police advised, "Sir, I'd use 'em, or you could wind up a hostage of communists wanting publicity."

In response to his arrival, Abakomov's greeting party was the firing end of Russian rifles. Six heavily armed officers encircled Frederick and, while his group was kept rooted to the sidewalk, ushered him inside.

"It was the most asinine show of Soviet belligerency yet!" said his interpreter later, "Judas, not one of us was armed!"

Frederick was fuming, and got hotter under the collar as Abakomov, refusing to shake his hand, abruptly asked what assignments Frederick previously held. Frederick gave a clipped account, firing off answers to questions that stopped once Abakomov satiated a curiosity about the weather in California. At that point Frederick said, "I reviewed a case of a U.S. corporal carrying an invitation to one of our Armed Forces band concerts who, trying to reach your PAO [Public Affairs Officer], was arrested by your men, and it took six days and God knows how many phone calls before the issue was resolved. Given the possibility of a mutual security risk and our messages getting misinterpreted, to avoid any delay of a cohesive response we should communicate directly."

"Nyet!" roared Abakomov, leaping from his chair and stomping out of his own office. Afterward, Frederick laughed, "I was startled, but angry enough to tell his interpreter-aide I had seen better behavior in wart hogs running wild. It is doubtful the aide took the trouble to translate this to his boss."

Like salt in a wound, the next day a U.S. soldier on a routine patrol, reported witnesses, was bodily shoved into the Soviet zone by Russian sentries, who promptly arrested him. Word of it reached Frederick at 6:00 AM, but he waited an hour to be sure Abakomov was in his office before blitzing his switchboard with phone calls, not one of which got past a front man. Infuriated, and giving his driver a case of jitters, Frederick insisted he ignore speed limits as they tore across Vienna to Soviet headquarters where—in knee-high boots and jodhpur-like trousers—four guards swung their rifles up at port arms to block Frederick's entry. He paused, then, like a sidewinder grabbed the muzzles of the inner two, pushed them aside, and burst into Abakomov's office, leveling, "Why was one of my men abducted?"

The Russian, jumping in surprise or fury—maybe both—listened to a translated version and snapped back, "The soldier trespassed."

"That can be proved false," Frederick replied. "Release him to me now, or I will return with enough force to persuade you."

It was never defined if this shortened by days or weeks the imprisonment of the G.I., who was hastily freed. But soon explicit, Abakomov would try to embarrass the U.S. commander; and Frederick, concluding the Soviet responded best to brink-of-battle diplomacy, would keep dishing it out.

At his first inter-Allied meeting, however, Frederick exerted quiet decorum, as seated around a conference table, delegates of the four occupying powers discussed the policing and rehabilitation of Austria.

Every statistic had to be broken down: How many shoes had been manufactured with rubber soles? With leather? Was the production of lubricant oil up? That of lumber? How about optical equipment? Could the daily quota of rations to Austrians be raised above 2,000 calories? Funding for Austria's recovery came from the Marshall Plan, a generous rebuilding plan hatched in 1947 by U.S. Secretary of State George

Marshall. Stalin had been asked to participate, but had refused, and the Russians were withholding food from Austrians, impeding movement of goods and traffic, seizing property under the guise it was war booty, and insisting that non-elected communists represent Austria's government.

Frederick was not a table thumper, instead making his opinions known in few, genial spoken words. But when Abakomov demanded Jewish refugees who had snuck from the Russian to British zone be returned, Frederick sent verbal arrows zinging across the table as he listed all the stipulations set forth in Potsdam in 1945 when Stalin had met with Truman and Churchill to shape Allied control of occupied countries. Then, calling it, "your malignant intentions," he bawled out Abakomov for "breaking every agreement in the Potsdam Pact."

What transpired at that, and each, meeting was sent in reports to General Keyes in Salzburg. Keyes' dealings with his Soviet counterpart and Frederick's with Abakomov worked with disarming effect. The two Americans greatly respected one another, and while Frederick ruffled Soviet feathers, Keyes, keeping a closer ear to Washington, stroked them back down in a measured, but firm, approach. Bounced between Frederick's riling reproachments and Keyes-induced control the Russians were growing confounded. Where was the weak spot? Where had acquiescent America found these two characters?

Socially there was seldom time the Americans could get together. Typically, when not attending Inter-Allied meetings or working at his headquarters, Frederick conferred with troubled populace groups, visited his soldiers at guard posts, and met with the magistrate of Vienna, Helmut Kramer, who was a fastidious cataloguer of any information he got hold of and, despite having no official role in running orphanages or military controlled camps for displaced persons, had recorded the number and ages of inmates at these places. Much to the delight of Frederick, who was scheming a solution to find homes for war orphaned children. With over 168,000 of its own, Austria was also the chaotic sanctuary for thousands of young refugees who, in contagious terror, ran alongside mobs fleeing their communist conquerors. But their plight was not part of Frederick's command duties—and if wags later accused him of stepping out of bounds to chase a pipedream, it was half true.

Yet, led by curiosity and compassion, he had gone by several orphanages, describing in a letter to Ruth: "There is such confusion in these young victims' eyes. Some were German work slaves, some just babies in the war, and do not know their names or nationalities of their parents. I have begun writing our friends to ask if they or anyone they know will be a family to at least one child."

He may wistfully have hoped Ruth would also accept the idea. He always wanted a son, though in Hawaii in 1940, Ruth had sent this yen of his soaring into oblivion when, shuddering at memories of caring for their motion sick daughters on swaying trains and bobbing ocean transports, she had explosively insisted he drop the subject forever.

In another letter to her, he mentioned shops were filled with old paintings and porcelain and, if ever he got free time, he would buy some. A Renaissance man, Frederick had a taste for European antiques, many of which were being pawned by Austrians forced to trade on the black market "because," he added, "Russian thugs are holding back on Marshall Plan handouts. They even steal Band-Aids slated for hospitals to build an image the U.S. is dishonest and stingy. Unless our politicians stop paddling in the choppy waters of collaboration and dive into the murky depth of the turbulence, they will have us plunging into a new war."*

That was not the sort of missive he normally sent to Ruth. But it was not the sort a soldier sent to Washington either and, like so many of his colleagues serving in Europe, he had needed to get a few of the gritty details off his chest.

What socializing Frederick did get in was work related. When in June Field Marshall Bernard Montgomery arrived from London and said he wished to see an opera, Frederick escorted him. He also held a dinner for U.S. Armed Forces Committee members who came to observe the occupation, and took some of them to see the Lipizaner Horse show. Then one evening he accepted an invitation to a reception from Abakomov, and construing it to be a labored attempt at diplomacy, only upon getting there realized "I made a mistake." With his host at his side,

---

*And indeed, within two years U.S. politicians were pulled to the "murky depth" when no longer able to ignore the U.S.S.R.'s spread of communism by scaring up hate against America and attacking through satellite nations—the sinker being Korea.

he was handed a crystal glass of dark liquid. Raising it, he got a whiff of rancid olive oil as Abakomov, smirking, held aloft an identical glass for all to see and made a display of drinking it. Thinking it an absurd test of who owned the stronger stomach, but not about to give him the edge, Frederick followed suit, in his mind resoundingly naming every state capital to keep from gagging on the slimy stuff.

Rows of Soviet officers watched intently as a second glass was handed to the generals, at which point Frederick edged up toe to toe with his contestee and swilled down the oil. Abakomov, compelled to do likewise to save face, wretched and, knees buckling, sunk to the floor. Nodding grimly at the onlookers, Frederick strode out, and brought up the oil on the outside steps, ruing he had accepted the invitation "but really relishing," as he put it later, "that the SOB ended up on on his rear before his own men."

All hell broke loose the next day when now *Allied* peaked as a parody of discord. Frederick had got to his hotel suite at 1:00 AM—after a session with wailing emigres wanting asylum in the U.S.—and been asleep an hour when wakened by a call from the night detail in his office. The news was an inter-allied patrol of soldiers had been forced at gunpoint into Soviet headquarters. Bolting out of bed, and pounding on the doors to rooms housing most of his staff, Frederick created a ruckus that roused most U.S. civilian delegates too. He had intended to alert his staff he was contemplating an armed foray to retrieve the soldiers, but instead, the bathrobe-clad crowd out in the hall argued heatedly until, at dawn, the State Department group begged, "Please! For OUR sake don't threaten the Russians!"

It so happened the four powers were to convene that day, and as the English language newspaper *Basic News* reported, it was: "an extraordinary meeting. For six hours the American, British, and French commanders protested the abduction early this morning of an international patrol...but the Russian member refused to admit the holdup took place."

Or that he had simultaneously arrested Austria's Chief of Security on a trumped-up charge of espionage against the Soviet army.

"General Abakomov," growled Frederick, "try remembering we as occupying powers are here only to maintain law and order, and we can not level indictments against Austrians on their homeland."

The perfidious ally smiled. The arrested Security Chief already had been deported to the Soviet Union to spend (along with countless high officials who disappeared) what remained of his life in a political prison. Out on the streets, mobs of angry Viennese were in an uproar, decrying the arrest as "part of a reign of Stalinist terror."

But the extent of Soviet offenses was not fully bared to Americans back home until the next day (23 June) when, in Berlin, Germany, the Russian occupiers blockaded all land and transit routes, leaving the Germans and displaced persons of war trapped in Berlin to face dire shortages of food and supplies. And in Vienna that day, as if to test the U.S. commander, gun toting Russians again nabbed one of his men. But this time Frederick calmly reached for the telephone and rang up his M.P. station to request three M-8s—fast moving armored cars with four man crews, turret mounted 37mm guns, and rear mounted machine guns—be at his headquarters at 9:00 AM. What he planned would have horrified the U.S. political bunch if they had gotten wind of it, for no one knew what with the crisis in Berlin, did the Soviets need only a little nettling elsewhere to trigger World War Three?

Frederick's tiny convoy of M-8s raced through the streets, and by prearrangement came to a snappy side-by-side halt facing Soviet headquarters. Frederick stood at the turret of the center M-8 and aimed the hefty-sized 37mm gun at the door.

"Tell your General Abakomov," he yelled at startled sentries, "I will wait twenty minutes for him to deliver the imprisoned American to me before I start firing."

The sentries no doubt grasped little English, but the array of weaponry directed at their vital organs demanded rapidly involving their superiors. A frenzied throng of armed officers and police appeared outside, listened to Frederick repeat his message, scurried back in, and before long a car careered up to the firing line—and out popped a harried G.I.

A loud cheer went up from the American task force.

"Oh Lord! Oh Lord!" exclaimed one soldier. "It feels *so* good being part of our tough rustler's reprisal!"

But what if, Frederick was later asked, his bluff had been called?

"That was not possible," he answered. "The Soviets are expert bullies, and a bully's tendency is to just sulk when having little chance of getting the upper hand."

As for the U.S. State Department, his actions sent shudders down more than a few spines, though apparently no one suggested muzzling him. There was, in fact, one grateful State worker, Jean Carlton, who wrote to Frederick: "I pray to God every night to keep you safe from harm. Thank God that we still have men like you."

As to those serving with the occupation force, they relished relating, in years following, that no other American was snatched while Bob Frederick was in Austria. "The Soviets," said one veteran of the times, "were terrified of our commander."

Through summer Vienna remained tense, its population fearing a fate like the Berlin Blockade. But at Inter-Allied meetings, bucking a slew of altercations, now every member was pulling on the same oar to steer Austria to stand on its own, a feat not unnoticed in the U.S., mainly due to an Associated Press article that asked:

> How can the vagaries of Russian occupation be explained? In Berlin the four power setup ceased months ago to function. The city is beset with disorder which may bring about an extremely ugly situation. In Vienna, on the other hand, all is sweetness and light, and now relations there at a high point of cordiality. Responsible for the existing harmony is Maj. Gen. Robert T. Frederick, America's representative on the Inter-Allied Council, and at 41, one of the youngest to hold that rank.
> Such a contrast in conditions in the two largest capitals in Europe, in each of which are the same occupying powers!

But "harmony" had not eased Frederick's goal to keep order, and it was always late at night when, in his suite, he pursued relocating orphans, using his uniform hat box to hold a pile of letters to friends. He even again tried to nudge Ruth to accept a child, and she had written back his effort was "admirable," then deftly avoided the subject by dwelling on the muggy weather in Washington. She was readying to move with their daughters to Piedmont, California, "where," she wrote, "we will wait for you in the house vacated by your great aunt Hattie, who is in a nursing home."

It was not that there was wholesale apathy toward war orphans; there was a Committee for Care of European Children, and the International Refugee Group, both strenuously recruiting adoptive parents. But a pertinacious technicality stood in the way of Army families wanting a child; hopscotching from post to post, or separated by dint of military duty, they fit no agency's requirements of a permanent address and guarantee of school location. And so Frederick, doing a fandango around the requirements, was offering himself as sponsor, his mother's ranch as a permanent address, and to arrange each child be accompanied to the U.S. by returning Army personnel. The first day of autumn he mailed out six dozen of these conspiratory dispatches.

By then the air was crisp and trees ablaze in fall colors, but to the Western Allies the real glory of the season was that for the first time a prickly situation left them doubled up in laughter. A French delegate had been stopped by Russian guards outside Vienna for driving with an expired pass, and climbing in his car the guards ordered he drive to Abakomov's headquarters, but on reaching Vienna he had sped pell-mell in a swift detour to the English headquarters, where the astonished Ruskies were arrested for entering British territory without a permit.

News of the captors-made-captive spread in the Westerners' zones with knee slapping roars of hilarity. Strangely though—it seemed to Frederick's staff—the one who ought to enjoy it most responded with a wan, brief smile. But then they could not read Frederick's mind. He was worn out, his mental, spiritual, and physical expenditures in war at last catching up with him. And he was homesick.

It is a statement of his high demands on himself that no one in the U.S. delegation was aware of his condition, but had, in fact, been surprised when weeks back he uncharacteristically complained his right leg shot up in Rome ached constantly. More than that, however, he felt the sacrifices had grown weighty, particularly—as comes to the mind of any tired warrior—the longing for a stable family life.

Thus, at the end of September, driving from Vienna north to Salzburg he met with Keyes, to explain he had pondered remaining in Austria, saw it as undue compulsion to "hold the fort"; had contemplated asking for temporary leave, saw it equivalent to abandoning his command; and consequently had settled on the remaining alternative, telling Keyes, "I have started proceedings to get a compassionate retirement."

Keyes said nothing, though his eyes, dampening with tears, spoke volumes. Possibly better than most combat leaders he knew the phenomenal strength it took in the war for the young general to handle his array of jobs normally given, one at a time, to older men. Finally, slowly, he said, "I will miss you tremendously—but understand and will back up your request."

Whereat, Keyes cabled the Department of Army (DOA):

THE OFFICER I RATE EXTREMELY COURAGEOUS, INTELLIGENT, CONSCIENTIOUS HAS REQUESTED RETIREMENT FOR COMPASSIONATE REASONS, AND I OKAY IT, WITH RELUCTANCE.

Not so the DOA. Back came a cable:

DISPROVE RETIREMENT OF OFFICER THAT [sic] IS VALUABLE TO SERVICE. OFFICER HAS OUTSTANDING WAR RECORD AND GREAT FUTURE IN ARMY.

It had typical anonymity. Yet while not revealing if Frederick's request was bucked up to the top, someone apparently hoped to pacify the Army's bright star, and it most likely was General Omar N. Bradley, who had replaced Eisenhower as Chief of Staff earlier in the year. Bradley, a combat officer—he had commanded 12th Army Group in north Germany, as Frederick was channeling the 45th Division along southern routes in the Rhineland—was an astute assessor of a man's capabilities. In any case, soon somebody issued the directive, "Give Frederick any job he wants."

Meanwhile, unaware of this, and resigned to his adverse stroke of fortune, Frederick doggedly kept working, and it was luckily a relatively calm period in Austria. Even Abakomov could not expunge the peace when declaring at one meeting he would no longer allow prisoners jailed in the Russian zone pending their trials to be removed. Which, offering no dissent, Frederick ignored. For Abakomov had created, as the *London Times* put it:

"...a totally absurd situation, the only courthouse for all trials of all prisoners being in the American zone."

But before the Soviet wormed his way out of that by rescinding his decree Frederick left Austria. In the U.S. attention already had turned away from Europe to a political contest between Truman and the Republican presidential candidate John Dewey. It was 1 November, and Frederick, getting word ten days before, was to report to an interim posting on 4 November. There happened to be no opening in the job he said he wanted, after the Pentagon pressed he express his wishes, and he had responded, "If to remain in the service, I wish to be in the field with troops." However, for temporary duty he was not too disheartened to be going to Field Forces Headquarters at Fort Monroe; the chief of field forces was Devers, who held Frederick "in highest esteem and genuine liking"—and that was mutual. On the Vienna airstrip, as he approached the plane that would carry him out of the Soviet sector, a small girl firmly clasped one of his hands, her brother his other hand. Headed to a new family, they had been preceded by 11 orphans for whom he had found homes in America.

As much revelational as historically noteworthy, two hours after Frederick departed Soviet soldiers in Vienna brutally yanked a U.S. delegate (a Mr. Ross) from his car and murdered him. Though startling news to Americans at home, the old hands in Austria shruggingly accepted the inevitable, that with the "tough rustler" gone the Russians could again unleash their siege of fear.

"Frederick was the only one," recalls a State Department ex-official who asked he remain nameless, "to, in that half decade after the war, stand up to Russian aggression."

15

"Don't be Complacent"

As General Jacob Devers had been anticipating, he soon lost his new field forces advisor when, in less than four months, Frederick relayed that he was leaving to assume command of Fort Ord, in California, along with the 4th Infantry Division based there and Ord's subpost—the Presidio of Monterey and Army Language School at the Presidio. It was the Fredericks' seventeenth move since they had married, but this one, Ruth noticed, provoked in her husband feelings both of joy and nostalgia. Fort Ord, the Army's largest training center, had 28,000 acres of ocean front dunes and wooded hills perfect for waging mock combat; and was also—back when known as the Gigling Reservation—where, as a perjurious fourteen year old private, he had spent part of a summer with a National Guard unit.

Getting settled into quarters at the Presidio, then from his headquarters at Ord, Frederick arranged for Emil Eschenberg, who had served with the First Special Service Force and the 45th Division, to be the training officer, and Ken Wickham to be chief of staff of the 4th Division. By an ironic twist, the first piece of official mail Frederick received was from the North California U.S. Army Recruiting District. Addressed "To Robert Tryon Frederick," it read:

"1. You have been called to active duty in the grade of second lieutenant in accordance with circular 330, Department of Army.

2. Retention of your reserve status is contingent on your successfully passing a physical examination and completion of basic instruction. For this reason, do not purchase any uniforms.

You will be paid the pay of a second lieutenant. The base pay with no dependents is $180 a month, plus $21 subsistence allowance. In addition, with dependents a second lieutenant is paid $60 rental allowance."

Blinking hard, Frederick reread it. Yet like a fossil, his name had been unearthed by someone digging into old records of reservists, "which," he grumbled to Eschenberg, "if typical of how that district operates, will cause much confusion in a crisis." But it would take a greater inefficiency to prompt him to rebuke; instead he sent in reply a whimsical: "Frankly, while the chance to enjoy the life of a second lieutenant has a certain appeal, due to financial and other reasons I prefer to remain in my present grade, rather than avail myself of the opportunity you offered."

The next letter to reach him, however, required no response, as it read:

My dear Frederick,
I have always had great confidence in you. You were one of the outstanding combat leaders, and since shown real executive ability. I am certain you are going to the top.
Warm personal regards,
  [signed] 'Jake' Devers

What did it mean? Was the high echelon already contemplating Frederick for the top job as chief of staff of the U.S. Army? As he had just turned forty-two—and that position was usually held by men in their late fifties or sixties—Frederick saw in Dever's comment no prophetic implication. Anyhow, now that he was back with troops he was too busy to speculate. Believing work should never be delegated without careful inspection of the results, he was seen roaming Fort Ord and the Presidio of Monterey at all hours. Remembered Wickham, "Frederick often worked through the night, going out with M.P.s on patrols in their jeeps, or to the telephone center operated by civilians to chat with them and, in the process, find out what was going on at the grass roots level. Or he'd be at the guardhouse at midnight and ask for an inventory of knives and a countdown of prisoners, then go to the mess halls at four AM when the first cooks showed up, and casually ask what the menu was, and sometimes it was not what it should be. It made the regimental commanders very nervous, because they knew he knew more of little things happening in their units than they did and, in a day or two, they would chase me down, and plead, 'Can't you get the General to come see me now that I have everything in order?'"

As to the 20,000 G.I.s under Frederick, "We can't get away with anything," one of them groused. "He's got eyes in the back of his head."

Meanwhile, thinking beyond accepted methods for training men, Frederick had originated a new regimen. To be the architect of any military program was to court trouble. But he had been worrying over how peacetime breeds lower standards and, to boost effectiveness, from his incalculable well of imagination had come up with what in a report to the Pentagon he called "Division Faculty Training." It entailed, instead of a unit's overhead teaching every subject to its members, a faculty of experts on particular subjects teach each unit, to ensure each received the same high level of instruction.*

He also ordered that training be realistic—tanks rumbling out of the darkness of night toward soldiers, explosives popping, smoke screens— as men clawed their way past barbed wire obstacles. Never before tried in peacetime, the benefits were huge: for it accustomed his soldiers to using teamwork, and it developed leaders who had no prior skill in directing troops in combat conditions.

And he acquired for the M.P.s, "to give them pride in their uniform," he said, *blue* helmets (unheard of back then), which in spite of initial heckling as "Freddie's blue bonnet boys" the M.P.s soon found instilled a sense of proudful distinction. But just as good an example of Frederick's leadership in peacetime was that described later by Wickham.

"The entire 4th Division was on parade on the large formation ground at Ord when, leaning toward Frederick, I asked if the pattern of troops

*And soon after, re-labeled "The Division Faculty System" by the Pentagon, it was instituted at every training installation.

was okay. He answered he hadn't noticed, that all he looked at were those troops doing eyes right, to catch the eye of as many as possible to make a personal contact. He knew that meant a lot to the men—who usually only know a general as a name giving out orders."

Frederick's respect for soldiers was legendary and, so too, his efforts to help any man he thought worthwhile. And now in a case come before him, one sergeant had stolen money from another sergeant. The court had sentenced the thief to six years in the penitentiary when Frederick called in the sergeant's wife, who related they had four children and were living in a tent because they hadn't enough money for rent.

Frederick looked at her fixedly a long while.

"Well," he finally said, "you will have to go to work, and to control the money you receive. But first, your teeth are in terrible shape, so I am sending you to the dentist."

Next, he phoned a realtor in Monterey and said: "You have cheap places to rent, and I have someone needing a cheap place, and with all we do for the community, the many civilians we hire, I am sure you will turn up something in return."

He then suspended the sergeant's sentence; the family was kept together; and the sergeant repaid the victim of his crime.

This was command at its best, a general looking out for the welfare of individuals. And true to that trait in human nature to show ownership of insightful appreciation, one soldier wrote *The General Frederick March*—which the band at Fort Ord practiced and played at every opportunity with martial pomp and energy.

Early that September Russia exploded an atomic bomb, making the job to maintain world security—which America had inherited at war's end—much more difficult. On top of that, now in China a communist government was in power. George Marshall had resigned in January as U.S. Secretary of State due to a bout of illness, and been replaced by a former State Department assistant, Dean Acheson, and to Frederick both these men were too soft on containing communism. But it was Truman, who had decreased military spending, and his Defense Secretary Louis A. Johnson, who had further shrunk defense funds, that he directed a momentary flash of anger, telegraphing to the two of them:

IT IS NOT POSSIBLE FOR CURRENT MILITARY
SPENDING AND THE ARMED FORCES STRENGTH
NEEDED TO MEET CURRENT INTERNATIONAL
THREATS TO BE SYNONYMOUS.

Though his official duties kept him out of the public eye, asked
often to speak at functions covered by newsmen, Frederick, in his soft
spoken way, now appealed to Americans, "to shake off inertia, a liability
we indulge in to avoid reality, but may lead to disaster. For this is a
dangerous world, and we cannot achieve security by clutching to
philosophies alien to the foundation of this country."

Of course, no military man could publicly flail at government policy
without consequences, but throwing a bracing shot, his voice growing
strident, he closed with: "Those on whom the responsibility falls to chart
our nation's course need your guidance. Don't be complacent!"

It was pretty strong stuff; or as one newspaper, the *Los Angeles
Examiner*, screamed out in a headline, "Quit Dreaming Of Easy Way To
Security, Frederick Warns!"

Aside from Dean Acheson, in a shift of jobs now General J. Lawton
Collins was Chief of Staff of the Army; Mark Clark was at Fort Monroe
as Chief of Field Forces (Devers had retired); and Al Wedemeyer, who
Frederick knew from his War Department days, had taken over Sixth
Army at the Presidio of San Francisco. And on all of them, Frederick's
actions in the next eighteen months was to have an immense impact.

At the start of 1950, weary of worrying "how our weakened army"
could supply sufficient forces, Frederick sped up the fighting ability of
troops by shortening basic training at Ord from fifteen to six weeks, and
this, too, besides causing more than a little heartburn in his training
officers, had not ever before been done in peacetime.

Soon after Universal Military Training was again in the news. A bill
to legislate UMT was pending in congress, and as Chief of Staff, Collins
phoned up Frederick, to request he address civilian groups and "advise"
they convey their support of the bill to politicians. Collins then asked
what he planned to say.

Frederick answered, "To prevent agitating the public, I will approach
the subject kimono style."

"What in hell does that mean?" rapped Collins.

"There are three styles of speeches," replied Frederick. "The bra type touches only salient points, the corset type sticks closely to the subject, and the kimono type is flowing, and not so likely to alarm people that the army is desperate for troops."

But it was. Yet its manpower, in some instances, was wastefully used. For a second time Frederick had had to blink hard to ascertain he correctly read a message that came in; sent from the office of the quartermaster general it relayed:

"OQMG requests information whether your installation is or has harvested ice for issue or sale under provision of Army 2280. In this connection request following information:

A. Period ice last harvested.

B. Purpose for which harvested ice is used.

C. Measure taken to ensure water from which harvested ice obtained is potable where issue made for human consumption."

Bristling at the idiocy of it, as an aide meticulously wrote down his reply Frederick dictated: "To OQMG: a. available information indicates ice not harvested in this vicinity since the Glacial Epoc of the Quaternary Period in the Cezonoic Era. b. careful research fails to disclose what purpose harvested ice was used, nor evidence of any measure taken to ensure water was potable in that epoch."

The OQMG was not heard from again. Of course, messages of great import also routinely trundled through army channels and, in March (of 1950), one of special note warned that Soviet equipped troops were amassing in North Korea. But was this a war tocsin? And if so, where did those marshaled troops plan to attack?

The answer came on 25 June. Howling down mountains and hills, in a murderous surge the North Korean Communist Army invaded South Korea. Two days later Americans rushed to find atlases and maps, as Truman announced he had ordered U.S. naval and air forces to defend South Korea. Then, on 28 June, the United Nations declared its members would lend aid—to head off chances of a U.S.-Soviet confrontation—

but that American ground forces must bear the lion's share of knocking
the communists back into North Korea.

The U.S. Military was unprepared, and woefully shrunken thanks to
Truman, who with peculiar recall now extravagantly committed U.S.
ground troops to Korea. There were not many ground troops—and half
of those in the Army on occupation duty in Germany and Japan.* So in
fits and spurts, that summer naming General Douglas MacArthur to head
the U.N. command in Korea, Truman frantically tried raising one million
troops, first by calling up National Guard and Reserve units, then by
ordering the Army stop being volunteer and revert to the draft.

In the circumstances, Frederick was angry and frustrated; yet he
found apprising the immediate impact of the Korean crisis on Fort Ord
less a necessity than an exercise. He had already imposed realistic combat
training, sped up the regimen, and his popular Division Faculty System
was in full gear. The only change was his 4th Division was now
redesignated the 6th Infantry Division. But with no way to determine
how many draftees would be sweeping into Ord, and at what intervals,
"future plans," he told his staff, "are as unstable as water." And though
knowing he had answers for most contingencies, his staff had no reason
to suspect he would soon initiate the revolutionary abolishment of one
of the Army's thorniest and most illiberal policies.

As the first U.S. troops sent to Korea suffered tremendously, Truman
sweated under the glare of criticism for shortages of men and supplies.
Then, in September, his cagey political antenna waving, he threw all the
blame on, and fired, his secretary of defense, Johnson. He then named
George Marshall, who had regained good health, to replace him. By then,
eleven U.N. countries were involved in Korea, but nobody in Truman's
cabinet had a definite plan for how to conduct the war.

Frederick, overhead wondering aloud, "Is the aim to eject the
communists or defeat them?" had, meanwhile, in response to a dilemma
at Fort Ord, implemented a definite plan of his own. For by then, too,
drafted soldiers were pouring in at Ord; but never knowing how many in

*Plus eighty percent of the Army's reserve of arms was unserviceable,
and it had received no new vehicles or equipment since WWII.

each rapidly arriving contingent of inductees would be white, how many black, he had made a daring decision.

"It is ridiculous to try arranging adequate numbers of segregated barracks, mess halls, units, and training groups," he told Collins during a phone conversation.

The Chief of Staff had called to say that he was pre-treating the war long range, and preparing the Army "to keep fielding troops, for God knows how long."

Thinking about the vagueness of the administration's war plans, Frederick replied he was reminded of a line in *The Prophet*, "a book by Kahlil Gibran: 'Pity the stag cannot teach swiftness to the turtle.'"

"As for here at Ord," he added, "I have eradicated the policy of segregating soldiers, and am mixing the races."

This was beyond radical. In units in Korea integration had begun due to casualties and a need for troops. But it was not accepted as a social change, and certainly not done on military bases.

True, Frederick was not sure "colored" troops (as they were called those days) were much good in combat. But he had seldom seen any at a frontline, only heard of instances where they had fled when a battle heated up; and overriding this, his desegregating troops harmonized with his positive belief that the higher the "colored" soldier's morale, the better he would perform.

The media was strangely quiet, as if waiting for an ax to fall on Frederick's neck and racial riots to erupt. Within Fort Ord, however, the support was overwhelming—one black soldier writing to Frederick, "We Negroes have never been so proud, so full of hope"; and one white soldier writing him, "General, what you've accomplished is a national landmark.." And it had a domino effect. As 1950 drew to a close, not unaware of the tranquil reaction at Ord, commanders of other training bases started to follow Frederick's lead and integrate their troops.

By now in Korea, after some successes, U.N. forces had met with disaster, and hopes of liberating South Korea from the communists vanished. For China's Fourth Communist Army had swarmed in on a 300 mile front, had cut deep into U.N. lines, and had a nearly limitless supply of manpower. As U.S. troops withdrew to new defense lines, Americans at home let loose a tornado of anger: "Our boys are being beaten because all of you commie lovers in our government let China go communist after we fought for its freedom in WW Two!"*

Plus, now it looked like the war may grow into a global conflict as, with a slip of the tongue, Truman accidentally revealed to newsmen that he was considering using atomic weapons in Korea.

None of which personally, of course, impacted Frederick, except for the fact he could not help wondering if, in the following spring after two years at Fort Ord, he would end up in Korea.

In January 1951, the Frederick's eldest daughter, Jane, married a captain at Ord who was being transferred to Fort Benning, Georgia, and, right after the wedding, the bride's father caught the first of many planes to carry him around the country, on orders from the Pentagon, to oversee his Division Faculty Training System of instruction at every U.S. training installation. Upon his return, he found assigned to Fort Ord was an assistant division commander—which he'd not had—Brigadier General Gerald J. Higgins, who had a distinguished career as a parachutist and, like Frederick, was young for his rank. Everything went swimmingly well—for two days.

"Then," observed Wickham, "Higgins seemed to do nothing. I told him General Frederick was not a big brother to everyone who served under him, that he judged people by how they performed, and I handed him a three volume study of Fort Ord's capabilities and problems the staff had compiled. Higgins took it into his office, and in fifteen minutes brought it back, so he couldn't possibly have read it."

Not long after, Frederick again left to, in Europe, attend a conference on ground defenses. Before departing he asked each of his staff to make out a daily information sheet outlining what they did in terms of contracts or decisions during his absence. On the day following his return home, calling in Higgins he said, "I did not get your sheets telling me what you have been doing."

"I haven't done very much," Higgins answered.

---

*Even one loyal Democrat (then congressman), John F. Kennedy, was moved to criticize, "What our young men saved, our diplomats and our president have frittered away."

"That is my impression, too," said Frederick, frostily. "But I would like you to start putting it down on paper."

Recalled Wickham later: "Frederick was really irritated, and he wrote Higgins a letter, and in it told him he had 'violated every rule between an officer and commander, and between general officers, and shown a lack of basic courtesy.' For a full week Higgins sulked in his quarters, though the *raison d'etre* for him being at Ord was to help Frederick, who had little patience with officers who caused difficulties."

Especially now. For just arrived was one of those quintessential galaxies of politicians that fly about on inspection trips. The group represented the Senate U.S. Armed Forces Preparedness Committee, and was headed by Senator Lyndon Baines Johnson. For three days the men from Washington minced about firing ranges and training grounds in their city shoes, investigated medical facilities, barracks, and mess halls, questioned unit leaders and troops, and witnessed the "smoothness," as one put it, "of desegregation." As they prepared to depart, LBJ—a man once described as having the grace of a hound dog—lopped up to Frederick and said, "The way soldiers here are being trained—are you a warmonger?"

Demurring from exposing his thoughts, Frederick replied blandly, "Have a safe journey."

Then going to his office, from a desk drawer he pulled out his diary— a grey-covered book with ruled lines, the kind school kids took notes in. Plenty of generals scribbled furiously in diaries or journals, recording each activity, every reason for their decisions, who they met, and what they ate; George Patton even lectured to himself in his accumulation of writings, at one point putting down "I must be a great general."

On the other hand, Frederick seldom remembered he had a diary, and only occasionally recorded in it some detail or concern needed for future reference, or an opinion he did not intend sharing with anyone. Such as now, as (easily assumed in regard to) he jotted down, "The damn idiot doesn't know defense from offense."

However, the Senate probers' rating of Fort Ord was glowing, and nationwide, newspapers published the results that "Ord is 'superior,'" the only use of that word in Senate rankings of bases; [and] as to integration:

"...eighty percent of the men at Ord are draftees from widely different environments, and it is a remarkable tribute to our democracy that such disparate groups have welded together in a harmony we could have never expected.'"

The report went on to praise "the faculty instruction system," and concluded with:

"All this is due to the outstanding personality of Maj. Gen. Robert T. Frederick—a quality reflected throughout his command."

But it could not have been a worse time for Frederick to receive such laudatory recognition. Just days before, he had been felled by a 103°F fever in what he thought was flu, when from Washington he got a directive he was to now make a whirlwind trip to every army base "to explain ways they can reach Ord's level of efficiency." Frederick later recalled thinking, "What I need is a week of rest,"and the strain of the trip was quite evident when he got back to California. Worn out, and pale, he had lost weight. But there was no relief from his hectic schedule as now, from the Presidio of San Francisco, Al Wedemeyer arrived to get, presumed Frederick, a look at his command.

From a (then) lieutenant in the public information office at Fort Ord, Dave Clark, we get a partial account of what ensued:

"During the welcoming ceremonies, and as Frederick escorted him around the base, both generals were stoney faced. But when it was over they walked to the Officers' Club and, once inside, grinning and hugging each other, they sat down and reminisced—like a couple of next door neighbors talking about how to mow a lawn. I will never forget how easy going and relaxed they were, yet when the occasion called for formality they could shield every emotion.* Later that day, Wedemeyer went to Frederick's quarters to continue their visit, and to dine with his family."

---

*Called the "mystification of command," it's the art of letting the men under him see only what a leader wants them to know.

Soon after, it became obvious Frederick was swiftly weakening physically. Whereupon examined by his doctor, it was determined he had long been suffering from infectious mononucleosis and an enlarged spleen, and he recommended he lay flat on his back in bed for seven days.

While trying to recuperate, surrounded by newspapers, maps, and a radio, from afar Frederick watched fascinated as a political fray sprung up in Washington. Six days before (on 5 April 1951) General MacArthur had sent a letter to the President criticizing his policies in Korea—policies that, initially waffling, then hamstrung all chances of beating the communists; and now (on 11 April) Truman, feisty in even the best of times, relieved MacArthur of his command. His replacement, a West Point classmate of the Army's Chief of Staff, was fifty-six year old Lieutenant General Matthew B. Ridgeway, who had been leading the Eighth Army in Korea; and the Eighth was to be commanded by Lieutenant General James A. Van Fleet who, age fifty-nine and a former classmate of Eisenhower's at West Point, was on duty as the Chief of the U.S. Military Aid Group to Greece. Who would fill the job vacated by Van Fleet had not yet been settled.

Truman's popularity had plummeted months earlier, but now as Americans bitterly opposed his firing MacArthur, his Republican opponents were tripping all over each other to quickly declare their candidacy for the presidential election in 1952. Leading the pack was a right wing "isolationist" senator, Robert A. Taft, with whom Frederick had got acquainted on one trip to Washington when called to testify before Congress about communism in Austria. But of most interest to him, however, was the action in Korea; and as hourly he kept track of this from bed, Ruth Frederick grew uneasily aware her husband was pining to get in on the fight.

After a week Frederick's spleen was again normal but, returning to work, he had no energy and rapidly fatigued, both notorious and prolonged residuals of severe mononucleosis. Pushing himself, yet not able to ignore his exhaustion, he already was feeling downcast when a directive arrived that he had been named Chief of the Joint U.S. Military Aid Group to Greece, and Commander, Army Section. Vastly disappointed, he had been hoping to go to Korea to command a corps, which as a headquarters unit coordinates the military operations of three or more divisions.

"He was the most logical choice," recounted Wickham later. "He was an outstanding division commander in wartime, and in peacetime—but nepotism was at work. Only older major generals who were long time friends of the Chief of Staff of the Army were being awarded corps commands."

Had Frederick read an Officer Efficiency Report that Wedemyer had sent off to Washington subsequent to their visit his mood may have lifted; OERs are something every general had to submit on other officers, and Wedemyer had written of Frederick:

"Unquestionably subjected to terrific strains, as evidence his brilliant WWII record...noted in him tenseness...admonished him relax; confident he is striving [to] follow my advice."

What Wedemyer was not made aware of at the time of his visit, a doctor had prescribed Frederick take Benzedrine to shake off that lethargy caused by his 103°F fever, and it had made him nervous as a cat chased by a dog. Anyway, that did not diminish his capabilities, and as stated previously by others, Wedemyer ended his synopsis of Frederick with:

"[He] is appropriate material to be the next Chief of Staff of the Army; one of the finest officers and gentlemen I have been associated with in the service."

So why was he going to Greece? To quietly groom him for the top job? To fill out his resumé? Certainly his position in Athens would hone his skill at handling the outcome of battles and uncertainties of peace, for Greece was reeling in the aftermath of a civil war. But of all the rending transitions in his career none so distressed him, for Ruth was not going with him; she had decided it best if their youngest daughter finished high school in the U.S.

"His leaving," remembered Dave Clark, "was hard on everyone. He was revered at Fort Ord and at the Presidio of Monterey, and at the Language School—I don't think he even realized how many men were very proud to be serving with him—and how many drafted soldiers very proud to be training in his 6th Division."

Having vacillated over how to get to Greece, still bereft of energy Frederick had settled on taking a ship, to get in a few days rest, when he left his family at 4:00 AM on 1 May. And not looking back, consoled himself that Greece was a perfectly decent place to work, and his job perfectly suited to better acquaint him with the untruths and compromises in U.S. diplomatic and foreign policies.

16

"Free Men"

A hot sky gilded Athens white and gold, the city shimmering in the glow when the U.S. naval ship slipped into port and, disembarking, Frederick was whisked downtown in a command car to a sumptuous suite reserved for him at the Grand Bretague Hotel. Wasting no time, he unpacked his uniforms and arranged to meet with all his staff.

For an aide-de-camp he hadn't far to look; he had brought along Major William Stein, an astute officer who had held the same job at Fort Ord. As to an orderly, also accompanying him was Corporal Daniel Delahanty, who had been with him since 1944. Every general has an orderly, and Delahanty had often been a pain in the neck—but a likeable one—when after a night off he would show up hung over. But he ironed Frederick's uniforms impeccably, and was a fairly good housekeeper.

That evening, at a dinner hosted by the Prime Minister of Greece, Sophocles Venizelos, Frederick was the guest of honor. Going alone, it would have been no benefit to take Stein along, as neither of them knew a word of Greek. Fortunately Venizelos spoke English, and in a lengthy toast to Frederick, he couched in the language of diplomacy that Greece was "awash in troubles."

It was a great understatement. For seven years, Greece had been a pothole of human wretchedness and mendacity. At the start of World War II Nazi troops had occupied the country, but Greece's Communist Party, Socialist Party, Royalist Party (that supported then-in-exile King

Paul and Queen Frederika), and sundry other parties had been too busy
fighting among themselves to fight the Germans. Then in 1944, because
it was in the British Theater of War, Britain had liberated Greece; whereat
the Communist Party, using weapons from neighboring Bulgaria and
Albania, tried to overthrow the government. Frederick had read up on
the history, and found that, depending whose view one believed, the
Greeks had valiantly resisted or, shrugging, let the British fend off the
communists, who murdered thousands of unarmed civilians and carried
off over 28,000 Greek children, holding them captive in mountain border
areas to "educate" them in Marxism. By 1949, however, Britain could
no longer afford to supply aid, and so America had begun funneling in
millions from the Truman Doctrine treasure chest set up to "protect
democracy" in Greece (and Turkey). And in the three years since, the
government of Greece had changed hands three times.

Actual fighting had ended months before Frederick's arrival, and it
was now not bands of communists but feuding, corrupt politicians
hectoring the country and affecting every U.S. diplomatic decision. But
politics would not, Frederick figured, impinge on his job as Chief of the
Joint U.S. Military Aid Group (JUSMAG) to advise Greek Armed Forces,
oversee their training, and monitor supplies. As a soldier he had no
freedom of political expression, anyway; he was to serve without question
or bias.

Yet prior to his departing the U.S., he had received a dispatch from
U.S. Secretary of State Dean Acheson:

"The duty of the Chief [of JUSMAG] is to make decisions in
accordance with State Department policies."

If that wasn't politics, wondered Frederick, what was? For it meant
putting aside years of training to make snap decisions and give orders,
and learn to walk a tightrope in the constantly shifting winds of U.S.
diplomacy.

In two days Frederick had gone by the U.S. Embassy to get a current
accounting from U.S. Ambassador John E. Puerifoy; had attended a
meeting of the High Military Council composed of Greece's minister of
defense and senior generals, where—passing notes back and forth to his

interpreter-aid—he told them what he expected of them; had inspected army training centers on the island of Crete; and ridden a tiny donkey into mountains in northern Greece to visit soldiers manning outposts to prevent a resurgence of communist guerillas. As for the donkey, it represented a big goof when at the start of America's benevolent mission to Greece, 500 Missouri mules had been sent over to carry weapons to the Greek army in the mountains. The mules were too wide for the narrow mountainous routes; only scrawny Greek donkeys could traffic those paths, "and so we had to spend months trading with Greek farmers," remembers one fellow there at the time, "all of these hundreds of massive mules for their puny donkeys."

It had been called a "Greek solution," a term Frederick would soon come to know meant the way to get things done in Greece was to propose: I will do this, if you do that; if you say that, I will say this.

Making himself conspicuous among the armed forces, he had got a feel for their situation and the dimension Greek generals owed their success to political backing, when he was invited by King Paul and Queen Frederika to the Royal Palace. He had met the King ten years earlier in London when they both had paid a visit to then-in-exile King Olaf of Norway. But he had not seen, only heard, that Queen Frederika, who was thirty-two and of English-German descent, was quite pretty; a fact she confirmed when greeting him, her dark eyes sparkling, she smiled, and said, charmingly, "We adore Coca Cola, General. Can you arrange cases of it to be delivered here?" Then abruptly swerving from the topicality of the moment, she asked, "How long is American aid to continue?"

Frederick replied about $127 million in military equipment remained to be delivered, but that, otherwise, he had no information. At which point King Paul revealed what they really wanted to know was his opinion of General Alexandros Papagos, the Commander-in-Chief of Greek armed forces. Answering, "I have been in your country only a short time," and getting a sense something was afoot Frederick hastened to add, "and formed no opinion."

That night, General Papagos resigned as head of Greece's military, then at 5:00 AM the next day, Greek soldiers attempted a coup in his name by surrounding all radio stations and the Parliament building in

Athens—and Frederick began to wish he was someplace far off, as now a door to the future of Greece swung open.

Firstly, a decree was instantly issued making King Paul commander-in-chief of the military, and as U.S. Ambassador Peurifoy fretted, "He seems to like the job." Frederick worried the ferment in the military would grow explosive if the King tampered with its staff. But of just as much a concern to him was the prospect of Papagos in any political role. The tall, sixty-seven year old Papagos was considered a hero in Greece's fight against Italy in WWII, but his record was not all glory. Captured by the Germans, he had spent most of the war in Dachau prison camp until Frederick, moving his 45th Division south in 1945, sent in troops to liberate the camp. Having since met with Papagos numerous times, Frederick found him abrasive, too ambitious, and extremely far right politically. And knowing firsthand that extreme forms of government create disunity—having experienced it in dealing with the Soviets in Austria—Frederick secretly thought the left-of-center government of Prime Minister Venizelos the more desirable of the two.

Secondly, the King had declared that he would not relinquish his role as C-in-C even if Papagos wanted it back. So Frederick, now hurrying off to the Palace, tried persuading His Majesty to change his mind, and got the response: "No! Papagos is mentally ill. But if Greece is admitted to NATO, I might find a place for him that involved his returning to control the armed forces."

"But if he is mentally ill," quizzed Frederick, "why do that?"

"I would lose face if I didn't," replied King Paul, "and besides, it would be sure to please American officials."

This was an obvious ploy. To be included in NATO would give the Greeks a psychological boost and greater security, and because Eisenhower, coming out of retirement, commanded the North Atlantic Treaty Organization, formed in 1949 to fight the Soviets, "every Greek with any power," remembered Frederick, "was trying to look as if he was behaving."

Meanwhile, efforts by Ambassador Peurifoy to reinstate Papagos as C-in-C also failed, and from Washington, Secretary of State Acheson wired over: "FEAR U.S. PRESTIGE WEAKENED." To which the U.S. Embassy cabled back: "WE ARE STILL AS MUCH LOVED AS ANY

SUGAR DADDY." But for how long? For now, in what Frederick considered a specious attempt to stabilize Greece, Peurifoy settled on the "Papagos solution"—to discretely back the rightist general in elections next September—on the premise because the Greek far right survived Nazi occupation in WWII by submitting to Germany's dictates, it would be a yielding conduit for American control. Frederick was infuriated. "Neither King Paul, nor Venizelos, nor Greek military leaders trusted or liked Papagos," he said later, "and wraiths of every political persuasion had been swatting away at him."

Nor did Frederick's anger lessen when from the State Department he got a message that directed: "Refrain intervening in Papagos entry into politics, except to deny Americans inspired it; privately, however, you are to minimize hostility of King and Queen toward Papagos."

No doctrine prescribed what a soldier is to do in a two-faced drama of diplomatic perfidy and double crossing. Luckily, he was to soon escape. Scheduled to fly to London to report to Eisenhower about the strength of Greece's military, after four days with Ike he went on to Washington where, before a Congressional committee, he argued forcefully against stopping aid to Greece the next year (1952), when the Marshall Plan expired. Many in the U.S. Congress were eager to lift Greece off the backs of American taxpayers; yet, as Frederick argued: "Greek forces have high spirits, but their equipment is far below U.S. standards, so you cannot expect them to keep participating in Korea's war, or to efficiently guard against communist expansion without our help."

On 24 June, returning to find Athens wrapped in sweltering heat (air conditioning not yet a commodity), he moved from the hotel to a small house on the coast "to get what faint breezes may blow in," he wrote to Ruth. Even less able to cope, his orderly Delahanty pleaded to be returned to the States and, sending him back, Frederick hired a Greek housekeeper, Effie, to take his place. And now, too, as tempers mushroomed in the torrid summer air, summoned by the Prime Minister, Frederick quietly listened to him rail against Papagos, who had made public that when (not if) elected he would "close down" all newspapers that criticized him, "punish" the chief of staff of Greek forces General Tsakalotos for not backing him, "strip the King" of any military power, and make himself "both prime minister and minister of defense."

Possessing good intentions not to violate his role as impartial military advisor, Frederick avoided giving any opinion, only to very soon have his conscience collide with his beliefs.

On 4 July 4 1951, at a ceremony to mark America's independence, Frederick spoke before a crowd of U.S. Embassy staff, legionaries, the U.S. military group, and friends. He asked they give thought to "all who have never known, or do not now have the freedom Americans know." Then mentioning the fight in Korea, and that every generation "must work for the principles of liberty," and "allow no dictator to control people through force and fear," he ended by quoting from the Greek anthem, in one line changing "all men" to "*free* men."

It created a huge rumpus in the press. Hammered especially by communist newspapers for "revamping our beloved anthem," making a gesture to atone Frederick sent out notices he had meant "just to stress the right to be free, not arouse national indignation"; but he was not remorseful.

"By golly, if I cannot talk politics," he told his chief of staff, Colonel Glenn Finley, "I will at least express cues to the main players."

He enjoyed better success when a bunch of U.S. senators arrived to examine Greece's economic situation. Feted by the King and Queen at the palace, they were also honored guests of Venizelos at a gala party, and at both affairs the Prime Minister raised up his glass and toasted "the distinguished soldier General Frederick, whose belief in freedom and great work and advice give us hope for the future."

Moreover, Frederick was quite popular in Greek armed forces, as with quiet dexterity he praised their abilities, advised how to cut expenses, watched out for their welfare, and visited wounded Greeks returned from Korea. Only once was this coalition strained—when American air operations in Korea killed a number of Greek troops. It gave communist propagandists a cause to blast the U.S., and radio stations operating out of Romania to transmit instructions to communists in Athens to subvert the Greek military. Frederick's reaction was to get in between the two by contacting General Tskakalotos (the Chief of Staff) to warn he watch for signs of commie propaganda permeating armed units. Next he rushed to the embassy to convey to Ambassador Peurifoy that Tskakalotos wanted to know should communist subversion blossom into a revolt, was the American State Department prepared to intervene.

Speaking rapidly—and with a frown, as if he already knew the answer—Frederick asked, "How would the embassy prefer I respond to that?"

"With a question," Peurifoy replied. "Maintain a noncommittal position capable of any interpretation, so no matter what happens we can say *We* told you so. The best course is to answer any question by raising the eyebrows and saying *Oh?*"

Far from pleased, Frederick felt this was a time when it was crucial the embassy issue a strong statement to help quell chances of a national uproar. Already impatient with diplomatic artifice that he described later "left no room for reality," he had grown equally tired of the ceaseless official functions, ceremonies, and less formal engagements. They included dinners with Papagos, Venizelos, and the Monarchy; and in turn he had to pour out hospitality to foreign and American officials. Nonetheless, after one evening, Peurifoy's wife sent a note around to him:

"Dear Bob, your dinner party last night with its delicious food, entertaining guests, and beautiful setting was a great social triumph."

Yet to Frederick it had been but another of too many social obligations crowding his schedule of running the Joint U.S. Military Aid Group, traveling to military bases, and of mordantly observing shady Greek politics and U.S. diplomacy subterfuge.

And now as elections neared more unrest flared across Greece. In one of many sordid events, General Tskakalotos, in cohorts with King Paul, planned to undermine Papagos' bid to be prime minister by staging maneuvers the day of elections to prevent soldiers and their unit leaders from voting. Frederick heard about it from an unimpeachable source— Tskakalotos himself—and it is fair to assume he thought the awful spectacle of Papagos in power no worse than tinkering with the democratic process. For he demanded Tskakalotos "stop all influence on the military to defeat Papagos," and then, on election day, with scrappy vigilantism he drove through every outlying area of Athens, and posted his staff all around the city, to ensure that no military personnel was deprived of voting.

Papagos lost anyway. Much to the chagrin of Ambassador Peurifoy, whose scheme to install the general backfired as, uniting in a common fury, now the Socialist, Leftist, and Centrist parties controlled the government.

As for Papagos, he was embittered and testily contrary. However Frederick had no cause to confer with him, but had another difficulty to attend to. He had failed to show up at his office one day, and his aide, Stein, had gone to his house and found his housekeeper, Effie, in hysterics. Frederick had fainted, had come around, and had fainted again. Since he had had mononucleosis he had lacked energy, and blamed it on the hot weather in Greece. But perhaps more significant, he had never once been granted leave since 1938, and had been feeling worn out not only physically, but mentally.

All the same, it had not stopped him striving to in his quiet manner bind his mission to strengthen Greece's military to Washington's goal to stabilize the country. And that month (on 27 September 1951, to be exact) Greece became a member of NATO, thus gaining a role in the West's defense network. Only to be unsettled by news the U.S. Congress had voted to slash economic aid by over $70 million. For four months Frederick had been expounding on the need to keep a level of aid that allowed the military to get new equipment, and paid soldiers enough so they did not worry about the welfare of their families. Now going to the embassy, he advised Peurifoy it was not worth risking the effectiveness of the military "to save 70 million."

Peurifoy agreed, and went on to say Papagos was insisting a new election be held. Then, in a bit of curtain lifting, he added, "I will exercise moderate influence, so as to not damage our relations with him."

"For heavens sake," Frederick protested, "why embolden Papagos? That is like supporting tyranny."

But Peurifoy opined he doubted the present government's "durability." Of course, Frederick was not privy to the intertwining vines of messages between the State Department and the embassy. But gambling his candor not be mistook as rudeness, he replied, "And neither does your choice of an alternative lend itself to faith and optimism."

Almost simultaneously, fighting a rearguard action to sustain in Greek forces a high efficiency, Frederick counseled every commander to keep a stiff upper lip. In the circumstances there was little else he or they could do; and in only one instance would he rock the boat—an unstalwart vessel—of U.S. State Department nebulous schemes to carve out the future of Greece. But though he did so inadvertently, it got him in trouble—hip deep in trouble.

Papagos, with his far right friends, was stirring up agitation for another election when now, hoping to appease him, the American Embassy held a reception to bring him together with all sorts of people involved in the Greek economy, politics, and security. As usual at diplomatic affairs, banquet tables were replete with sumptuous food, liquor, and wine, and Frederick, arriving late and hungry, was making his way to a tray of food when a voluptuous woman sashayed up to him. Introducing herself as Mrs. Reese, and saying she would like a drink, he escorted her across the room, and they spent a brief time exchanging pleasantries.

Mrs. Reese was a tall White Russian, and wife of a very short, very rich Englishman who owned the theaters and racetrack in Athens. At the end of the evening, again seeking out Frederick, she asked if he was free to join her the next week to see an art show put on by local artists. Considering it a moment, as they both were married, and he without his family to share Greek culture, Frederick viewed it as an opportune invitation and accepted; only to unluckily later learn Mrs. Reese had many shortages of character, one being honesty.

It began when, urgently called to the embassy, Frederick found Peurifoy in a state of great perturbability. Up to then they had had a good relationship, but it obviously now cooled, as Peurifoy spit out, hotly, "What were you thinking—going out with Nadya Reese!"

"It depends," Frederick said, taken aback, "what you are talking about. I was thinking it was kind of her to invite me, that apparently her husband was not able to accompany her, and I thought some of the artists were interesting. Why?"

Peurifoy's shoulders sagged; then, weaving words around the topic, he said Mrs. Reese had been "moonlighting," and that Frederick had created an "awful situation," and Papagos was infuriated.

"What," Frederick asked, puzzled, "has he got to do with it?"

Peurifoy sighed. "Nadya Reese is his mistress—and we cannot afford unwanted publicity of a candidate to run Greece affronted by an American. But he considers you a liability to his arrangement and has threatened not to cooperate."

To Frederick this was too preposterous to protest. And not all true. But the situation as Peurifoy saw it was not the way Frederick knew it to be; that a lapse of information had led to his trodding on Papagos' *personna honos*. "In fact," said his aide Stein, later, "Papagos was extremely interested in Frederick, and admired him not for his wartime exploits alone, but for stomping out General Tskakalotos' attempt to rig the last election."

As for Peurifoy, there is no record of his thoughts available. But could it be he regarded Frederick seeing Mrs. Reese as a try to sabotage his backing Papagos as the U.S. puppet to restore Greece? And worried about his own reputation if he failed?

For now, getting to the gestalt of his distress Peurifoy said: "You must not confide any of this to anyone, on the chance it falls into the hands of politicians hostile to Papagos."

Then, lowering his head to avoid Frederick's gaze, he added, "I have notified Acheson you are to be replaced."

Thunderstruck, Frederick left in a hurry and, that night, he walked the road on the lip of the coastline near his house, feeling more than a little angry, and alone.

Later, Lieutenant General William W. Quinn, who as a major had served with him in southern France, described, "Bob had a charisma and the good looks of a movie star, and beautiful women were always chasing him. But in Greece, he just hadn't run away fast enough."

And never mind he had moved gracefully and obediently, despite all that he had done in Greece had political overtones; and been a dedicated soldier-diplomat. He was now a casualty of U.S. State Department duplicity and hypocrisy.

Summoning up a reserve of deftness to weather the blow, he had regained his aplomb when two days later Army Chief of Staff Collins tore over to Athens.

"Everyone loved Frederick," recalled Stein, "and was worried about him—that went for Collins too, who nuanced that wrapped up in the melee of Greece and ignoring his health, Frederick needed a well deserved rest."

Collins also knew Frederick had earned great respect as Chief of JUSMAG. And assuring him he was "as valuable as ever," he backed it up by saying, "A position on my staff will be waiting for you to fill when you are ready."

Therefore, Frederick told him, first he would check in to Walter Reed Hospital for a thorough going over; and, responding "Take a month or more," Collins repeated. "The position will be waiting for you."

As Frederick proceeded to pack official papers and his personal belongings, a shock wave reverberated around Athens. From the Prime Minister and his cabinet, and Greek generals and foreign diplomats and politicians, dozens of messages of sympathy, and distress, arrived by couriers at his door. Venizelos wrote a lengthy note that included:

> It is sad to have to write farewell letters, but to have to write one to you in particular is a more than grievous occasion.
> It is to be deplored that we shall miss you in critical times....when the Armed Forces are being attacked by wicked Greeks seeking to promote their own interests the presence of an upright soldier is more than necessary.
> From the very moment of your arrival you made every effort to assist the Greek Army, and to get to know the Greek soldier in even the most outlying unit. The Greek government and I personally wish to express to you our thanks; the sympathy and love of all of us shall attend you always.
> We are sorry to be deprived of a personal friend....
> [signed] Sophocles Venizelos

General Tskakalotos was no less upset, conveying. "I am losing a beloved friend. But we will continue to try our best to keep out of politics, in spite of hard efforts from many sides towards contrary objective. With brotherly love...."

Amid other outpourings of emotion one that stands out came from the chief of Greek National Defense, General Grigoropoulis:

"My wife and I will live in fear now without your loyal support.* Your leaving is a tragedy for Greece."

On his last full day in Greece, Frederick was invited to lunch at the palace with King Paul and Queen Frederika. Then, early the next morning he boarded the USNS *George W. Goethals*. In an American Embassy press release it was announced: "The Chief of JUSMAG, General Frederick, praising Greek military and civilian spirit, left today for Washington, where he will accept a new duty assignment."

Which was, for a brief spell anyway, what Frederick thought too.

*With good reason. Greeks without power were behaving like an unrehearsed choir, some bellowing, others humming, but to the same tune: We will do anything to keep U.S. dollars flowing in. Thus, in the next election after Frederick departed, Papagos won. And even today Greeks still cringe at the memory of three years (1952-54) of his dictatorship.

17

Honorable Retreat

Like the inevitability of a sunset, Bob Frederick would soon be called back to duty. General Collins had made it manifest that, due to the caliber of the man, he would rise to loftier heights. It presaged that Frederick was still on somebody's favorite list to be Chief of Staff of the U.S. Army. However, some of his colleagues thought he was washed up: for he did not possess a personality that buttered egos, nor anything inside him that clawed to win notice or reward.

In the meantime, for over a month Frederick underwent a battery of tests at Walter Reed. And as doctors poked and prodded him it was determined again the culprit for his weakening health was his carbon monoxide poisoning at Anzio. His heart had further enlarged, and he displayed one other symptom, a difficulty to control the impulses of tenseness and impatience. In addition, tests showed he was severely deaf in his left ear, and moderately so in his other ear, as a result of acoustic nerve damage during his many airplane flights (no military aircraft, in those days, was pressurized).

And what was on Frederick's mind? Getting in a welcome rest and some socializing, he was philosophic. For years he had put above all else duty to his country, been an activist or nonconformist whenever occasions called for it, and had had experiences parallel to nothing in the civilian world. Taking a hard look at his situation, he cogitated was he willing to put up with more moves? Besides which, even should he eventually hold the Army's top job, though it was a position of glory, it was not always pleasant dealing with troublesome political superiors. But uppermost, he had already had a spectacular career, and he was satisfied with what he had accomplished. Sending a note off to Eisenhower, he began, "Dear Dwight....":

> I have no idea if you have heard any version of what brought about my recall from Greece, and can only say the episode was disheartening, though I have no sense it will militate against future chances I might have. However, granted time to rest up prior to returning to work, I feel strongly pulled to consider the requisite travel involved and separations from family.

He added that Ruth had been staying in Palo Alto, California, a town they hoped to one day settle down in—and he concluded with:

> "I have received a few offers from elsewhere in the civilian sector, but whatever the outcome, I have opted not to remain in uniform, but to retire."*

One could ask if his decision was a function of character, or of a thinking man. He was only forty-four years old, for God sake! Had all his years of acting on his independent thinking and creating historical changes overpowered his resistance to chafe at always being a pawn of the nation's political leadership? Many years later, when asked about this he refused to discuss it beyond saying, dryly, "I was exhausted."

Of course his leaving Greece had induced pantries full of rumors that ran the gamut from him inheriting a million dollars to stabbing a Greek, but good soldier that he was (unlike many removed from command for a cause, or as a scapegoat who proffer their own justifications) Frederick kept his mouth shut. Making his retirement equally piquant, as busy minds now crocheted and embroidered more stories—the truth

---

*And his retirement was granted based on 50 percent disability, i.e. his loss of hearing; but it would have gone through anyway because counting his four years in the Enlisted Reserve Corps while at West Point he had spent 26 years in uniform.

not enough for those who never experienced the pressures put upon a proven leader.

Then soon, adding to the hearsay, though customary to award the next highest rank to a retiring officer, Frederick was denied this.

"Because," said his old friend Wickham, "he'd *asked* to retire, plus a few in the Pentagon felt he was not old enough to have three stars."

But temporizing his disappointment, Frederick was looking forward to a new way of life—one that was to unfortunately, only in hindsight, be a paradoxical heaven and hell.

His path as a civilian led first to the Willard Hotel in Washington, as a guest at a dinner given by U.S. Senator Estes Kefauver, who introduced, and somewhat embarrassed, him as "a war hero worshiped by soldiers." Back when Frederick had testified to a congressional group on the need to continue aid to Greece, Kefauver had seen a similarity in their personalities. Neither man strutted or ranted, but got what he was fighting for by quiet perseverance; and, at the time, he had informed Frederick, "If ever you leave the Army, I want you with me. You get things done without stirring up a bit of dust."

Kefauver, known widely for chairing a probe into the mafia, was described by his foes (politicians professionally hurt by probes into their connections with organized crime) as "an ambition-crazed Caesar." Now wanting to be the Democratic Party's nominee for U.S. president, the Senator was lining up support. The next election was not until November 1952. But Truman's unpopularity had grown because of his firing MacArthur, while waiting in the Republican Party wings as potential candidates were two generals, MacArthur and Eisenhower. Hoping to offset public opinion that firing a general was "a democrat's disease," Kefauver now had asked that Frederick speak out in support of him, starting at a rally in Miami.

Not that Frederick was a sudden convert to the Democrat's side; indeed, he was quite conscious the only rapport he felt with Kefauver was he had expressed a mutual concern, "that the Soviet Union has the offensive in the cold war, by searching the globe for soft spots to impose communism."

Even so, that week purchasing a car, Frederick drove to Miami and delivered a brief talk about Kefauver's wariness about communist expansion. Afterward invited to a dinner hosted by the organizer of the rally, at the end of the meal Frederick may have been thinking he was not a political person, but certainly was thinking he had no stomach for it, as a waiter mistakenly handed him a bill for expensive steaks the organizer had ordered for all those present.

Aghast at the totaled cost, Frederick remarked, "We must have eaten Ferdinand the Bull."

"Oh, no problem," responded his host. "We can slip it into the national debt as a senatorial expense."

Finding it took all he had to exit without replying, angrily (as he said later) "That is an odious deception to most Americans," the next day, bowing out unhesitantly of all things political Frederick drove to Fort Benning, Georgia, to visit his daughter Jane and his first grandchild, a baby girl. Then from Benning, he headed to North Carolina to explore a position offered to him, to be superintendent of a military prep school. Only to realize he could not wrap his mind around the job—not unnaturally: for a man who had led combat troops, held commands at army and air force schools, and trained divisions, to superintend a few hundred teenagers lacked the mental and physical challenges he desired.

So next, heading westward he arrived in Denver, Colorado, where he had been offered directorship of a chain of resorts. But here some bad news caught up with him. Mrs. Frederick, Sr., in her mid-sixties and still running the walnut ranch, had fallen during a rain storm at the ranch and broken one of her legs. Like a dutiful son Frederick sped to California to assist her, and to assume, in essence, the life of a gentleman farmer.

In Palo Alto he and Ruth bought a large, stately house, to from there commute to the ranch an hour and a half northeast. Having moved twenty-three times in two dozen years, they had accumulated oriental rugs of varied sizes that when thrown down had, with furniture marred by numerous moves, made many a set of Army quarters a home. As had a trunkful of curtains which, if seldom seeming to fit windows in most quarters, had been held on to just in case. Such as now, as moving to the first house they owned, Ruth said, dismally, "Not one of the forty pair of curtains in this trunk works at any window in this place!"

That summer was the laziest Frederick had ever spent. Going to the ranch three days a week to prepare it for harvest, and to check on a new ranch house he was having built on the property, he and several business persons in Palo Alto had got together to form The University Club, a club where they could meet over lunch for scholarly talk and raise funds for scholarships for needy college students. (It since has expanded into a country club, yet even today, Frederick's name is on a plaque at the entrance as a founder.)

But mostly content to stay at home and tend to the apricot and lemon trees in his backyard, and listen to his favorite recordings of classical music, only twice did Frederick become restless. The first time was when a FBI agent paid him a visit. Five years earlier (in 1947), the American Embassy in Greece—in conjunction with intelligence gathering by the FBI—had begun collecting the names of U.S. citizens who wrote the Embassy in protest of death sentences Greece meted out to communists. Which in turn had led to investigations of Greek-American organizations, as fear of communists infiltrating U.S. military bases and political institutions grew. Leading the search was FBI chief J. Edgar Hoover, one of whose minions had come to ask Frederick could he assist the bureau by identifying Greek-American commies?

Replying he had never been privy to embassy intelligence data on U.S. citizens, afterward, thinking like a soldier, Frederick spent a few restless days fending off regrets ("not very easily," noticed Ruth) that he was not out in some field searching for an enemy.

Then from Korea came ominous news of many casualties, and this time Ruth found Frederick pacing the floor in restless ire that U.S. troops had now been subsumed to a defensive role against marauding Chinese troops as Truman, deciding to settle for two hostile Koreas—north and south—sought an "armed peace." Adding to Frederick's distress, his son-in-law, Captain George C. Fee (West Point class of 1948), had just been transferred from Benning to Korea.

Meanwhile, a newfangled apparatus—television—allowed Americans to watch politicians in action, and Kefauver, who had come onto the scene like a comet, had fizzled out. The Democrats' nominee for U.S. president was Adlai Stevenson; the Republicans', Eisenhower. And come November Frederick, up to then expected as an army officer to serve in silent subordination of political leadership, for the first time voted, for Ike.

Then the following January, as Eisenhower was sworn in, though on speaking terms with him, Frederick chose to send him a note that said, in part:

"As you face the tremendous task before you, I take heart you as a soldier know that only a well-prepared military can cut the horrendous costs borne by troops, particularly those who must fight when the country has an ill-defined purpose."

Thinking, perhaps, of his son-in-law, Frederick was a critical observer as negotiations to end war in Korea droned on; and not until 23 July 1953 was an armistice signed. By then Joseph Stalin was a dead tyrant; Russia had a nuclear bomb; and after enduring eight years as an obscure modality of nonconventional fighting, a small unit of special forces had again been formed in the U.S. Army.

"That is better than none," said Frederick, exuberantly, to one former colleague who kept in touch. He then added *sotto voce*, "But it will take someone keener on the concept than Ike is to push to build large special forces teams to use as a backbone of strength for both combat and maintaining peace."

Besides numerous ex-colleagues who stayed in contact with him, so did a great many ex-G.I.s; each week at least three letters reached him addressed to "General Robert T. Frederick, Palo Alto, California," or "Somewhere in California.* One veteran wrote to complain:

My wife keeps saying I act as though you are my father, and I have to keep telling her it is because it is you who taught me honor, humbleness, honesty, courtesy, and courage.

And while such communications may have lessened any angst Frederick felt over leaving the Army prematurely, so had the fact he had gained more time to share with his family.

---

*Which was part and parcel of that truest of bonds—the bond of loyalty formed by soldiers in battles.

It was now 1955 when, up at the ranch, on 15 February Frederick drove a pickup truck through the orchard and, with no hint of tragedy, headed down the nearby highway to attend a meeting of walnut growers and the Blue Diamond Nut Company. As witnesses told it he leaned over to roll up the passenger side window, and the truck careened off the highway and, with a loud crunch of metal, slammed into a tree. Thrown through the windshield and hitting the tree, Frederick lay unconscious in a bloody heap, glass embedded in his head, his left arm fractured in four places. Rushed to a small local hospital, there doctors sewed up his gashes, set his arm, and diagnosed he had severe brain damage, and needed to be moved to Letterman Army Hospital in San Francisco for neurological surgery.

As newsmen got word of his accident it spread across the nation and overseas. "You would think the Pope died," one telephone operator in San Francisco told a reporter, "Hundreds of calls are coming in from all around the globe from people asking about the General's condition."

And from the White House, put in direct contact with the chief neurologist Eisenhower instructed him, "Do everything possible for Frederick."

Twice doctors opened up his skull to relieve the pressure of blood pooled on his brain, but Frederick remained in a coma eleven weeks. Then in May, he opened his eyes—and began an agonizing recovery. He had lost most of his memory and power of speech. For a man who had fought and worked hard and talked easily, his infirmities were an endless frustration; and lurking frighteningly was the unknown in his future.

Soon after, taken home by ambulance to Palo Alto, he steadily rallied, but once fluent in French and German he knew not a word, and fog clouded other parts of his past. Some days Ruth and their youngest daughter, who had married and lived close by, walked him round and round his den to build up his strength, and showed him dozens of photos to spark his recall. All the while, he had added encouragement from old comrades whose thinly disguised affection for him came through in their letters, one being from Eisenhower, who wrote on pale blue White House stationary:

Dear Bob,

I was grieved to hear of your accident, but as my recent inquiries bring the news you are on the mend, it is with just as deep-felt emotion I am pulling for you, and wish you a speedy recovery.

Yours, respectfully,

 [signed]Dwight

That summer, with Ruth at his side Frederick sat in his yard, his face warmed by sunshine, when reflecting back he recalled how rays of sun streaming in stained glass windows in the West Point chapel would warm him on winter days. So many dreams had lay ahead of him then. After a few more moments of reflection, with unexpected levity he said, "I remember the date we married, June ninth."

Drawing on a remarkable resolve, by the start of 1957 Frederick was again a man of action. And while always to have occasional speech difficulty or a tempest of agitation (which is common both from brain injury and with heart damage), he had the confident persona of someone ready to surmount hardships in his life. Which, though certainly not as exciting as before, offered new avenues for new ideas. He designed and got a patent for huge wooden crates that locked snugly onto the platforms of truck trailers to haul walnuts from growers to buyers. He was the first to build canvas-sided cottages for migrant workers. He formed a rental company, whereby equipment he and others owned was pooled for use at harvest times. And he became a regular at the Commonwealth Club in San Francisco to hear statesmen and authors talk—to catch up on what had been news during his forced hiatus. Not all of which pleased him.

For one thing, Russian troops had crushed an uprising against communist rule in Hungary; and again Frederick felt stirrings of anger at the State Department, "that persists," he wrote an army friend, "to wimpily ignore that communism, even when cloaked in sheepskin, has fangs." He was also disturbed that Ike, who had easily won a second term, championed a nuclear arsenal to provide instant retaliation to a Soviet attack. True, America was at peace, was booming economically, and everyone in dread of being atomized by Russia. But Eisenhower's defense doctrine was sucking away money from conventional military forces "that will always be needed," wrote Frederick, "in the culmination of any conflict."

It is likely his concern of diminishing funds for conventional defense was fueled in part by a ceremony he had just attended. A tall granite monument honoring the 45th Infantry Division had been erected in Oklahoma City and, asked that he speak at the dedication, he had talked of how the monument was "as firm and strong as a 45th soldier," but could not relay: "the confusion of combat, the chaos and despair that blots out all but the iron will of a fighter, or the lift he gets when the enemy gives way."

One reporter on the scene had noted:

> Frederick isn't as heavy as when he led the Thunderbirds to victory to Germany. Neither is he as husky as when he commanded the First Airborne Task Force, nor when he organized, trained, and led the First Special Service Force in the Aleutians and Italy. But the seven oak leaf clusters on his Purple Heart ribbon bar may have something to do with that...[for] this was a fighting general.

Elsewhere in the press were frothy attempts to explain why the U.S. was getting burned by a "boiling unrest" of anti-Americanism in Greece. Yet it gave Frederick no joy to know he had been correct that Ambassador Peurifoy's stratagem to back a Rightist would backfire.

But it did give him a huge sense of complacency.

The following autumn, the Fredericks made a sentimental journey to Staunton Military Academy, then going up to West Point, for a week they relived times spent together there. On returning to Palo Alto, Frederick received a letter from the Department of Army that asked would he be the guest of honor at a ceremony in Fort Bragg, NC, and personally pass on the colors and battle streamers of the First Special Service Force. For finally, after always being on the fringes of the military, special forces had been expanded into three groups, and become a separate branch of the U.S. Army.

As Frederick arrived at the ceremony, however, his legacy was even more apparent. The insignia for this newest Army branch was the crossed arrows worn by his commandos in WWII; and on its arrowhead shaped shoulder patch, an upturned dagger representing the fierce stiletto that Frederick designed in 1942. Before an assembled crowd, striding across the main parade ground, he proudly transferred the lineage of the FSSF, and was officially recognized as the "father" of Special Forces.

By the time he again got home it was November, and the nation's political pendulum had swung back to the Democrats. Voters had elected as the next U.S. president a big fan of the Green Berets, John F. Kennedy; who at his inauguration on 20 January 1961 made a promise "to pay any price, bear any burden" in the Cold War. Whether it would be favorable for Americans was yet to be seen. But soon after Kennedy increased the number of special forces teams his predecessor had sent to South Vietnam as advisors to assist in that ally's fight against communist guerillas.

As for Frederick, who had with Ike's departure lost a pipeline to a president's mind, now only able to learn what was occurring in Vietnam from the news, not till the summer of 1964 would he get his dander up at the Commander in Chief. In the meantime, with his usual reserve, he led a simple life and was a doting "grandpa" to his eight grandchildren. Who—a few at least— he took each summer to the coast, or to Blue Lake in north California, his car loaded down with inner tubes and fishing rods. And sometimes he was seen in the bleachers at a little league baseball game, if one of his grandsons was playing that day.

"That's where I ran into him," recalled Dave Clark, who had been a Public Affairs Officer at Fort Ord in the 1950s.

"I had moved to Palo Alto, and gone to a game with my sons when Frederick spotted me and said, 'Clark, how are you?' I was astounded, because at Ord I had been in his headquarters just a few times to ask what he wanted done with the press. It shows how much stock he put in remembering names, as he looked you right in the eye and said something to you that made you feel you'd had a very special day. That's a natural leader—and he had it all the time. After he left Ord, all people kept saying was 'Golly, wish General Frederick was here.' He never did anything by the book if there was another way he could achieve the same goal and make people in on the project feel good about themselves. He lent something special to everything he did—and did it instinctively."

And it was not until three summers later when Frederick got really angry at the current administration, as heightening America's heavy mood over the assassination of Kennedy the previous November the new president, Lyndon Johnson, tossed fuel onto the fury and the fire in Vietnam.

Johnson, who on a tour of Fort Ord (in 1951) had irked Frederick with his "warmonger" comment, was now on the warpath. Two U.S. ships had been fired on by North Vietnamese patrol boats, and to retaliate, Johnson had endorsed piecemeal bombing of North Vietnam whenever there was "an attack against forces of the United States."

Frederick knew what terror felt like; knew much about the combat man's life; and despised war. "But to run a war limited to reactions of what the enemy does is sure to fail," he vented to a few friends in that tribal band of West Pointers.

"Our civilian leadership has obviously learned nothing from the past, as it has no plan of action except this stunningly flawed bombing campaign that with frequent pauses gives the enemy time to rebuild defenses and come up with new countermeasures."

Willing to burden his argument by more criticism he continued, "Not one combat trooper should be sent to Vietnam until a decisive strategy for victory is laid out."

Instead Johnson, to apply gradual pressure, kept on doling out bombing targets until, at the end of 1965, lurching into his next phase he ordered ground combat troops to Vietnam. At the time, some Americans protested U.S. involvement in southeast Asia—and for the next two years mass anti-war demonstrations grew in ferocity. In one case 100,000 people had marched on the Pentagon when Frederick, disgusted, brooded over how anyone "can dismiss the reality the military did not send itself to Vietnam, the present administration ordered it there."

On a crisp fall day soon after, however, he was pleasantly distracted. A newspaper editor, Robert Adleman, and a retired colonel, George Walton, arrived in Palo Alto to interview him for two military history books they were working on. As he dug through cartons of old field orders, maps, and correspondence, they remarked his "paper past" should be preserved. It was the impetus for Frederick to—working with an archivist—donate select items to the Hoover Institution on War, Revolution, and Peace, at Stanford University (where they reside today in eight boxes labeled "Frederick Collection").

Not too long after, he received from the authors copies of their first joint effort, *The Devil's Brigade*, a book about his First Special Service Force. As it happened, the Hollywood producer David Wolper planned to make a movie from the book, and in a telephone call Ruth Frederick took, she learned the actor William Holden would star in the role as her husband.

"Holden?" Ruth responded. "Why not Gregory Peck? He looks a lot more like Bob."

But Holden it was; and for Frederick the coming year was filled with activity as filming got underway. Flying to Utah, where mountain combat scenes were recreated, he served as a technical and factual advisor, the latter "rather futilely," he remarked, "the Hollywood tendency being to gussy up some facts, abbreviate or outright distort others."

Then, on the eve of the movie hitting theaters, its publicists arranged a grueling tour that involved he appear at the premier of the film in Chicago, Detroit, Salt Lake City, New York, Los Angeles, Montreal, and Winnipeg. And then on to London, where for the first time in twenty-five years Frederick met up again with Lord Louis Mountbatten.

"It has been a long while," said Mountbatten.

"Yes," acknowledged Frederick; and from that feeble beginning they enjoyed a long visit, sharing news about their families. When a reporter interrupted to ask Frederick for some of his wartime memories he smiled; such painful memories—the spilling of blood, the dead comrades, the loneliness of leadership in combat—he continued to smile, and shook his head.

The media meanwhile had latched onto the movie with wild enthusiasm:

"The best war epic!" "To forever be remembered!"

"Frederick had an iron hand in a velvet glove, his diffident smile and soft speaking voice contrasted with his innate gift for command!"

And in every city he was interviewed either on the radio or on television, and set upon by people wanting his autograph. In his bold, slanting hand he signed their pictures of him, and was embarrassed by all the fuss.

"He is consummately modest," offered one of the hundreds of WWII veterans attending post-movie receptions for Frederick, who showed his affection for them with a ready grin and warm greeting. "In fact his modesty and shyness," the veteran told a reporter, "are in themselves epic."

But Frederick was a rare cat, a *living* legend, and thus drew more publicity. To his chagrin he found it physically exhausting, and headed home quite eager to pursue his interests in music, in growing prize tomatoes, and collecting antique weaponry. What ironically is true, he had never aspired to gain distinction.

But already the press was at his door. As he graciously ushered each newsman into his den, where lining one wall were photographs of generals he had worked with—Marshall, Collins, Omar Bradley, Devers, Patch, and Eisenhower—invariably each fell into a few minutes of silent awe as he read the inscriptions on the pictures. As for instance on that of Ike, who had written, "To Bob, with my deepest and my unending respect and trust, Dwight." One newspaper, the *San Jose Mercury*, ran a full three page story about Frederick, and he was feted at a ceremony in Palo Alto, where the mayor decreed a "General Robert Tryon Frederick Day."

But no matter the occasion, he refused to yield to anyone the answer to had he "ever regretted he was no longer in uniform?"

In 1969 the authors Adleman and Walton sent him their second book, *The Champagne Campaign*, which dealt with his airborne force and his own action in the south of France invasion. But by now WWII seemed fustily passe. Collectively grabbing the mind of America was a policy to prompt South Vietnam to reestablish a stable government, to allow U.S. forces to withdraw. The year before President Johnson had had an epiphany: all the bombings on the north had accomplished nothing. ("Hell," groused one retired Army officer, "Bob and his ilk could've told him that several years earlier.") But though changing his war strategy, it had not allayed public rebellion that Vietnam was a quagmire sucking up American lives, and Johnson had announced he would not seek re-election. And now Richard M. Nixon, beating out the Democrat Hubert Humphrey, occupied the White House.

"At last," Frederick wrote Ken Wickham, with almost accidental mirth, "we have seen the end of war crafting that was part fanciful pipe-dreaming, part political bunkum." And he already had written an epitaph for the conflict in Vietnam: A classic in indecisive limited warfare that corroded American's unity.

But sadly, very soon after, Frederick faced the grim task of choosing his own epitaph. Doctors at Letterman had told him that he had, at most, a year to live, that now, short of breath, his pulse irregular, he was dying from congestive heart failure. He took the news with the same stoicism he had shown in grisly situations in wartime—at least initially. He still had a manager on the walnut ranch, but tiring of indeterminate issues like inclement weather and market prices for walnuts he sold the property. Next he bought three huge photograph albums, and in them chronologically compiled hundreds of WWII pictures given to him by admiring armed forces photographers.

But did he realize how many lives he had touched?

As word spread that he was physically fading, his den overflowed with cards and letters. Soldiers who once served with him wrote that he set examples they had endeavored to follow for life; black soldiers wrote to thank him for fomenting a revolution to integrate races at training bases; still others expressed how they found they could not accept that his legendary iron will did not make him indestructible; and more than a dozen babies had been named after him.

So perhaps now he did realize his impact.

About four months later, Frederick drove up to San Francisco to select a grave marker, and to instruct that it say only his name and rank. He also chose a plain G.I. coffin and arranged, rather than at Arlington, he be interred in the National Cemetery at the Presidio of San Francisco, where as a boy he had got his first taste for soldiering. And it was only then that he decided to put up a fight to prolong, or ease, what time he had left.

Contacting a team of cardiologists at Stanford University Hospital, who agreed with him that a pacemaker might help to regulate his pulse, he underwent the surgery, afterward expressing amazement to have "come out okay." But two days later, suddenly racked by fever and nausea, closing his eyes, his face relaxed, on 29 November 1970 Frederick slipped from his earthly bonds.

"His heart, great and kind and full of love for all his fellow men," later wrote naval Commander Maxwell H. Hamilton, "had simply taken all the battering it could handle."

News of Frederick's death swiftly reached all of North America, and at his funeral service in the main chapel at the Presidio there was standing room only, while outside under dark clouds, TV camera crews waited to film the final rites for that night's newscasts. By the time the hearse carrying Frederick's casket moved slowly down the road to the cemetery a steady rain was falling, rhythmic to the subdued rumble of funeral drums, as the long procession of mourners walked side by side to the gravesite. Among them were over a dozen generals, seven West Point classmates, a representative from the Canadian government, two from the FBI, members of the First Special Service Force, and many other veterans who had traveled very great distances.

An honor guard fired a volley of rifle shots, the sharp sound rolling up the hill and down through the trees to San Francisco Bay. Then, from a knoll above, a lone bugler played taps—the words to its sorrowing tune familiar to all in the military—

Day is done
Gone the sun
From the lake
From the hill
From the sky
Rest in peace
Soldier brave
God is nigh

As Ruth Frederick braced to receive the American flag covering her husband's casket, beams of sun suddenly parted the dark sky. "It is a sign," a young army officer, tears running down his cheeks, said hoarsely, "of the heavens welcoming this bravest of the brave."

Appendix:
Frederick's Decorations and Awards

United States
Distinguished Service Cross with one Oak Leaf Cluster*
Distinguished Service Medal with one Oak Leaf Cluster
Purple Heart with seven Oak Leaf Clusters
Silver Star
Bronze Star Medal with one Oak Leaf Cluster
Legion of Merit with one Oak Leaf Cluster
Air Medal
American Defense Service Medal
American Campaign Medal
Asiatic-Pacific Campaign Medal with Bronze Service Star**
European-African-Middle East Campaign Medal with one Silver Service Star (equal to five Bronze Service Stars)
Army of Occupation Medal with Germany Clasp
World War II Victory Medal
Combat Infantryman Badge

*An Oak Leaf Cluster is the equivalent of another of the same award.
**A Bronze Service Star is a decoration for heroism or meritorious action in the specified campaign zone

Foreign

FRANCE: Legion of Honor with *Croix de Guerre* with Palm

FRANCE: Legion of Honor with *Croix de Guerre* with Palm (2nd award)

GREAT BRITAIN: Distinguished Service Order

ITALY: Order of the Crown, Degree of Commander

ITALY: Silver Star for Valor

MONACO: Order of St. Charles, Rank of Grand Officer

NORWAY: Liberation Cross of King Haakon VII

GREECE: Grand Commander of the Order of George the First

Bibliography

Books

Adleman, Robert H., and Walton, George, *The Devil's Brigade*. Philadelphia: Chilton Books, 1966.

Association of Graduates U.S.M.A., *Register of Graduates and Former Cadets, 1986, United States Military Academy*: West Point, NY, 1986.

Bishop, Leo V., LTC, Glasgow, Frank J., Maj., and Fisher, George A., Maj., eds. *The Fighting Forty Fifth, The Combat Record of an Infantry Division*. Baton Rouge, LA: Army and Navy Publishing Company, 1950.

Blumenson, Martin, *The U.S. Army in WWII: Salerno to Cassino*. Washington D.C.: Office of the Chief of Military History, Dept. of Army, 1965.

_____, Anzio: *The Gamble That Failed*. Phildelphia: J.B. Lippincott Co., 1963.

Britt-Smith, Richard, *Hitler's Generals*. San Rafael, CA: Presidio Press, 1977.

Brown, Keith E., *When the Odds Were Even: The Vosges Mountains Campaign, October 1944-January 1945*. Novato, CA: Presidio Press (date unknown).

Burhans, Robert D., LTC., *The First Special Service Force*. Washington, D.C.: Infantry Journal, Inc., 1947.

Chace, James, *Acheson, The Secretary of State Who Created the American World*. New York: Simon & Schuster, 1998.

D'Estes, Carlos, *Fatal Decision: Anzio and the Battle for Rome*. New York: HarperCollins Publishers, 1991.

Devlin, Gerald M., *Paratrooper! The Saga of U.S. Army and Marine Parachute and Glider Combat Troops During World War II*. New York: St. Martin's Press, 1979.

Dupuy, R. Ernest, *Men of West Point*. New York: William Sloan Associates, 1951.

Dziuban, Stanely W., Col., *Special Studies: Military Relations Between The United States and Canada, 1939-1945*. Washington, D.C.: U.S. Army in World War II Series, 1959.

Garland, Albert N., LTC, and Smyth, Howard M., *The Mediterranean Theatre of Operations*. Washington D.C.: (publisher and date unknown).

Ladd, James, *Commandos and Rangers of World War II*. New York: St. Martin's Press, 1978.

Love, George E., *The Age of Deterence*. Boston: Little, Brown, 1964.

MacGregor, Morris J., Jr., *Integration of the Armed Forces 1940-1965*. Washington D.C.: Center of Military History, United States Army 1985.

McMichael, Scott R., Maj., *A Historical Perspective on Light Infantry*. Fort Leavenworth, KS: U.S. Army Command and General Staff College, 1987.

Nelson, Guy, *Thunderbird: A History of the 45th Infantry Division*. Oklahoma City: The Oklahoma Publishing Company, 1969.

Papandreou, Andreas, *Democracy at Gunpoint: The Greek Front*. New York: Doubleday & Company, Inc., 1979.

Perret, Geoffrey, *There's a War to be Won: The United States Army in World War II*. New York: Ballatine Books, 1991.

Pyle, Ernie, *Brave Men*. New York: Walker and Company, 1944.

Prange, Gordon W., *At Dawn We Slept: The Untold Story of Pearl Harbor*. USA: McGraw-Hill Book Company, 1981.

Robichon, Jacques, *The Second D-Day*. New York: Walker and Company, 1969.

Starr, Chester G., *From Solerno to the Alps*. Washington, D.C.: Infantry Journal Press, 1948.

Trevelyan, Raleigh, *Rome '44: The Battle for the Eternal City*. New York: The Viking Press, 1981.

Weigley, Russell F., *Eisenhower's Lieutenants: The Campaign of France and Germany 1944-1945* (Volume II). Bloomington, IN: Indiana University Press, 1981.

Wilt, Alan F., *The French Riveria Campaign of August 1944*. Illinois: Southern Illinois University Press, 1981.

Wittner, Lawerence S., *American Intervention In Greece, 1939-1949*. New York: Columbia University Press, 1982.

Newspapers and Periodicals
Chosen from pertinent issues too numerous to list, the following were used for specific quotes or descriptions:

Newspapers
Army Times, May 15, 1951
Cincinnati *News*, date unknown
Denver *Post*, Clark Lee, date unknown
Kansas City *Star*, Newbold Noyes Jr., June 4, 1944
Los Angeles *Examiner*, April 7, 1949
Minneapolis *Tribune*, Joseph Hennessy, May 7, 1966
Montreal Daily *Star*, Sholto Watt, April 6, 1944
New York *Sun*, August 22, 1944
New York *Times*, June 29, 1945
Salt Lake *Tribune*, May 17, 1968
San Francisco *Chronicle*, December 5, 1944: September 24, 1945
San Francisco *Examiner*, February 14, 1945; September 24, 1945
Stars and Stripes, George Dorsey, November 6, 1944
Washington *Post*, Frederick Painton, October 1, 1944
Winnipeg *Tribune*, August 13, 1965

Periodicals
American Legion, date unknown
Army, September 1982

Life, Robert Capa, June 26, 1944; June 19, 1944
Newsweek, Paul Malone, February 14, 1944
Reader's Digest, November 1944
Retired Officer, Lt. Comdr. Maxwell Hamilton, October 1981
Time, September 4, 1944
Yank, August 1944

Collected Papers and Documents
Hoover Instituion on War, Revolution, and Peace, Stanford, CA: Robert
    T. Frederick collection, consisting of his field orders, reports,
    correspondence, memorandums, and speeches.
United States Army Military History Institute, Carlisle Barracks, PA:
    completed questionnaires from men serving with Frederick in WWII;
    interviews with Frederick, BG Charles E. Saltzamn, Gen. Lucian K.
    Truscott, Jr., BG Raymond S. McLain, MG Fred L. Walker; oral
    history of Gen. Paul D. Adams.
National Archives; Military Archives Division records of the U.S. Coast
    Artillery Corps; Civil Archives Division records of the Civilian
    Conservation Corps; State Department Files, Foreign Service Post
    Files, Greece: State Department Files, U.S. Foreign Relations 1951,
    volume V.

Written and Oral Interviews
Interviewees:
Adams, Paul D., Gen.
Clark, Dave
Coons, George E.
Coswell, Jerry
Crouse, Marion W., Col.
Diestal, Chester J., Col.
Forward, Eugene A.
Freyer, Fred R.
Grey, C.B.
Hart, Charles E., Lt. Gen.
Hessel, Emil
Kurtzhal, Merle J.

Jablonsky, Harvey J., Maj. Gen.

Jones, Geoffrey M.T.

Mardiros, Armen N., Col.

Mauldin, Bill

McCall, George N.

McLain, Raymond S., Brig. Gen.

McGowan, Glenn J. Col.

Moore, Robert S., Col.

Parks, James P., Maj.

Petrie, Glynn

Prugh, George S., Maj. Gen.

Quinn, William W., Lt. Gen.

Ramsey, Robert A.

Rickey, James H.

Saltzman, Charles E., Maj. Gen.

Somerville, Duncan S., Col.

Stein, Evelyn

Tedford, Roy P.

Thompson, Paul M.

Walmer, Richard, Lt. Col.

Warren, James C., Jr.

Wedemeyer, Albert C., Gen.

Whitney, Richard W., Maj. Gen.

Wickham, Kenneth G., Maj. Gen.

Woods, Eugene

Additional Sources

The Frederick family collection: it consists of records of Frederick's early school years and voyage to Australia; his official military record; personal letters to and from Frederick and family members, and from the following general officers: Paul D. Adams, Mark W. Clark, Dwight D. Eisenhower, Albert C. Wedemeyer, and Kenneth G. Wickham.

Index

The Supercommandos
First Special Service Force, 1942-1944
An Illustrated History

Robert Todd Ross

Chronicles the organization, training, and combat operations of the First Special Service Force during its brief but exhilarating history. Full-color maps, Order of Battle graphics, charts, and numerous noteworthy original Force documents are also included. Over eighty full-color images of authentic First Special Service Force uniforms, insignia, weapons and equipment. An invaluable resource for any collector, reenactor, veteran, or historian.

Size: 8 1/2" x 11" ■ over 600 b/w photographs, over 80 color photographs, maps, documents ■ 320 pp
ISBN: 0-7643-1171-9 ■ hard cover ■ $59.95